P R I D E *of*
F A M I L Y

PRIDE *of* FAMILY

FOUR GENERATIONS OF AMERICAN WOMEN OF COLOR

CAROLE IONE

AVON BOOKS ◢ NEW YORK

AVON BOOKS
A division of
The Hearst Corporation
1350 Avenue of the Americas
New York, New York 10019

Copyright © 1991 by Carole Ione
Published by arrangement with Summit Books
Library of Congress Catalog Card Number: 91-11761
ISBN: 0-380-71934-7

The Summit Books edition contains the following Library of Congress Cataloging in Publication Data:

Ione, Carole.
    Pride of family : four generations of American women of color / Carole Ione.
       p.   cm.
Includes bibliographical references.
1. Afro-American women—Biography.   2. Ione, Carole, date— Family.   3. Whipper family.   4. Wheeler family.   5. Lewis family.
I. Title.
E185.96.157   1991
920.72′08996073—dc20   91-11761   CIP

First Avon Books Trade Printing: February 1993

Printed in the U.S.A.

OPM   10   9   8   7   6   5   4   3   2   1

*Those who are dead are never gone,
they are there in the thickening shadow.*

—AFRICAN POEM

For my family, may our past wounds be healed.

Contents

FAMILY TIME LINES

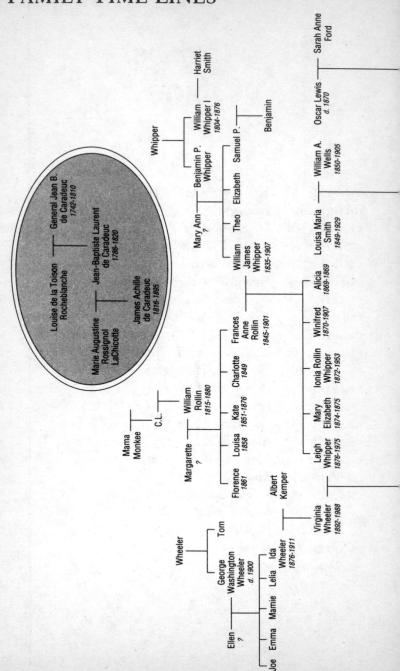

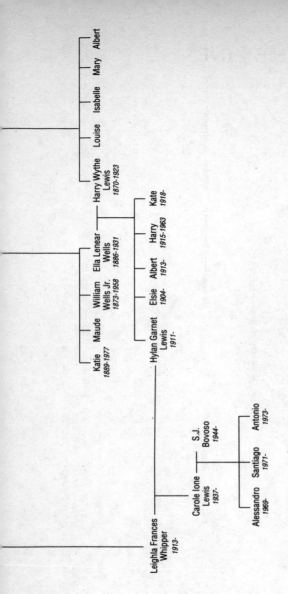

Albert

Mary

Isabelle

Louise

Harry Wythe
Lewis
1870-1923

Kate
1918-

Harry
1915-1963

Albert
1913-

Ella Lenear
Wells
1886-1931

Elsie
1904-

William
Wells Jr.
1873-1958

Maude

Katie
1889-1977

Hylan Garnet
Lewis
1911-

Antonio
1973-

S.J.
Bovoso
1944-

Santiago
1971-

Carole Ione
Lewis
1937-

Alessandro
1969-

Leighla Frances
Whipper
1913-

Preface

THE TRUTH IS, I knew I was female before I knew I was black.

I was raised by three singular women—my mother, my grandmother, and my great-aunt—and all my life I studied them: their smooth faces, the enigma of their bodies. Strong, proud, secretive, like the mythic beings in my storybooks, the women in my family presented themselves to me fully formed and without much history to speak of. They were simply there, with their hankies and hairpins, high heels and furs, perfumes and pianos, racing sheets and stethoscopes.

My gambling grandmother was a high-kicking dancer in the great chorus lines of the 1920s and '30s, and she loved to play the numbers and bet the horses. My dignified great-aunt was a medical doctor and a social reformer. And my mother was a journalist and a writer of murder mysteries, who also composed tropical songs. I hoped that one day I would be like these women—that they would accept me as one of them, that I would bask in their love and understanding and would share in all their secrets.

There were, of course, men in the family too. We saw them every few months, or, in times of relative truce, more often. When they were not around they were spoken of with pursed-lipped exasperation; yet I could often detect traces of reluctant admiration in the women's voices. The men in the family had made their mark. There was my father, a sociologist, and my grandfather, a respected actor whose own father was a Reconstruction-era judge. My great-grandfather's uncle was a nineteenth-century moralist, lumber merchant, abolitionist and publisher, from Philadelphia, whose life I could read about in history books.

I was raised to be proud of the accomplishments of our family, to feel that we had a special place in the world. As I grew older, however, I began to notice something that I'd been hiding even from myself: underneath the pride, I sometimes felt ashamed and afraid. Each of the women who had raised me had passed on certain rules about living: "Always have some money of your own. You can't trust a man"; "Always put cold cream on your face at night"; "A woman never tells her age. Be vague about dates." But I started to realize that there was something essential they weren't telling me; some reason why it was so difficult for us to feel at home with one another and with our lives. I was a rebel daughter, not knowing that my mother and my grandmother had each, before me, also been a rebel daughter.

Home for us, as black women, was never simple. In the distant past, our ancestors had held allegiance to lands as disparate as Europe and Africa, precolonized America and the island of Hispaniola. And in the United States, as if to echo the diaspora of our ancestors, home for us has consisted of different houses in different cities. Individually, we each traveled to distant places on a quest for home—my mother to Mexico, my grandmother on the vaudeville circuit, I to France, Spain, California.

Our foremothers had also struggled to feel at home in the world, but I didn't know this. Like most Americans, I had little concept of history in connection with my family—no idea how recently, in fact, we had become "Americans." Through four generations we had been called by a number of names: Indian, colored, Negro, black, African-American. . . . Yet, to my mind, none of these fits. Each merely serves to keep us from feeling truly at home in America. My grandmother and mother never talked about the past. My mother hated everything reminiscent of family history; she even refused to sleep in an antique bed that had been in the family for generations. My great-aunt died before I was old enough to ask her about her life, about *her* mother.

I knew very little about the three women I grew up with, and less about the women who came before them. In our family, the men's lives were well documented, but the women's were shrouded in mystery.

In 1973, I was struggling to balance marriage, motherhood, and a writing career in New York City. I was in my thirties and had three small boys. It was a hopeful time: women and black writers were coming to the forefront, and inspired by the women's movement, I decided to write an article for *Ms.* magazine about the women in my family. I remembered that my mother had once mentioned a diary written by her grandmother, Frances Anne Rollin—whom she had described as "an ancestor, a terrific woman, a writer." I wrote to her and asked her to send it.

From the moment I read the words Frances Anne Rollin wrote in Boston on January 1, 1868—"The year renews its birth today with all of its hopes and sorrows"—she became my beacon, the foremother who would finally share with me our collective past.

Born into a free family of color before the Civil War, my great-grandmother was an abolitionist and a feminist. She wrote about issues of race, class, and womanhood over a hundred years before me. I was enthralled but also puzzled. Why hadn't my mother told me about her while I was growing up? This question, with many others, sparked a search that went on for two decades. My children grew up during this time, and so did I.

I came to understand that it was the pride of family that kept secrets and told lies—the pride that told of the men and not the women, the fair-skinned and not the dark, the privileged and not the poor—which had kept me from home.

1

The Women in the House

511 FLORIDA AVENUE. THE address conjures tropical colors and ocean views, but there was actually a certain austerity about the narrow three-story row house in Washington, D.C. In the thirties, its front windows opened to the screech of metal against metal as the streetcars lurched and sparked their way down the sooty avenue. Its rear windows looked out on a tangle of faded back-alley porches and stairways—a landscape that seemed to me even as a child to contain all the unexpressed sadness of the neighborhood. And darkness reigned in between, accentuated by my great-aunt's insistence on painting the interior walls of the house brown. We, too, were varying shades of brown, and I can still see and feel us there, each with a certain weight and substance, yet somehow suspended in the murky interior.

In 1937, there were three women in the house, four with my arrival. A litany of resentments and grudges between my grandmother and my great-aunt had been placed on hold—my birth was, after all, a joyous occasion. We women, it seems in retrospect, constituted an inner sanctum, despite the presence of my father.

My great-aunt, Dr. Ionia Rollin Whipper—a staunch figure in Washington's black haute bourgeoisie—was Sister Onie to my mother and to the St. Luke's Episcopal Church Club women. She was Tant'Onie to my father (his shortened version of the Tante Onie she suggested) and just plain Onie to her brother, Leigh, and her closest women friends. But she was always Sistonie to me. More than just an aunt, she was a *great*-aunt, a force to be reckoned with.

My grandmother Virginia Wheeler, by contrast, was a breezy VA or Ginnie or even Ginger to her show-business friends. My father began calling her VV, which became Be-Be to my child's tongue. Be-Be was ideally suited to a career in show business. Five feet one, she had the compressed energy, the tight, lithe body, and the shapely legs of a dancer. Her fine curly hair was cut provocatively short, setting off her aquiline nose and high cheekbones, her pointy chin and almond-shaped eyes. She loved to gamble and drink beer, and had been dismayed to find that Sistonie, having long before taken an oath that alcohol would never pass her lips, had issued a decree forbidding any form of it in her house.

My mother, Leighla Frances Whipper Lewis, was by this time a graduate student in English at Howard University, drawn to the poetry of Byron and Milton, and president of the Stylus Literary Club. A small, delicate-looking woman in her early twenties, she had prominent eyes, a heart-shaped face, and skin called *café au lait* by her many admirers. There is a picture of her taken around the time of her marriage in which she looks so vulnerable that I cannot bear to look at it for very long. I see in her face the dreams she had, and in retrospect I fear for her. Yet I know that my mother is tough, tenacious, a survivor.

My father was Hylan Garnet Lewis, a young instructor of economics at Howard who switched to sociology after meeting E. Franklin Frazier there in 1935. He was a handsome man, with light chestnut-gray eyes inherited from his mother. Named after the black educator Henry Highland Garnet, he shortened his name to Hylan in high school. He would sometimes say that his initials, H.G.L., stood for "Happy Go Lucky." An excellent student—and with a talent, since childhood, for what were called "declamations"—he was a champion debater and orator at Virginia Union University. It was as a research assistant at Howard that he spotted my mother on campus.

After courting Leighla for two years, my father got up the courage to ask Sistonie for her adopted daughter's hand. By that time, though, my father knew that the formidable Dr. Whipper was well disposed toward him—once she had come upon the young couple embracing in the vestibule and, to my father's amazement, discreetly turned away.

The fact that Sistonie knew my father's family helped. My father's father, Harry Wythe Lewis, had been principal of the Garfield School in Washington. His grandfather on his mother's side, William A. Wells, Sr., had worked his way from being a porter on the Pullman cars to an appointment as private secretary to George D. Meiklejohn, assistant secretary of war under President Wilson, the first person of color to hold such an office. His son, William junior, was a colleague of Sistonie's, holding degrees in medicine, pharmacy, and law from Howard.

Gratified that Leighla was joining forces not only with a personable young man but with a well-thought-of Washington family, Sistonie gave her blessings.

After a St. Luke's wedding in the fall of 1935, my father continued to teach and my mother to work toward her master's. They lived frugally so they could attend shows at the nearby Howard Theater, where they listened to the music of Fats Waller, Duke Ellington, Cab Calloway, Fletcher Henderson, and Jelly Roll Morton. My mother got a job as a reporter with the *Washington Afro-American* and once landed an interview with Mary Pickford, in town to promote a film. Eventually Dr. Whipper invited my parents to live with her, both to keep her company and to help them make ends meet.

By 1937, the year of my birth, the worst of the Great Depression was over, but its aftermath lingered cloudlike over Washington and the house on Florida Avenue. It seemed to express itself in the shapes of buttons and the drape of fabrics worn by the women in the house. It seemed to lurk in the linoleum that lay beneath the rugs, and in the cheaper cuts of meat that made their way from the butcher's to the kitchen. Yet among some politically active blacks, including my mother and father, there was a sense of cautious optimism. President Roosevelt's New Deal was gathering momentum, and there was informal representation to policymakers via the so-called Black Cabinet, which operated through the influence of Eleanor Roosevelt and Mary McLeud Bethune. It was the first time since Reconstruction that such a feeling of possibility existed for blacks in America.

*   *   *

Mine was an easy birth—my mother wrote me years later—because of her "good hips." She named me Carole because Carol meant "song of joy," and the added *e* evoked Carole Lombard, the glamorous blond movie star. My middle name, Ione, was a concession to family, a simpler, more modern version of Sistonie's "Ionia."

In the hectic mornings after my arrival, my grandmother would watch in astonishment, yet with a certain amount of respect, as my great-aunt made her descent from the upper floor in a mist of powder and perfume. She would be magnificently dressed and coiffed, her hat poised at a stylish angle, gloves in hand, her pocketbook containing the requisite white handkerchief, her ample bosom replete with pearls.

This daily vision was all the more distressing to Be-Be since she was doing all of the washing, cleaning, cooking, and caring for my mother and me. "Your aunt was never dressed for any kind of housework," Be-Be told me, adding with a touch of pride, "I was used to it." And Sistonie seemed to expect it of her, even though there was a hired girl who helped with the housekeeping.

My great-aunt's imperious manner with my grandmother may have owed something to the fact that she was a doctor accustomed to giving orders and seeing them carried out by a staff of nurses. She was, in fact, on her way to Freedman's Hospital on those regal mornings. She had even taken a pediatrics refresher course in order to be prepared for any eventuality concerning me. (My mother, wanting to preserve her independence, had opted not to have her aunt deliver me, but Sistonie and Be-Be were both present at my birth at nearby Carson's Hospital, and my great-aunt was the first to cradle me in her arms.) Be-Be resented the fact that Sistonie's pronouncements about my welfare seemed to come down from on high. The source of my "six-week colic" was declared to be the richness of my mother's milk, and I was put on a formula. Small doses of bicarbonate of soda and cod-liver oil were dispensed with precision, according to Sistonie's instructions.

Perhaps Sistonie could not help but treat my grandmother as a wayward girl; she was used to working with unmarried mothers who didn't know how to take care of their children or themselves and who had no access to public assistance in the segregated Washington system. (The Florence Crittenden Home was limited to white women only.) Sistonie had taken some of them into her own home to teach them cooking and hygiene; the girls often did housework as repayment. Her manner with them was stern, yet her compassion was real.

Sistonie had difficulty extending the professional compassion she showed strangers to personal warmth for my grandmother. Perhaps she considered her commanding manner therapeutic. After all, even though Sistonie's beloved brother Leigh had had an equal part in the matter, Be-Be—like Leigh—had been in the theater.

Sistonie was very much a product of her times. Many middle- and upper-class blacks, emulating the Victorian mores of prosperous whites, looked askance at what they considered the immoral world of the theater. And for blacks bent on disproving whites' myths about our race—that blacks are loose, immoral, uncivilized, even animals—such distinctions were that much more important. It seemed necessary to be even more conscious of propriety than whites in order to prove good social standing—a propriety that often became confused with skin color or free birth. Many Washington professional and social organizations fostered a class snobbery based more on lightness of skin than on any particular merit. And many—Sistonie among them—spoke proudly of having descended from free families of color, families who had never been slaves.

Be-Be made it clear to me many years later that she was more bitter about the discrimination she and her fellow actors had received at the hands of other colored people than that which she had experienced from whites. "It was worse than Jim Crow," she said, still bristling with anger. Some of the better black boardinghouses in Washington turned actors away, and even at Howard, members of her touring company had been made to eat in a separate room from the faculty.

Despite the animosity between them, however, my grandmother and my great-aunt had a few things in common besides those that brought them together that May—their love for my mother and the desire to be there for the birth of her first child. Both, for example, were aware of the value of charm, and neither was averse to using it to mask an underlying iron will. Both had sudden, flaring tempers, though they expressed them in different ways: Sistonie was slow to anger and usually outwardly composed—until the moment she descended on the unsuspecting like a cyclone; Be-Be was quick and impatient, proud of her mercurial nature. "When I take a notion," she would say then and for many decades to come, "I just get up and go!"

Yet as hard as it was to share a house with Dr. Whipper, Be-Be had no intention of leaving 511 Florida Avenue before she was certain my mother and I no longer needed her. Though she bristled, she put up with all Sistonie's rules and regulations. Still, there was a limit to her patience. One day, as the Washington heat grew unbearable, my grandmother, exhausted from cooking and caring for the baby, dropped everything, hurried down the street to the grocery store, and bought two bottles of ice-cold beer.

Back at the house, she sat down at the table with one of the bottles and a tall glass. She kicked her shoes off and settled back for a refreshing drink. A few minutes later Sistonie came home and stood, frozen with disapproval, in the doorway. Her eyebrows arched, her jaw tightened. She opened her mouth to speak; but my grandmother's gaze was steadfast, her expression implacable. Wisely, Sistonie held her tongue. "Good evening, Virginia," she said evenly, and turned to go up the stairs.

"Good evening, Dr. Whipper," Be-Be called after her pleasantly, refilling her glass.

2

Wishing

IT SEEMS I WAS ALWAYS looking for my mother—waiting for her return. I had started traveling among the three women in my family at an early age, accompanied and—by the time I was eight—alone, on trains, subways, and buses. Later I remembered those years by associating them with years of school: I was living with Sistonie in Washington during part of second grade, and with Be-Be in Saratoga during the rest of second and all of fourth, fifth, and seventh grades. I was with my mother in New York City for first, third, sixth, and eighth grades and through high school.

Of course, while it was all happening, it was a collage of sensations and events: a snatch of music coming from an open window (years later I identified it as the Grieg Concerto), the reassuring yellow of a banana my mother left beside my bed one morning when we were staying at someone else's house, the rush of freedom as I dashed headlong down the glorious corridor of trees at the zoo. I remember, in particular, sitting in the tub at 511 Florida Avenue, my favorite place in the old house. I was five or six years old and visiting

Sistonie for a week, a month, a season. I wasn't quite sure. I was counting on the now-time of the tub to get me through. I watched, fascinated, as the water swirled down the drain, going round and round as I twisted a gold ring with a green stone on my finger, wishing and wishing and wishing for my mother.

The water was gone, and I was still wishing in the damp of the tub, when Sistonie came in. Her queenly presence seemed to precede her. In fact, there in the bathroom the scents of her sweet-smelling powders, emanating from a dresser drawer, always made her seem close by.

"What are you doing?" Sistonie asked, as she saw me sitting there in the empty tub. I told her, and her voice came lower, closer, piercing through my longing with surprising tenderness.

"Sometimes," she replied, "if you wish for something hard enough, it will come true."

What had Sistonie wished for? I find myself wondering. Had she ever wished for her own mother, only to have her suddenly appear? I never thought to ask.

Sistonie graduated from Howard Medical School in 1903, one of four women in her class; Howard was, in fact, the first American medical school to open its doors to women. In its early years, black and white women came from all over the country to study there. But unlike those of her colleagues who used their diplomas only to improve their salaries or social status, Sistonie—who had already spent ten years teaching in the segregated Washington schools—chose to practice.

After her graduation, Sistonie interned in predominantly male-staffed black hospitals, then became resident physician at Collegiate Institute of West Virginia, and later physician of girls at Tuskegee Institute. During these years, Sistonie kept diaries when she could. Two have come down to me: a leather-bound book titled *Day by Day: A Perpetual Diary*, kept intermittently between 1920 and 1929; and a spiritual diary dating from the late 1930s. The spiritual diary begins: *What it means to me to be God guided: Some say guidance is direct thinking. Some say it is the practical application of "Thy Will be done." Some say it is 90% hard thinking and 10% inspiration.*

The perpetual diary documents some very worldly difficulties: *June '22—I am very melancholy today. A note demanding 5 hours extra work is about to come to Drs. Dibble and Whipper. I am asking for afternoon off as soon as note arrives. My head is turned toward home today. . . .*

In the mid-1920s, Sistonie traveled through the South as an assistant medical officer for the Children's Bureau of the U.S. Department of Labor, instructing midwives. As she lectured on the rudiments of cleanliness and methods of taking care of mothers and babies under less than ideal circumstances, she often found herself in towns where many blacks still lived in conditions much like those under slavery. Some had never seen a doctor, let alone a woman doctor, and sometimes she had trouble making people believe she was one. And there were other indignities, some of which she confided to her journal.

Went to Waycross for blotting paper, while there, the clerk went to the storeroom for it, a white woman, presumably a relative of the proprietor, came to me—said, "Auntie, are you being waited on?" I stared at her, then replied, "Where did you get that Auntie stuff? You're old enough to know that I'm not related to you."

May 11, 1928, Haven Home for Girls M.E. Went to Independence in search of midwives. Called to give registrar several birth certificates. He came on porch followed by his wife. I told him I would like to speak to him. He told me to go around to the back. I repeated, thinking he didn't understand.

On another day she wrote: *was given a bed in Bay City—dirty bedding. I didn't find out until late, then I tore open two flannelette gowns and a silk slip which I used for sheets and a pillowcase. . . .*

While at Tuskegee Institute, an all-black institution, my great-aunt suffered from the tension caused by the Ku Klux Klan's frequent threats to come on campus. My mother retains a vivid image of Sistonie, who was plagued by migraines, rushing in the door to her on-campus quarters and throwing herself on the bed with a cry.

I still find my child self emerging from the shadowy rooms of Sistonie's house, pausing in the vestibule, where light filtered through the curtained glass panel of the front door. I would always look up the long railing that stretched toward the second and third floors, and usually Miss Reid or Mrs. Nelson, our elderly roomers, would be there. Miss Reid might have her hand on the third-floor railing, ready to enter her room. Mrs. Nelson might just have reached the top stair.

I never saw them anywhere else; they existed for me solely on the stairs. Each had something special to say to me: Mrs. Nelson, the grayer and stouter of the sisters (did it have something to do with the Mrs.? I thought it did), would intone, "This old knee," as she strained upward with her cane. And Miss Reid, thin and white-haired, more lighthearted than her sister, would call out in a high, bell-like tone, "Carole, you're a case!"

From the window ledge of Sistonie's office I could survey her big rolltop desk: its slatted hood, the loose paper, calendars, and notebooks strewn across it, prescription pads on which I wrote my own fake prescriptions for cod-liver oil, its long-stemmed telephone with tulip-shaped speaker.

One day I eavesdropped as Sistonie spoke on the telephone, her voice rising and falling. She was more excited than I'd ever heard her. The day before, she'd encountered a man downstairs. "I took one look at him and I knew it was Catoe," she cried. "You know, the robber who's been terrorizing the neighborhood."

She told of how she'd stood her ground, never taking her eyes off the robber, while she called to the top of the stairs: *"John! John!"* Then she watched as the man turned and fled, leaving the door banging behind him. Sistonie laughed heartily on the phone, congratulating herself for her presence of mind. The truth was, she said, that she'd been alone in the house at the time.

Often I'd accompany Sistonie on her house calls. We drove in her Chevrolet coupe, her brown leather bag on the seat between us or in back. I'd try to memorize her hand signals—the crooked arm for a right turn, straight for left—and I'd watch as she gripped the tall knobbed handle and efficiently shifted gears. I took note of the way she worked the pedals with her sensible black shoes, her legs clad in the thick beige stockings I'd watched her put on at home. She'd park somewhere on a quiet street, and I'd wait outside while she went in to care for her patients.

Or we'd go to Dr. Hillyar's house, where I would wait quietly in the parlor while my aunt and her best friend talked in the other room, behind heavy rolling doors. Breathing shallowly, as if to make the time last, I'd sit amidst a profusion of large glass bell jars filled with stuffed birds and fake foliage. The shiny surfaces of the glass dimly reflected the light from the windows behind me, presenting a dimin-

utive view of the room. Peering in, I could identify lacy lamp cover-
ings, tables, and cabinets filled with bric-a-brac, upholstered chairs
and stools, and occasionally something mysterious I hadn't noticed in
the real world of the room. My great-aunt never seemed to stay at Dr.
Hillyar's long enough for me to absorb all I wanted there. All I
remember of Dr. Hillyar, who was a prominent Washington phar-
macist, are the piercing eyes I glimpsed behind her thick glasses, her
mustache, and her low, gravelly voice.

"Come on, Carole, get ready. We're going to the country," Sistonie
would say, and the next thing I knew, we'd be driving out on the long
road to the Ionia Rollin Whipper Home for Unwed Mothers, on its
three and a half acres in the southeastern quarter of Washington. But
to me it was just "the country," or "the Home," and driving there was
the best of being with my great-aunt. Once, as we sped up and down
the ribbons of roads, dark blue in the summer sun, I asked about the
rippling rivulets of water down at the bottom of each steep incline,
and learned the word "mirage" as Sistonie sped matter-of-factly
through it.

In "the country" I wandered down by the duck pond behind the
house where the girls with the big bellies lived, and studied yellow
butterflies. In the mornings at breakfast I would listen to the girls
laughing and giggling—unless one of them had "gone" during the
night. Then the others would be discussing the event in hushed
tones. It seemed to be some kind of honor, as though they were
playing a special game and the one who "went" during the night was
"it." I wanted to be included, and sometimes the girls looked at me in
a special way, as though wondering how much to let me in on their
news.

On the same property there was a musty little building where
Sistonie taught me to sew. "Here, Carole, your eyes are good, thread
this needle for me," she'd say, as she worked on something I could
never identify—curtains, maybe, or a tablecloth. She'd stop every
now and then to teach me the stitches on a spare piece of cloth.
Perhaps she could have told me about her mother then, as it must
have been her mother who had taught her to sew. But Sistonie was
always silent as we worked.

In the evenings after school when I was in second grade, Sistonie would help me with my times tables. My mother had left me in Washington for a two-week visit, intending to have me join her again in New York, only to have Sistonie inform her that I was enrolled in school and "might as well see out the term." Meanwhile, my great-aunt tried, with little success, to make me understand that zero times any number was still zero. I sat puzzling out the numbers, unable to understand why they were of any importance. Sistonie would lose her temper and yell, "No! Three times zero is not three, it is *zero!*" Then, to my relief, she would give up and we would go to sleep in our separate beds in her room.

Sometimes I came home from school for lunch, letting myself into the house with a key that hung on a string around my neck. One day I brought a friend back with me. I led her through the vestibule into Sistonie's dimly lighted examination room and stood silently beside her as she stared wide-eyed at the imposing leather-and-chrome examining table.

"My aunt is a *doctor*," I said quietly.

Sistonie's patients were all women. "I don't treat men," I'd hear her say when an occasional unsuspecting male appeared at her doorstep; the interloper would be swiftly dispatched to a doctor of his own sex down the street. I had no idea what Sistonie did to women or for them; I only knew it had something to do with the bittersweet medicinal odor that my friend and I were breathing in. I knew that it had to do with the boxes and bottles in the cabinets, the needles and the rubber gloves, the cotton and the alcohol, the shining instruments gleaming in the semidarkness. And whatever it was, it was so frightening and yet so wonderful that I was never able to think about it for very long.

When I felt we had absorbed all the essence of the room we could bear, I led my friend back through the living room, where Sistonie stopped my twirling around on Sundays, making me hurry up for church at St. Luke's. I led her into the kitchen, where the back windows opened onto the alleyway. For a moment we stood there looking at the rickety wooden back porches and stairs, the hanging laundry, the garbage cans. But I had something else to show her. There was only one interesting thing in the kitchen, unless Sistonie was making a cake or tollhouse cookies, which only happened at night, long after the last patient had gone home.

I reached up to the shelf and carefully took down the Morton's

Salt box. There on its side was the familiar picture of the little blond girl with the umbrella. She was taking a walk in the rain, her own Morton's Salt box tucked under her arm, pouring out a steady stream of salt. And on her box of salt was another little girl strolling in the rain, with yet another box of salt. And on into infinity.

I did not understand the zero times tables, but infinity was within my grasp. I could still look at the picture and get inside it, the way I had the first time my mother showed it to me. I could feel the way the box under my arm got lighter and lighter as the salt poured out and melted on the wet ground behind me. "That is Carole," I told her, repeating the words carefully, exactly the way my mother had said them. I waited expectantly as my friend looked at the blond girl on the box and then back at me, at my brown skin—almost the same color as Sistonie's, a real brown, a true brown—and my dark-brown braids, so dark that they looked black.

"That's you?"

"Yes," I replied, with assurance. "That is 'Carole.'"

3

Air Sandwiches

WE SAT, ONE NIGHT, MY mother and I, waiting in the dark in a car parked on a country road somewhere in Alabama. I must have been sleeping, and found myself suddenly awakened by the cessation of motion, the words being spoken, the opening and closing of the car door. My father had just gotten out, and I could see a blur of brightness where he had gone, not far away. There was a terrible feeling inside the car. My mother was crying. I was sitting on her lap, close as I could be.

"He didn't want us to come in with him," my mother told me sometime during my teenaged years. My father, by then a prominent sociologist, elaborated, telling a story of wanting to spare us all some racial slight. He was just getting out to buy us something to drink, a bottle of Coca-Cola, perhaps, and she had wanted to go in with him. He told of how conscious he was that we were all of us black down there in the heart of Alabama in 1942, and on a dark country road; he thought we were safer in the car.

At the beginning of our stay in Talladega, the college put us up temporarily in a dorm. We ate at the college dining hall across the street, but sometimes I would feel hungry long after it was possible to get something to eat. I would sit up in bed and complain of hunger, the humid night air hot around me, a bright light overhead.

"Here, have this," my mother said. Her hand was reaching toward me, offering something. But there was nothing in it.

"Take it," she coaxed. "It's an air sandwich."

I reached to accept what was offered, noticing that she was munching, chewing heartily on one of her own. Soon I was chewing thoughtfully, looking at her with curiosity—aware that I was humoring her and that nothing was going to be as simple as I had thought.

That year in Alabama was the last year of my parents' marriage. "We were just too young," and "We didn't know what we were doing," I've heard them say on the rare occasions when, as an adult, I've seen them together.

A year after I was born, my father had accepted a grant for doctoral studies at the University of Chicago and had left my mother and me behind in Washington, where money was tight. My mother began talking to a lawyer about ending the marriage.

"Somewhat of a loner, in terms of making it," my father called himself when I asked him about it. He had wanted to do well so that we could all prosper. But even though my mother and father were together again between 1940 and 1942, that early separation apparently put a lasting strain on the relationship.

My mother later described to me the part of her marriage that became most intolerable to her—my father's moods. They would be sitting at the breakfast table in Talladega on what seemed a perfectly ordinary morning, and he would be reading, as usual; she grew to hate that. But the worst was his silence, which made her feel as if something terrible had happened, as if something had gone wrong with the whole world. The fact that something *had* gone wrong with the whole world, that a world war was imminent, did not make things easier. Even my grandmother, who always loved my father and urged my mother to stick it out, visited them once and admitted that the cloud of gloom that surrounded my father was indeed hard to bear.

My mother once mentioned calling my father on the telephone, long after they were divorced, and hearing him answer in a tone of voice that was open and excited, full of possibility, only to hear it turn flat and serious when he found out she was on the line. Whom had he been expecting to call? she wondered. Who would be the recipient of all that good feeling? She thought back then to their marriage and realized that *that* was a perfect example of what was wrong. It was that openness she had wanted, that feeling of being included in his life.

My mother and I left Talladega on a night train. My father returned to the empty house after putting us on the train and found two small dolls I'd been sleeping with, left behind under the pillow. He kept them, carrying them with him wherever he moved for forty years. Recently he gave them back to me—the cracked naked white baby doll and the little stuffed panda—and I only vaguely recognized them. But I imagine how it must have felt to awaken on the train in the morning, arriving in a whole new world without them.

I took the dolls home and washed them and tried to make them look less sad. I wrapped the doll in its doll blanket. The panda's eye fell out, and I replaced it with a shiny earring. For a long while I couldn't really look at them without getting upset. Though I couldn't really remember the night train, several times I did dream of being on a train. My mother was often on the train, too, but we were never headed for the same destination.

After we left my father, my mother and I went to live with my grandmother in New York at 18–20 St. Nicholas Place, a big old apartment building at the edge of Sugar Hill, the stylish middle-class black neighborhood above 145th Street. Lively and cosmopolitan, Sugar Hill was full of show folk, intellectuals, and sports figures. Kenneth and Mamie Clark, lifelong friends of my father and mother, who would become world renowned for their work with black children, were studying for their doctorates at Columbia and living in the apartment above ours. (Kenneth would make history in 1954 as the psychologist in the case of Brown versus the Board of Education of Topeka, Kansas, who showed that segregation was harmful to both black and white children. Subsequently the Supreme Court outlawed segregation in U.S. schools.) Harry Wills, the heavyweight boxer, lived up the street.

I was five years old, and it was wartime. We had blackout curtains on the windows, and Be-Be and my mother were mad because their friend Mr. Luckey's song "Moonlight Cocktails" was edged off the radio *Hit Parade* by "Deep in the Heart of Texas." Jobs in the Broadway chorus lines were growing scarcer, and Be-Be was often "on the road," waiting tables in the restaurant car for the New Haven Railroad. There are pictures of Be-Be in her perky uniform and cap, standing at attention at her station. But her stories of the road were filled with verbal battles with cranky cooks and demanding customers, battles that Be-Be always won. "Don't mess with Virginia" seemed to be the rule among her colleagues, and her customers soon learned to stay in line as well. I learned the word "anticipate" early from the punch line of one of Be-Be's tiffs with a man who wanted his toast crusts trimmed. "Am I just supposed to *anticipate* your every whim?" she'd said to him.

With a combination of her earnings from the railroad and money she won playing cards, shooting craps, and betting horses, Be-Be finally scraped up enough money to live in Saratoga, her "old stomping ground," as she called it. Her boss on the railroad had always let her reserve August—the time of the Saratoga races—for her vacation, holding it for her no matter what. "Virginia's got to go to Saratoga!" he'd say if anyone complained.

When Be-Be moved to Saratoga, she gave up her apartment, and my mother and I became roomers at 555 Edgecombe Avenue, next door to Joe Louis, who was then heavyweight champion of the world. But both my mother and Be-Be soon regretted giving up the apartment on St. Nicholas Place. My mother was looking for work as an actress, going to auditions, writing songs and trying to publish them. She took editorial jobs to pay our expenses, but money was always short. With contributions from my father and help from Be-Be, she took a series of rooms in other people's apartments. Essentially, it seems to me now, she was homeless in New York City.

During the times I was with her in these rooms, we both experienced the singularly uncomfortable feeling of not being in our own home; the constant fear of inadvertently doing something to provoke the disapproval of the person whose home it was. No matter how nice the people who owned the apartments, it was always a strain.

In an attempt to shelter me from the arguments going on in one of these places, my mother made arrangements for me to stay with a woman who lived in a nearby building. The woman's nephew lived there too—a boy who seemed quite old to me but must have been only twelve or thirteen. He seemed fine at first and I welcomed his interest in me. But soon, when I was alone in the house with him after school, he began to torment me, throwing pebbles that he found in the window plants, twisting my wrists, forcing me to take down my underpants and lie on his aunt's bed so that he could try to "do it."

Unsuccessful in his attempts to penetrate me, he hit upon the idea that I should come down the hall at night to his room once his aunt had fallen asleep. If I didn't go, he said, he would tell his aunt on me. For several nights I lay in a cold sweat on the couch, unable to move. I couldn't sleep, and staying awake was terrifying. I never figured out that he wouldn't tell his aunt what he wanted me to do; all I knew was that whatever happened, I would suffer. It would be my fault. I would see day dawning when I finally drifted off to sleep, shortly before it was time to get up for school. The next day I'd watch the boy's aunt fearfully for signs that he had "told."

One day the woman seemed to take pity on me. Perhaps she noticed that I didn't look well rested, or maybe she sensed what was going on. In any case, she said I could sleep in her bed if I wanted to, and I gratefully accepted.

It wasn't long after that that I went to live with Be-Be. I was glad to get to Saratoga, where I could let my secret sense of shame roll itself up inside me. But I wasn't the same anymore. We were staying over on Grand Avenue for a while, in a house my grandmother's friend Sammy Burke was living in; Be-Be didn't have a house of her own yet. I would go down by the railroad tracks that passed the house and bounce my rubber ball and talk with the retarded man who pushed a rag cart around town. His language was confused, but I took everything he managed to stammer out as a code and struggled to translate it. Things about games and something about the sky.

Time passed uneventfully until one day I entered the house to find my tormentor's aunt standing in the living room, talking with my grandmother. I was stunned into silence, but she immediately started teasing me, saying something about knowing all my secrets because I talked in my sleep.

Talked in my sleep? I had never thought of that. I didn't even know it was possible. Could I have told? I looked at the women, my mind racing, wondering if she knew—and if she did, wondering if she had told my grandmother. But Be-Be was laughing and the woman was laughing. Hating her, I ran back outside.

From Saratoga, I wrote my mother cheery letters, but usually I mentioned how much I missed her. "Be-Be and I are doing fine, but I have been getting very lonesome and wish to see you. Please try to write because it gets pretty lonely even with Be-Be here, and anyway it feels important to get mail and say have I any mail."

I missed the air sandwiches and the days in Talladega, when we would collect acorns and paint them gold and silver to make necklaces and bracelets.

Once, for some grown-up reason unknown to me, my mother and father and I were momentarily reunited at Be-Be's house. I felt we were all on the verge of some change. *Would it be possible for them to be married again?* I watched them emerge from the house into the dazzling light of the snow and asked them to sit on my sled. When they complied, I grasped the ropes and began to pull them slowly forward, noticing that they were big children, really, gliding grace-fully at my bidding. And I felt strong, stronger than any ordinary child, strong enough to pull their combined weight. I listened to the odd sound of their laughter, together with the familiar sound of the runners of my trusty sled over the hard-packed snow.

In recent years, I've found that there was something else bothering my mother during her years with my father—something that made his dark moods all the more troubling. His mother, Ella Wells Lewis, had died of an illness under circumstances that were always myste-rious to me and surrounded with an aura of shame. No one ever spoke of her. Later I learned that Ella Wells Lewis had died of cancer at St. Elizabeth's psychiatric hospital in Washington where her brother had admitted her because of their ability to care for cancer patients. She had always been prone to severe headaches, but after the birth of her last child, her illness intensified, and she would gather up the little ones—my father's brother Harry, a toddler, and his sister Katie, an infant—and roam the city, seemingly "lost" yet somehow at home in her own world, stopping sometimes to visit relatives or friends. They would take her into their parlors and, as soon as possible, gently guide her home.

In the back of my mother's mind, was a recurring thought that he might have inherited his mother's mental illness and that one day it would surface full force.

4

In the Kitchen with Be-Be

"THE LESS SAID ABOUT ME, the better. Just leave me out of it," Be-Be would say when I first began to ask her questions about her life. We were sitting on the green rockers on the front porch in Saratoga, looking out through the screen windows, past the hedges toward Case Street—Be-Be's favorite view and mine. It was early summer. Be-Be had filled the window boxes, and there was a big peach-colored begonia beside the screen door.

"Oh, Be-Be, please!" I pleaded. The pet name I invented for her as a child had stuck. Virginia was her real name—or so I thought at the time. In fact, her given name was Eva, which she now used as a middle name. I wasn't sure how old she was; she had set her age back so many times by then that everyone had a different figure. Records of her birth certificate were missing so there was no formal proof.

My exasperation with Be-Be was familiar from the days when I was growing up in Saratoga and she would tell me: "Don't run so fast. You'll trip over something and fall down and hurt your knee," or "Watch out you don't slip at the top of the stairs on an old shoe and fall down and stub your big toe." It was almost comical how specific she could get about the details of those imagined accidents. Even though, as a child, I had my share of scrapes and bruises, it was really Be-Be who would have already fallen down those stairs, or tripped and hurt her knee, because of her natural impatience to get on with things. She was the one who caught cold every winter because she would rush out into the deep Saratoga snow without her coat, chasing after the trash man or the paper boy. And she was the one who once almost poked out her eye with a cooking fork in her haste to rip open a package.

"You work too hard," she was always telling me when I grew up. "If you go too fast, you can't last." Yet she was the one who never stopped working; who, in her eighties, could be found tarring the latest leak up on the roof. (The coal man, arriving out front with a truckload for the old furnace, had advised her once, "Virginia, I can see everything you've got," and she liked to laugh about that.) Whenever I came to visit, Be-Be would exclaim, "What's all this you're carrying?" and I'd have to fight her to keep her from carrying my heavy bags.

Be-Be didn't seem to care about herself that much, knowing, I suppose, that she could usually effect miraculous self-healing with the help of a green jar of pungent Mentholatum. "I swear by it," she'd say emphatically. "It can heal just about anything. I'd almost put it in my eye." Mentholatum, combined with a strong hot toddy at night or a glass of sherry, could pull her through almost any disability. She didn't put much stock in other kinds of medicine. With these same tools and sheer willpower, she could heal us too—my mother, me, and later my three boys.

It was Be-Be, wearing some simple skirt and blouse and a pair of old sneakers, who taught me how to ride a bike during my childhood days in Saratoga. She and my grandfather were as far from the standard image of grandparents as they could be. Be-Be was fair-skinned and curly-headed, short and stylish in pumps and angled hats when she took me to the racetrack. My actor grandfather, on the other hand, had deeply dark skin and was dramatically tall and lean. He dressed elegantly in dark colors and wore wide-brimmed hats and thin, droopy bow ties. I described him to a few of my friends as a black John Carradine. You had to make an appointment if you wanted to see him. I used to like to tell people that.

My grandmother had never, to my knowledge, lived with my grandfather—I could hardly imagine them together—and she always kept any conversation about him to a bare minimum. Both she and my mother would visibly stiffen whenever he was mentioned, and I saw him only occasionally. But once in a while, when I was living with my mother in New York, I would come home from school to find him sitting in the living room talking with my mother or my grandmother, his deep voice and actor's presence taking up all the space in the room.

He was often talking about jewelry, discussing various stones and settings and a jeweler in Harlem named Jack, whom he trusted. As far as I was concerned, that seemed to be his principal connection to us. He arranged for me to go see Jack once to get a special ring with imitation stones. These, my grandfather said, would be replaced with diamonds once I was older, but I lost the ring before that could happen. However, at twelve I had my ears pierced in order to be eligible for his gift of diamond chips. I liked the earrings a lot, but the piercing was painful, and under the guise of an examination, the doctor had fondled my fledgling breasts. I went home feeling ashamed and abused—not exalted and grown up, as I'd expected—and stored this event in my file of information never to be told. I concentrated instead on the things I was supposed to be proud of. I was proud of my odd, glamorous grandparents and their quirky ways. But I suspect now that their very glamour kept me from the people they truly were.

Although her life had certainly *been* glamorous, Be-Be didn't exactly fit that description as she sat there on the porch beside me in 1973. She was wearing a floral-print cotton dress that was a little too tight and was ripped on the side because she had impatiently struggled to get into it. Over that was a white chef's apron, which was, like most of the things Be-Be wore during the daytime, somewhat the worse for wear. When she stood up to go inside, I noticed that her slip was showing. Her sneakers were worn down at the back. But this was her "working around the house and garden" self. There was always something for her to fix, something for her to plant—petunias, ferns, primroses, impatiens—and some kitchen duty waiting, and she wouldn't put on her good clothes for that. This didn't prevent her from scrutinizing my clothing carefully through the years, making me bristle with indignation or wince with hurt. "You're wearing that old thing again?" she'd ask. "Don't you have anything better?"

Waiting in her closet were a blond mink jacket and hat, which she would always try to get me to wear for special occasions. "You always want to look nice, you know. Let people know you have something." She also had a couple of special suits and some dresses my mother had brought up from Mexico. Her perfumes, Chanel No. 22 and Toujours Moi, awaited special daytime activities: a trip to the track, an occasional lunch out in the country, a wedding, or a friend's funeral. For nights at the Spuyten Duyvil—the restaurant she created in Saratoga—she'd "pull it all up" by donning one of the Mexican dresses, running the Coty powder puff across her face, and adding a dash of deep-red lipstick.

I followed my grandmother into the cool of the house, carrying the potatoes I'd been helping to peel. She carried a bowl of string beans and her favorite long-stemmed glass, still half filled with Amontillado sherry. We moved through the living room, crowded with assorted fifties furniture much too big for it, through the small middle room, where her oak bed was set up, through the room that served as pantry in summer and family dining room during the rest of the year. From this room an open door gave onto the empty restaurant-bar. We could see the barstools, the stocked bar with gladiolas on it, and part of the big round table at the back. From the pantry we passed into the kitchen, the heart of the house.

I sat down at the old enameled table, which, like everything else, took up too much space. You always had to maneuver around it to get to the sink or the stove. I had a big red notebook then, a three-ring binder, for my talks with my grandmother, my mother, and my grandfather. There was, as well, a section for my ongoing journal. I opened the book to Be-Be's section, while my grandmother busied herself at one of the two stoves along the back wall—one a professional stove for the restaurant, the other a combination gas and coal-burning stove for family cooking. She was preparing macaroni and cheese, ham, string beans, and potatoes for dinner much later in the day.

It was embarrassing to be asking Be-Be questions when she clearly put more importance on the day's dinner than on my research. She'd often call me early in the morning at my New York loft, and I would talk to her about whatever was important to me at the time: a poetry reading that was coming up, perhaps, or a new writing assignment. "But what are you fixing for dinner?" she'd ask.

I tried to coax my grandmother into talking by evoking the details of her life that I knew. I knew that as a child in West Virginia, she had always wanted to know what was on the other side of their mountain. The image had stuck with me since I was a child. When I sang "The bear went over the mountain to see what he could see," it was always Be-Be I saw in my mind's eye—a curly-haired little girl, barefoot, with a broad-brimmed hat and a loose-fitting dress. I saw her deciding to go over the mountain, just as she'd told me she'd done, then standing at the top looking out over a vast mountain range, finding that there were yet more mountains to climb. "I'd try another day, another mountain," she said when I asked her how that had felt.

And because her cooking was so important in my life, I knew that Be-Be had started making her delicious biscuits when she was just a little girl. I knew that in West Virginia they always had fresh buttermilk, and barrels and barrels of butter. "I hate people who are stingy with butter," Be-Be would say. She always slathered her pancakes with butter while they were still cooking on the grill, drenched the stack with melted butter afterward. "Give that child some butter on those pancakes!" she'd cry, or "Butter those biscuits while they're hot!"

The older she got, the more butter Be-Be used, as though it would ease children's quarreling, my mother's discontent, my discontent. "I don't see why you can't stay here," Be-Be would say to my mother or to me. "Settle down in Saratoga. I don't see why you have to be running around to the other side of the world."

I would remind my grandmother that I had tried living in Saratoga. And my mother would tell her, "I have no friends here. It's different for you. There's Miss Margaret and Biddie. You can play cards. There's nothing for me to do here in the winter."

"Mmph," Be-Be would say. But she never gave up thinking that we would change our minds.

My mother and Be-Be had other running tiffs, like whether we should have potatoes or rice for dinner. Be-Be was partial to potatoes, part of her West Virginia heritage. My mother loved rice, a staple of the Creole cooking she'd eaten while growing up with Sistonie. She tended to like dishes like okra and rice, Spanish omelets, assorted shellfish, and hot, exotic spices. Be-Be didn't care much for fish of any kind and rarely used garlic. What was food for the soul for one was bland or distasteful to the other. Be-Be started making both rice and potatoes whenever my mother was present. When we were alone, she'd just make potatoes and comment, "I like potatoes better with chicken, don't you agree?" And my mother would murmur when Be-Be was out of earshot, "I don't see how anyone can eat anything but *rice* with lamb, don't you agree?" This was too serious an issue for me to take sides.

Once or twice, as a child, I found myself asking an oddly piercing question: "But, Mommy, who is *your* mother?" I would have been looking at my mother, trying to figure it all out. . . . Let's see now, she is my mother, she really is my mother. And Be-Be is . . . well, she's Be-Be. But who is my mother's mother?

I'd start remembering the answer even before she could reply. But in the meantime my mother's eyes would narrow. Intuitively, I knew I wasn't really supposed to ask direct questions—certainly not this one. After a pause, my mother would reply, "Why, Be-Be, of course."

"Oh yes, of course. I forgot for a minute," I'd say, averting my eyes and puzzling about why I'd forgotten. My grandmother seemed more like my mother than my mother did, and particularly as I grew older, my mother seemed a lot like a sister to me.

Yet since Sistonie had mothered my mother from the age of four on, she and Be-Be had come to each other again quite late, when my mother was in her late teens. They were close and not close. Ironically, the past history of separation between them had become their bond. Both of them felt, I think, that Be-Be still had mothering to do, years to make up for. Unconsciously I must have sensed what was true, in a way—that my mother and I were growing up together, and Be-Be was a mother to us both.

Be-Be slipped the ham into the oven. "There," she said. "Now it can be told!" This didn't mean she was ready to talk to me. It was one of her old expressions, meaning she could breathe easier once the ham was cooking. "We always had a ham," she liked to say.

I thought of the proud tone in her voice as she placed large orders with the butcher. When there was a ham in the house, Be-Be felt more secure, no matter what was going wrong: whether she was trying to scrape together the money for the liquor license, or whether she'd discover another hole in the roof, or whether she hadn't heard from my mother because of the impossible Mexican mail. I could always imagine the thick slabs of ham they must have eaten in West Virginia, and I could sense the shadowy shapes of the pigs Be-Be told me were kept "out back." I knew Be-Be's grandmother and grandfather had let her do just about anything she wanted to do. "I was just a little lump of gold, come down from heaven," she said. "Nothin' but a little lump of gold."

But Be-Be, as far as I remembered, had never told me her mother's name, and there was just about everything else that I didn't know about her life.

"Your great-aunt, and all that swell family—now, they accomplished things. Write about them," she'd say. And she'd tell me what she'd heard from my grandfather and from Sistonie:

"Sistonie's grandfather's name was William Rollin. He was French. He had two wives; one was colored and one was white. Sistonie's grandmother was the colored wife. There were two brothers, and one was governor. Sistonie's grandfather's brother was governor. Her mother's mother soaked tough meat in vinegar. It was West Indian cooking; they ate a lot of okra. They lived down there in Beaufort and owned a lot of property. The tide had taken a lot of line, though. Leigh said he lived in a place called Whipper Barony."

I latched onto these words, playing with them, turning them around in my mind, trying to make them yield a lifetime of information. Governor of what? Where was Beaufort? What did "a lot of line" mean? Be-Be was vague about details. Many years had passed since she had heard these stories.

"Your great-aunt brought up an old trunk that time she came to stay up here. It was full of Confederate money and old slave papers, and it was out there in the barn until Fasig-Tipton came and tore the barn down and took it away to the dump," Be-Be said, and I despaired at the thought that there had once been a trunkful of information in the barn, right behind me as I played on the swing set Be-Be bought me. What slaves? Whose slaves?

"Your grandfather told me that his mother had such a dignified walk that the neighbors would come out to watch her walk through the backyard—the toilets were in back then, you know, and she'd be walking to the outhouse."

I tried to imagine Frances Anne Rollin Whipper's walk. My

grandfather had told me at my high school graduation that I had "the Whipper walk." It had never occurred to me that he might be talking about his mother; I had assumed he was referring to the prestigious male ancestors she often held up as family icons—"the magnificent Whippers."

At the end of my visits with Be-Be, she would pack up leftover turkey and dressing sandwiches and ask me what else I needed. Money? She might help me with the bus fare back to New York. Butter? Beer from the bar? Some of that daiquiri mix I used to like? Maybe a big piece of the ham? I'd gather my care packages and leave Saratoga again, heading for archives and more research. I did find out more about my great-grandmother; more, in fact, about my family than I ever dreamed of knowing. But it was to Be-Be that I kept returning.

5

Spuyten Duyvil

"I GOT THE HOUSE FOR YOU," Be-Be would often say to me, "so you would have a home." 157 George Street was a short walk from the Saratoga racetrack, on the east side of town, where many of the more affluent Saratogans lived. It had belonged to a friend of Be-Be's, and she had bought it on tax sale. "A broken-down shack," she called it. Sometimes she'd laugh when she said that; other times she'd just shake her head. It was the beginning of forty years of turning "this old *shack*—this broken-down *joint*" into a home—and a business.

"Tell 'em again about the name, Carole," Be-Be would say over the years, and I'd go through the whole thing once more. Be-Be had been trying to think of a name for the restaurant she wanted to open, and I came home from school with a story about a place north of New York City called Spuyten Duyvil. As an adult, I would hear various translations of the archaic Dutch, including "Spitting Devil," but I related the story as I understood it from our textbook: a Dutchman had had a devil of a time getting across some rapids, and once across, had named the place "In Spite of the Devil." When I offered the name up to Be-Be, she had laughed and said that that was it—the perfect name for our place.

For a couple of years before that, we had lived in another house in Saratoga, with Be-Be's husband at the time—a dark-skinned man named Nesbitt, who smoked cigars that Be-Be couldn't stand. As far as I was concerned, he made little impression on our lives, and Be-Be's only comment about him once he was gone was "He didn't take enough baths." Speaking more generally, she would often say, "Men don't take enough baths for me."

Neither that husband nor that house lasted very long, and soon we were in the company of an endless assortment of handymen, fix-it men, part-time carpenters, and plumbers, all of whom gradually got things on George Street in more or less working order. Despite her feelings about men in general, Be-Be would often say, "Get a man to do it," and reach for the phone. They'd come in their plaid shirts and baggy pants, their hands dirty from some previous job, and stand scratching their heads as they looked at the roof where it was leaking, or the floor where it was sagging, or the plugged-up sink. Be-Be would remember whatever their favorite whiskey or beer was—"Sit down and have a drink, old top. I've got your bottle over there"—and when they were hungry she'd dish out a plate of whatever was on the stove.

At night Be-Be and I would sleep together in the big oak bed she'd bought at an antique sale, buried under several blankets, with down pillows to comfort us after the harshness of the day's work getting the place together. Be-Be would always be up and out of bed before me, and if it was a weekend and I didn't have to go to school, I'd lie there and listen to her voice in the kitchen. She might be talking to the iceman, who brought fifty-to-one-hundred-pound blocks of ice for the icebox onto the back porch—the iceman who later killed his wife and then himself. Or she might be talking to the milkman out front, or the vegetable man, who would come by with a horse-drawn wagon full of produce. All these men were white, but there was another circle of visitors as well.

"Come on in, this is a colored place," my grandmother would say. The older I got, the more embarrassed I was when she said it. Our black friends would smile or laugh out loud as they came in. Be-Be would laugh, too, and get them a beer, or maybe send me for ice and glasses and the bottle that was their favorite whiskey. "Gimme a little

V.O., V'ginia," they'd say to her, or "A little Seven and Seven will do it," their voices sweet and thick with black talk. "How ya doing, VA?" they'd ask. "No use kickin', it only hurts your toe," Be-Be would reply. "How are *you* doing, old top?"

Sometimes the "colored" visitors to the house would talk about Florida, where Be-Be cooked for white families some winters. A few of her friends went down there in the wintertime to work as butlers or maids or chauffeurs, and if Be-Be didn't already have work, they would find her a cooking job. They would all have a good time down there, it seemed making money and playing cards, then they would come back north in the spring.

Be-Be was not like those cooks in the movies named Beulah or Jemima: Be-Be was beautiful, and she could still dance. She had pretty legs and little feet just slightly bigger than mine; I always marveled at the rhythm of her two steps to my one when we walked downtown together. I sometimes heard her at night showing her card-playing buddies an old step she used to do, the "Black Bottom"— a boomp, a boomp—a boomp, boomp, boomp!—or the Charleston. Her voice would be full of excitement as she told them: "We were doing the nightclub number, the *cabaret* scene, you know, and Henri Michaux said—he was kind of *crude*, you know—'Now all you *ugly* gals get in the back, and all you good-looking ones get in the *front*.' "

And everyone knew, including me, listening from the bedroom, that the ugly gals were the darker-skinned, blacker-looking ones, while the good-looking ones had light skin and "good" hair like Be-Be.

I wondered how some of the dark-skinned people sitting out there playing cards really felt about that, but they were laughing. I wondered how Be-Be could be so proud that it was a colored place, when in the morning she would be pulling and tugging on my hair (especially the bit way at the back, behind my ears, that she called "the kitchen"), saying, "You don't want to look like a little pickaninny, do you?"

I did not. "Little pickaninnies," I found out, was what slave children were called, and I had to be constantly on the lookout for breaks in the very fine line that separated me from them. One day I took a pair of scissors and cut "the kitchen" out. Be-Be wasn't as mad as I expected she'd be. I guessed that she thought she might have done the same thing if she'd been born with hair like mine.

Like Be-Be, my mother had "good" hair. Shoulder length and

glossy, my mother's hair featured prominently in the publicity photographs she called "cheesecake"—photos that appeared in the "Negro" papers in New York when she was in a play or singing at a club. Once she was singled out in a magazine as having "the perfect heart-shaped face." When her calypso songs were published, her glamorous photographs were on the covers of the music books, showing her wearing something like the sarongs that Dorothy Lamour wore in the movies. In one she sat sideways on a small Grecian pillar, her hands clasping one bent knee, the other leg outstretched before her. Her breasts were thrust gently forward and her dark hair, framing her face—which was coquettishly turned toward the camera—caressed her bared shoulders. Sometimes we would study these pictures, and she would explain to me how to get the best results from cheesecake, which always made me think of the creamy smooth dessert we sometimes ate at Lindy's counter.

In order to make my own hair as shiny as my mother's and Be-Be's, I had to go to the beauty parlor—the most truly colored place I knew—where dark-skinned women in white uniforms straightened hair with hot irons. Balancing their cigarettes in ashtrays on cluttered counters, they worked in a haze of smoke and grease, talking to each other or, worse, to me, over the metallic click of curling irons and the sizzle of frying hair. "Are you tenderheaded?" they would ask.

"No," I would always answer, no matter how much it hurt. "I'm not tenderheaded." Even if they burned me—which they sometimes did—I would never admit to such a thing. I could take it.

Sometimes, instead of going to the beauty parlor, I'd have my hair done by a woman across town. As the only customer there in the woman's own kitchen, I found it harder than I did in the beauty parlor to convince myself that it wasn't really me—not the true me anyway—going through this odd procedure. I also had to be extra polite, since the woman probably knew my mother and grandmother, and I'd have to pretend extra hard that I liked the way she had done my hair, even though I hated the greasy curls and demeaning styles she came up with.

As soon as I was out of sight of the hairdresser, I'd put a cap on my head and rush home. Then I'd spend the next few hours in my room in front of the mirror with a brush and comb, trying to make it look better.

Afterward, I was glad my hair was straight, but though it took several hours to have it done—from the untangling, washing, and drying through the sectioning off, pressing, and styling—the straightening never lasted long. It "went back" no matter how careful you were. If you perspired in the summer heat, or got caught in the rain, or went swimming, it "went back." So I never learned to swim, and instead sat on beaches or beside swimming pools pretending I didn't really want to go in.

But in the early days in Saratoga, I rarely had my hair straightened, and it was my real "gone back" hair, unshiny and thickly prone to snarls, that Be-Be pulled into braids as I sat between her knees in the living room. My mother, after her divorce, tended to say that I looked like my father. And when I looked in the mirror I could see that my lips were thicker than hers, as his were. "The Lewis lips," she called them. My skin color was also closer to my father's, and my hair, too, was from his side of the family—I knew without her saying so that it was the Lewis hair. When I was moody in the mornings, or when I sulked, she would say it was the Lewis side of me coming out. "And don't stick out those lips," she'd add.

It was during my first year in Saratoga, at school, that I learned in the girls' coatroom that the word "nigger," as in "catch a nigger by the toe," had something to do with me. I realized this only because one of the girls singing "eeny, meeny, miney, mo" came over to me to apologize. My earliest friends in Saratoga were white. They knew about things like race, religion, and ethnicity, while I hadn't a clue. Elizabeth, who was Italian, had skin that was darker than my grandmother's; Carol was Jewish and very fair-skinned. But all three of us were confused. "The Jews are stuck up; they think they're better than anybody because Christ was Jewish," Elizabeth told me. And when I dressed up in my short gypsy outfit for Halloween, Carol and Elizabeth pointed out that there was no point in my wearing a costume, since everyone would know me by my brown legs. There was no disguise for my color.

Sometimes Be-Be would say that the two or three black friends I finally found in Saratoga dressed like little pickaninnies or that they were low class. I was indignant about this and would fiercely stand up for my friends. One of my best friends was Jackie Lewis, who wore a colorful rayon scarf tied under her chin. I begged for one like it instead of my woolen cap, but Be-Be said it looked cheap.

"She doesn't know about color yet," Kenneth Clark had told my mother when she asked him why I was leaving the skin blank in my coloring books. (Later I experimented with new versions of skin and hair coloring, filling book after book with multicolored children.) But by the time I was eight and we were living on George Street, Peter O'Brian awaited my return from school so that he could aim high-flying ice balls at me—with deadly accuracy—while he chanted "Nigger! Nigger!"

One winter day, after dodging Peter once again on my way home from school, I stood on the heating grate to remove my snowsuit, listening to the hiss as my encrusted mittens dripped melted snow down on the furnace. Be-Be was grabbing the old coat she always kept hanging on the cellar door and slipping her bare feet into a pair of boots. She was about to run out the door to speak to Peter's parents. "Poor white trash!" she said as she left the house. "They're nothing but poor white trash!"

I went and sat in the kitchen, as far as possible from the front door, and fearfully awaited her return. I thought of the Westerns I'd seen in which white settlers huddled together in fear of the Indians. Only, of course, it was just the opposite—we were colored people staking out a home in a white neighborhood. I was terrified of an anger that could be so fierce from a boy who didn't even know me. I'd seen Peter's mother, and she looked pretty mean to me, pasty-faced and redheaded like him. But Peter's parents were never home when Be-Be went over, or as Be-Be thought, they just didn't answer the door.

In general, however, time passed fairly peaceably on George Street. The backyard had an apple tree and a crab apple tree and my swing set. Be-Be, wearing a professional apron over her housedress, liked to sit on the porch to the right of the screen door, where she was hidden by the flower boxes from passersby but could see out and nab unsuspecting dogs heading for her ferns.

I'd sit nearby reading a comic book or writing in my diary. *Be-Be can't find her girdle* was an early entry my grandmother particularly liked. Be-Be was always leaving her girdles somewhere, and I was proud of my ability to find them. They were like the ones Sistonie wore—circular tubes of satiny peach-colored elastic with garter loops and hooks or even a zipper that I would be called upon to do up. Usually Be-Be's girdle or pocketbook had fallen between the bedboard and the mattress or was buried underneath some clothes on a chair. Later it was her teeth I'd be sent to find, or her glasses, but these items proved more elusive and could sometimes manage to disappear from the house altogether.

One reason we had such a hard time finding things was that Be-Be and I would move from room to room in the house whenever we'd "take a notion." In autumn we might sleep in the twin-bedded room upstairs. In winter, when there were no roomers, we would close off the upstairs except for baths and sleep in the warmest room downstairs—the middle room, with the oak bed in it. I'd awaken in the morning and see branches piled high with new snow, hear the reassuring early-morning sounds of Be-Be in the kitchen. She would have already gotten a fire going in the wood-burning stove, and my underwear and shoes would be heating on the oven door. We'd listen to the radio to make sure it wasn't a snow day, and then, after hot cereal and cocoa, I'd pull on my snowsuit, mittens, and boots, grab my books, and be off to school a few blocks away.

Biddie, Be-Be's good friend, came by the house every Monday to collect for the numbers. Biddie always had a big grin on her long face, so that when she said, "How ya doin' Beee-Beee?" it came out sounding warm and funny. A tall, amiable woman, Biddie would stand in the middle room and pull out her pad to enter our order. "In the box or straight?" she would ask. If it was in the box, you could hit any combination of the number that came out, but if it was straight you had to have it exactly right. Sometimes Biddie would pull out her dream book, which had a number for just about anything you'd dreamed.

Most of Be-Be's friends would sip their drinks sitting on the porch in the rockers, or on the glider, talking and gazing out through the screens. Be-Be would always have a bottle of Ballantine's beer beside her—this was in the years before she switched to sherry—and she might have a bowl of potatoes to peel and slice thickly before she peppered them liberally and home-fried them in bacon drippings.

Sometimes the visitors would talk about which horses looked good: "I've got my eye on somethin' good in the fifth." Be-Be had been following certain horses for a long while and knew what they'd done at different tracks around the country and just when to play them.

"It's time for him to come in the money," she'd say. I hardly ever saw her studying the racing sheets; she had much of that information in her head. Now and then during the course of the summer, someone would have a hot tip from a trainer and Be-Be would rush out the door. "Watch those beans on the stove!" or "Turn out the oven in half an hour," she'd cry, undoing her apron and throwing it on the rocker, dropping everything to run over to the track and place her bet.

The first morning of Saratoga's racing season, in August, Be-Be would say, "We've got horses!" and later in the day, some shiny new foreign car would career up George Street. The horses would have been arriving at night for a while now, calling to each other as they were led directly beneath my bedroom window. I'd sit up and look out at their shadowy forms as they moved by. Then I'd turn over and sleep again, a wonderful sleep, knowing they were there.

"They're all standing on their eyebrows now!" Be-Be would tell me, and send me to the corner for another bottle of beer. Our rooms were ready for roomers, with freshly ironed curtains at the windows. Crisp clean sheets and towels and white aprons and green kitchen uniforms for Be-Be had arrived from the linen service and were crammed into the upstairs closet. Everyone we knew was creating spare rooms to rent. Every backyard within a few miles of the track became a parking lot, and every child became an entrepreneur, calling out rates, flagging down cars, waving them in. Lemonade stands flourished. I became a waitress and a publicist as well, twirling on the sidewalk as people began to stream out of the track after the seventh or eighth race, waving the new menu that I had printed by hand. Broiled Chicken, Roast Leg of Lamb, Prime Ribs of Beef, Porter House Steaks, Parsleyed Potatoes, Fresh Corn, Ripe Tomatoes, Delicious Pies and Cakes. A full dinner cost $2.25.

"They're rolling out the red carpet!" I'd hear Be-Be say to a deliveryman, or "August means Saratoga and Saratoga means August," she'd comment cheerily to an old friend, and I'd know she meant "and that means money."

Each night of the season at the Spuyten Duyvil, I would fill pitchers of water from a big earthenware cooler, set the tables, and place the flowers in the center. I had candles in readiness to create *ambience*—a word my mother had taught me—once darkness fell. When the customers came in, I'd rush to fill their water glasses, then return to take their orders. Then I'd hurry back through the pantry to the kitchen, where Be-Be was mashing the potatoes, testing the roast, or lifting an enormous turkey from the oven. Every pot we had would be simmering, and the oven would be radiating a fierce heat.

In late 1948, most of the stable hands who came up from Kentucky and Virginia with the horses were black men and boys—unlike now, when most are white and many are girls. One morning Be-Be went out back to ask the stablehands if they wanted to board at the Spuyten Duyvil. She offered them group breakfast and lunch rates, and the "boys," as they were called, began to come over daily. But then one day, two of the owners wandered into the place, looked around at the cozy decor—simple tables and chairs, checkered tablecloths, and a bar that Be-Be had gotten from the illustrious old Grand Union Hotel—and the Spuyten Duyvil was "discovered." It wasn't long before the rich and the superrich started pulling up in Mercedeses, limos, and sports cars, coming to sit in the garden where I used to play.

Be-Be would take a few minutes out from cooking to listen from the porch to the wild roar of the crowd as the horses approached the finish line. The announcer's sharp crackling voice would ebb and flow, but when the wind was just right, we could make out exactly which horse was winning. But most often the crowd's cry would rise on the air, reach its peak, then suddenly drop, and in the silence after the race Be-Be would speculate as to which horse had won. Sometimes friends would place her bets for her during restaurant season, and I could usually tell from a distance whether they were coming back with good news or bad.

"Saratoga . . ." Whenever Be-Be said the name, it was always with that edge of excitement, her voice lingering on a high note. And whenever she said it, I knew she was recalling Saratoga in its "glory," when in the teens and twenties she would go there as a dancer in a show or between jobs. There was a horse room and a bookie on practically every corner, and a floating crap game available at all hours.

"Saratoga was always the place to *be*. You could shoot any kind of craps," Be-Be would say years later, pointing to the bottle of Dry Fly sherry that had replaced the Amontillado that had replaced Ballantine's beer as her favorite drink. "Pour me a little something in that glass," she'd say, looking at me askance if there was not enough in it. "I said *something*."

"You could play mostly any kind of card game," she continued. "There were clubs all over the place. The casinos were out around the lake. All the big shots were here. Newtie would be out on the corner, 'waitin' for the word.'

" 'Hi, Newtie!' we'd say, and he'd tell us 'Yes' or 'No.' Jimmy Leary was then the big boss of Saratoga. Everything depended on him. If he said 'Go!' you did go. He was the police, a gangster. He wasn't supposed to be, but he was. Newtie was the lookout man. Sometimes he'd be running his little crap game right there on the corner of Congress and Cowan. That was his corner. If it was 'Yes!' then you could go in and shoot on the table, the big crap table. It was a lot of fun. Every single morning, as soon as I woke up, I'd go out to play."

When I asked Be-Be where she got the money to play with, she looked at me incredulously. "Why, I got it from the day before. I was always lucky."

"Gambling was wide open in this town," Be-Be said wistfully. "All the big shots supported it." But this was before the cataclysmic moment in 1942 when Thomas E. Dewey became New York's governor and, as Be-Be put it, "sold the town down the river."

Even when I was growing up there, I discovered that the most ordinary local could turn out to be, underneath it all, a typical Saratoga rogue. I listened to the milkman reminiscing with Be-Be about the days when he delivered bathtub gin to special customers, fresh from his own still. The vegetable store owners turned out to have been among Saratoga's biggest gamblers. The families of important lawyers had unsavory histories. The bus station attendant had been a notorious bookie. But the town had "dried up," and Saratoga was like a beautiful old ship in dry dock. The charred remains of the big casinos could be seen around the lake, with their crumbling signs, "Fontainebleu" and "Piping Rock," evoking the extravagance of another era. "It's disgusting," Be-Be concluded.

Still, when I was growing up, Be-Be and her friends played cards as often as they could get a game together at someone's house, usually weekly. "Where's the game?" I'd hear her ask. "Anything happening this week?" Sometimes it would be poker, other times blackjack, pinochle, or craps. Be-Be was good at all of these. I knew that she was lucky; we could be walking downtown and she'd wander to a patch of grass, bend over, and pluck a four-leaf clover. One day she and I found a whole patch of four-, five-, six-, and seven-leaf clovers in the backyard.

I was lucky too. Be-Be won one hundred dollars more than once on a horse or a number I'd suggested. She won on 903 when I heard the number on a Raleigh cigarette ad on the radio. Once, down at Jim Scott's horse room on Congress Street, Be-Be took my advice and played a long shot named Johnny Boy, whom I'd picked because I was taken with a neighbor we always called "little Johnny Schnell." That day the winning favorite at Pimlico was disqualified, and Johnny Boy came in the big money, 19 to 1.

The luck that Be-Be and I had was tricky, though. I learned the hard way never to say "Good luck" when Be-Be left for a game, because that was bad luck. One night I let it slip before she left for a game across town; I'll never forget how I felt the next morning when she came home after playing all night, trying to win her money back. Be-Be taught me how to play blackjack, which I played instead of solitaire, since playing solitaire brought the police. I never ate peanuts or whistled in the house, because both were bad luck. Be-Be said these things were bad luck when she was about to go on stage, and I guess she figured the old theatrical superstitions probably applied to the house as well. As I look back on it now, it seems as though we were always "on stage" in some way.

When the game was at our house, I would lie awake in bed and listen: I can still hear the slap of cards on our dining room table, the click of chips, the almost palpable silences while people studied their cards. "What's trumps?" "Who dealt this mess?" "I pass."

6

From My Mother's Window

IN 1947, MY MOTHER AND her new husband, Norman, invited me to come live with them in New York. My mother had put her name on the long waiting list for Riverton—a group of brand-new buildings in East Harlem constructed after blacks were turned away from Stuyvesant Town—and an apartment had finally come through. The Riverton apartments were prized in a city in which middle-income housing for blacks was in scant supply. Although it abutted low-income projects and looked somewhat like them from the outside, Riverton was not a "project"; it was a "development." Those who lived there were proud of this distinction.

My mother, overjoyed to finally have a place of her own, set out to decorate it like a tropical island. Chartreuse dishes with bamboo borders graced our dining room table. Chartreuse vines climbed beige bamboo on the living room wall. Our apartment was an exotic jungle, which I loved. But beyond our island environment was another reality. After the comparatively sedate and sheltered Saratoga schools, P.S. 24, a few blocks away on East 128th Street, was a shock to me.

The first few weeks of school I'd hurry home up Madison Avenue, hugging my books to my chest, followed by most of the sixth-grade class.

"Chicken, chicken, come on and fight!" Roselyn, the biggest, ugliest, and, yes, blackest girl in the school, was saying as she loped along beside me. The others would pick up the chant, adding their own insults and cheering Roselyn on.

It wasn't only me, with my neat clothes and good grades, that they disliked: it was Riverton itself. They had been chased from our private playgrounds by our guards, they had seen Riverton's well-dressed, "stuck-up" residents heading off for work in the mornings and returning home in the evenings. I represented everything they hated. At age ten, I knew this, though I didn't quite understand why, or why I was expected to fight. I had been taught *not* to fight. So for about two weeks, we all made this journey as soon as school let out.

My grandmother was visiting, and she and my mother would both watch from the window for my return. I glimpsed them there the day my classmates grew bold and crossed the invisible barrier of 135th Street. Roselyn had sworn she'd follow me all the way into my building; but as we walked over the sparse grass toward the door, I saw my mother and grandmother, no longer at the upstairs window but right there in front of us, wearing their sternest faces. Embarrassed, I went over to them, and the children stopped in their tracks, but their jeering continued unabated.

"Had to get old mama and grandma down!" they cried as the women led me toward the building. "Next time we'll fight them too!"

I turned briefly, long enough to see Roselyn's big balled fist shaking at us. "You'd better watch out tomorrow! Tomorrow I'm gonna get you!"

My mother and grandmother were talking as we entered the building; I heard the words "ragamuffins" and "hoodlums" and "police." But I didn't want to listen to them. As we went up in the small elevator, I stood as far away from them as I could, feeling the cold metal of the wall and railing behind me. I was thinking about the day when I would have to fight Roselyn and trying to figure out how I was going to do it.

I told my mother a couple of days later that I *had* to fight. There was no way for me to continue living without fighting. Finally, my mother said, "All right, tell Roselyn you'll fight her, but I have to be there." I was mortified, but had enough sense to realize that having my mother there was better than not doing it at all.

Roselyn always passed notes to me in class containing dire threats and demands for a fight. The next day, I sent back a message accepting the challenge. The fight was set for the following day after school, at the corner of Lexington Avenue and 129th Street. At the appointed hour, I found myself standing on the corner facing Roselyn. My mother had arrived on schedule and stood not far away, indicating that she was there only to observe and would not interfere. Roselyn was accompanied by about twenty other kids, who had come to watch. There was a trick I had seen in some movie that I was planning to use, and the thought of it had, in fact, given me some confidence. Someone gave a signal, and the fight began. Suddenly we each had hold of the other's hair. But there was no time to feel pain. As I'd planned, I put one leg between Roselyn's legs to trip her up, but it didn't work. Roselyn was sturdy and didn't budge. We tugged at each other some more, and then it was over. For some reason, Roselyn seemed satisfied that we had fought. So did everyone else. They backed away, crossed the avenue, and headed off in the other direction.

I felt relieved and bewildered as my mother and I turned toward Riverton. "Well, you fought Roselyn," my mother said, and she must have been relieved herself. Things were easier for me in school afterward.

In the afternoons, when I got home from school, I would practice at our blond piano. Later, when she came home from work, my mother would sit there, too, for an hour or so, singing and composing calypso songs. Their lilting rhythms evoked the carefree islands of the Caribbean, and their simple, sensual lyrics usually dealt with the love of saucy Creole girls and the men who pursued them. I learned early on from these lyrics that soldiers and sailors could be trouble—you might never see them again.

There was one song, written by someone else, that I would often ask my mother to sing for me: "I got an island in the Pacific, and ev'rything about it is terrific. I got the sun to tan me, palms to fan me and . . . An Occasional Man." This was heady stuff. I loved the defiant pause before the last three words, and the idea that a woman could be that independent. What exactly would happen if *I* were stuck on a deserted island with a man? My ideas on the subject were vague, but I developed a scenario in my head, complete with movie fade-out at the critical moments. I wasn't good at drawing men, but I began to draw pictures of grass huts and beautiful long-haired women in sarongs who were destined to meet—an occasional man.

The man in our lives then was my stepfather, whom I called "Pop" to distinguish him from my father. My mother's second husband was "a diamond in the rough," as I'd heard her say, and I liked him. Pop had style. He had a soft, gravelly voice and rolls of bills in his pocket. I knew, though, that the roll of money and the way he peeled the bills from it were part of the show he had to put on at Wellsworth Tavern, the bar he managed near 125th Street.

I got a quarter each for ironing Pop's cotton shirts and for touching up the nylon ones. But though he lived in the apartment with us for a couple of years, his hours were very different from mine, so I didn't get to see him very often. Sometimes, though, Pop took us for drives in his green fishtail Cadillac. He took us up to Saratoga in it, and on picnics to Hunt's Point. Once we went to Atlantic City and ate soft-shell crabs in the car before the long drive back to New York. Another time he took me to see a Dodgers game at Yankee Stadium, suggesting as we entered the stadium that I be "nicer" to my mother. I didn't know exactly what he meant, but I told him I would try.

I liked to listen as Pop recounted the silly bar wagers on which hundreds of dollars hung in the balance, or as he and my mother teased each other. One of their ongoing debates was over female movie stars—my mother was dismayed that his favorite was Alexis Smith. "So cold," she would say. Why couldn't he pick someone really sexy, like Rita Hayworth? One day she showed me the famous photograph of Hayworth in a satin nightgown, kneeling on a bed. "*She's* a real woman," my mother remarked, her voice full of admiration.

A real woman was what I wanted to be. I had pestered my mother to give me the book she had promised on the "facts of life," and she finally produced it. But after scrutinizing every sentence in it, I was disappointed to find that it provided no information at all about love-making with the perfect man.

It must have been around this time that my mother told me about my great-aunt Winifred, Sistonie's sister, who had not known what was happening to her when her periods began. Frightened by the sight of blood—so the story went—she had jumped into a tub of cold water. To me there was a connection between the cold she subsequently caught and her early death from tuberculosis. My great-aunt Winifred's fate, I knew, would never be visited on me. For one thing, we were modern, my mother and me; and what's more, I knew that when I got my period, I would welcome it.

One day in Saratoga I was running up the back stairs when I suddenly felt faint. As I felt myself wilting down the steps, suddenly Be-Be was there, before I fell and I was being lifted effortlessly and carried up to the front bedroom. "Be-Be's got you," she was saying. Lying in bed, I heard her whisper to someone outside that I must be *changing*. That I was growing up. But I was not growing up fast enough for me.

When I finally got my period, months of wishing later, I was eleven years old and at Roseland Studios for my Saturday-morning ballet class with "La Sylph," my aging, white-haired teacher, who had been a famous ballerina. I hurried home on the subway, feeling as though all eyes were on me. As I came rushing into the apartment, my mother thought at first that something was wrong, but when I told her what had happened, she settled me in bed and went out to get me the sanitary belts and pads I had longed for. I lay in my room with the blinds drawn, not sick, but emotional to the point of tears.

Pop was home and on his way to work. He peered into the room. "Congratulations," he said shyly. "You're a woman now."

I was very proud and not embarrassed at all. I cried a bit and went to sleep, on the threshold, it seemed, of everything I wanted in the world.

From my mother's window I could watch her whenever she went out. I'd rush to the window after allowing her the exact amount of time I'd found it took her to get down in the elevator. Then I'd watch her crossing the street, teetering on her ultrahigh heels. She had always been by far the most beautiful mother of all, with her long dark hair, big eyes, and stylish clothes. I would look in her closet when she wasn't there, letting the scent of her perfumes waft over me as I examined her handsome suits, soft day dresses, shiny sequined evening gowns, silver fox fur, big hats, and rows of sling-back heels and pumps. I loved her fox tails biting end to end, her bedroom with the blue smoked-glass mirror on the dresser, the subdued gray furniture with brass handles, and her window with its blue venetian blinds. On the dresser sat her perfumes: Prince Matchabelli, dark and almost evil in its fat crown-shaped bottle; flamboyant Shalimar; and sedate Chanel No. 5. Then there was Madera de Oriente, with its stick of fragrant wood inside, brought from Spain.

My mother made her first crossing to Europe, on the old *Île de France,* when I was in high school. I loved her letters with their big pastel stamps, loved imagining her in different cities, wearing the pretty new translucent nylon dresses I'd seen her pack. I could see her in Paris, where I'd heard that Frenchmen, maddened by their exoticism, ran after beautiful black women on the Champs Élysées. And I could imagine Venice perfectly, where the bells from the church next to her pensione woke her up; and Rome, where a blond Italian man had rushed up to her on the airport runway and invited her to dinner. "Why didn't you go? Why didn't you go?" I squealed when she told me about it.

Although she was always glamorous when she went out, at home we'd sometimes play a game I called Monster, in which, after she'd creamed her face for the night, my mother would lower her lids hideously and stagger down the hall after me until I got so scared I'd have to beg her to stop.

My mother had been a newspaperwoman, most recently with *The People's Voice,* which had its offices on 125th Street. She'd interviewed the hard-to-reach and controversial black spiritual leader Father Divine. She also performed for a time with a local West Indian dance troupe, singing and dancing to some of her own songs. I went alone to see her perform, and sat in a seat on the aisle. When my mother came out on stage—still the prettiest of them all—I couldn't contain my enthusiasm. I tapped the woman next to me and said, "That's my mother."

For her other jobs she took the Madison Avenue bus downtown (the avenue had two-way traffic then) to the real world, a world in which very few black people existed. In those days, when we ventured below *our* downtown, which was 125th Street, to shop at Macy's or look in the shoe stores along Thirty-fourth Street, we might spot one or two other black people, who would stare curiously, as if to say, So you're down here too. Who are you? It was unimaginable that one day there would be whole areas of the ground floor of Macy's devoted to black cosmetics—that black and Hispanic people would be considered *real* in the world of commerce.

On her way to work, my mother would watch from the bus windows as the blocks changed character, from black slums to Hispanic slums to run-down white and then to wealthy white neighborhoods. She said it was always difficult for her to come back up to our stop at the end of the line, and when at night she lay in a swoon of fatigue and anger on the sofa, I imagined that she was thinking about that.

In the real world downtown, my mother was an editor with a literary agency that offered assistance to would-be authors in the revision of their manuscripts. Meanwhile, she was writing her own stories, mysteries in which she would enjoy "killing off" people who had crossed her in one way or another. Then she created a female assassin, a professional killer with no feelings at all. Years later she would publish a story that revealed the reason for her assassin's lack of feeling—her only daughter had been raped and murdered. I would feel my heart pounding when I read it.

In late 1949, Pop bought us one of the first television sets. There were virtually no black people on television yet, but I loved to watch programs like *The Continental,* in which you'd hear the sound of a doorbell, not unlike our own, and then the door would be swept open by a man in a smoking jacket, with a thick European accent. He would speak directly to the camera, giving the illusion that he could see you—that you were a naughty but nervous woman standing at his door. "Don't be afraid, my darling. It's only a man's apartment," he would say. Ceremoniously he'd open champagne, pour a glass, and hand it out toward the camera for you.

There was also *I Love Lucy.* Ricky, like Pop, worked at a club, and he was Latin, which made him more like us than any of the white families on television. I'd watch programs while doing my homework or drawing. Meanwhile, my mother might ask me to "do" her toe—that is, rub her toe with cold cream or smooth her toenail with an emery board—before she fell asleep on the sofa.

For a while after Pop and my mother separated, I'd "start out" sleeping in my mother's bed with her and she'd get me to "do" her back, scratching lightly, and then she would sometimes do the same for me. But as I plunged deeper into adolescence, I couldn't bear to be that close. My mother began to lock her closet so that I wouldn't disturb her things. One day, as a kind of a joke, I started calling her "Mother" instead of "Mommy," and somehow I never went back.

In my freshman year at the High School of Music and Art, I studied both Spanish and French. My mother had mentioned that our ancestors came from Santo Domingo. Spanish was the language of Santo Domingo, and I knew that in its neighboring country, Haiti, people spoke French. I liked the idea of trying to get back to my island roots.

My mother was described as Creole on one of her album covers, and as I understood it, Creoles were a beautiful island people of mixed race—African and Spanish, French, or Dutch. I wanted to be Creole too. I began to listen to the rhythmic Afro-Cuban music that was becoming popular; and I began falling in love with the good-looking Hispanic people I saw on the Madison Avenue bus. My best friend, Yvonne, was part American black, part American Indian, and part French. We liked to pretend to be Puerto Rican. We'd take the bus down to 112th Street, in the heart of Spanish Harlem, and as we pulled the cord to be let off, we'd spout memorized rapid-fire Spanish phrases, thrilling to the idea that the other passengers were thinking of us as Spanish girls as they continued down Madison Avenue. We later learned that our Spanish was practically unintelligible, but by that time we were both in new phases.

From my mother's window I could scan part of the Riverton playground across the way, hoping for tantalizing glimpses of boys I had crushes on—Marx, with his sandy, curly hair, and John, who was so good at basketball, and Ivan, who had dark-chocolate skin.

I also watched older girls below—the ones with breasts and hips and school sweaters and boyfriends. One of these was a girl I'll call Beverly, the daughter of two of my mother's friends who lived in another building. One afternoon after school, I received an urgent call from her—she asked me to come to her house to help her pack. She'd had a big fight with her parents and needed to leave before they returned.

In her room I found stacks of shirts and pants, still on their hangers, spread across her bed. "I'm a lesbian," she told me. "Do you know what that is?" I'd never heard the word, but I had found a book of short novels by Colette on my mother's shelves, from which I had surmised that women could love women intensely, much as they loved men. And I knew that I loved Yvonne very much. We were inseparable. We squealed at the same spots in the same Johnny Ray songs. It seemed to me that this was what Beverly was talking about, and I assured her I knew all about it.

Painstakingly, Beverly showed me how to fold her numerous men's shirts and ties, and extracted a promise of secrecy. For the next year I was her only link to Riverton, and I received sporadic evening telephone calls, during which she related her activities in the gay underworld of New York. One night she told me she was being kept by a wealthy woman on Park Avenue. She said she wore only silk shirts now. She had to whisper from a separate bedroom for fear of being overheard. The last time I heard from her, she told me proudly that she was the only woman in a well-known traveling show of men who performed in drag. Her name was changed by then, and no one would recognize her, she said, for she looked and dressed just like a man.

My mother spoke darkly of certain girls—usually the girls I admired, the attractive ones with breasts and hips—as the kind who had to be "sent away." "You don't want us to have to send you away, do you?"she would cry if I stayed out later than usual, or if she caught me essaying what I thought was a sexy, breathless voice with boys on the phone. One night, using the similarity of our voices to get the information she wanted, she pretended to be me on the phone. A boy I liked a lot was calling to ask what I meant by a note I'd sent him, which contained the line "I'm no angel" (which I'd spelled "angle"). My mother revealed who she was and bawled him out. Terrified, he swiftly hung up, and we steadfastly avoided each other from then on.

After Yvonne moved to New Jersey, I became part of a social club of five girls we called the Continentals. None of us was allowed to go out on dates, so we devised club meetings to which suitable boys were invited as guests afterward. As children of prominent members of New York's black society, we were called "socialite teenagers" in an *Amsterdam News* photo caption that marked a party we gave. One Sunday, three of us cooked up the idea of having the boys meet us inside the Loews 116th Street Theater. When I told my mother we were seeing a movie there, she asked why we were going so far away, and I made some vague reply like "Just for a change." She was silent for a moment and then, to my surprise, acquiesced.

A few hours later, we were sitting in the balcony of the darkened movie theater, each with a boy beside us. Jimmy Dallum, the boy I liked, tried to put his arm around me, and I took it away. I noticed a man sitting behind me with his feet up on the seat next to mine. The feature was just coming on when I saw the shadowy figure of my mother, walking along the aisle, looking for me. Panicking, I jumped up and ran out the other way, only to find myself trapped in the mezzanine, my mother coming toward me, my stepfather approaching from behind..

I learned that the man who'd been sitting behind me had been my stepfather, and that my mother had telephoned ahead to a friend who was manager of the theater, getting his cooperation.

As I sat dejectedly gazing out the window of the back seat of the green Cadillac, Pop seemed to be taking the whole thing much more lightly than my mother. "Why did you take that boy's arm away?" he asked me.

When I went to Saratoga in the summer, I used all my teenaged skills to try to make it an interesting place, but already I was feeling that my true life lay elsewhere. I was growing older. I sat at the screen window in my room, and instead of looking at the horses, I looked out at the stableboys, yearning for their attention. "I saw you from my window," I told one of them, and to my surprise, he replied, "Yeah, I saw you too." So many years of window watching had made me feel I was invisible. One evening at dusk I wandered up the alley for a secret rendezvous and was wetly kissed by that same boy. A bit shaken, for I had never imagined such a thing as an open-mouthed kiss, I returned home, contemplating the passionate feelings racing around inside me.

I wore dirndl skirts or tight jeans and developed a sultry stroll. One morning in August, I passed the spot where Be-Be and I had discovered our lucky clovers—they were still growing there. A man in an idling white convertible, sitting beside a glamorous blonde, stopped talking to a trainer long enough to give me a hot, passionate look. I discovered a short while later that he was Aly Khan, soon to marry Rita Hayworth. Walking back to the house, I was already beginning to revise my fantasies, turning them forever away from stableboys.

A couple of years earlier, my mother and I had been on the Madison Avenue bus together, heading downtown. Two derelicts, a man and a woman, were talking in the seat behind us. "We never slept apart in twenty years!" the man announced, for all the bus to hear.

I felt my mother shuddering beside me. "How dreadful," she whispered, no doubt imagining the unkempt couple facing one another each morning for so many years—and, I thought, horrified by the very idea of such a long-term commitment.

But *I* wanted the kind of relationship that could last for twenty years; something no one in my family had ever had. I was smitten with the concept of romantic love as only a thirteen-year-old can be, and I wanted my mother to approve. After the couple had gotten off the bus, I must have said something like "I think it's nice. They really love each other." My mother and I sat staring at the passing slums without speaking, and then she said, her voice thoughtful and distant, "Well, yes. I wish that for you. Yes, I do."

"Leighla always thought that a knight in shining armor would appear and carry her off to live happily ever after," Sistonie said to Be-Be one day when they were both visiting us at Riverton. I suppose the comment had something to do with the breakup of my mother's relationship with Pop. Sistonie was shaking her head sadly, as though the thought had been weighing on her mind.

I was coming from my room, slowing my step and lingering in the hallway just in case there was some interesting conversation going on. Usually I was spotted fairly quickly, and the women would break off their discussion. I always hoped they were talking about sex and romance. More likely, they were talking about the anger and disappointment in their lives, and that is what they wanted to keep from me.

In any case, this time I had actually overheard something valuable. Moving as nonchalantly as I could, I entered the living room and headed toward the dining alcove, pretending I hadn't heard, while my mind was whirring away.

For the first time I had caught a glimmer of something other than the *fait accompli* of our lives together. I suddenly realized that my great-aunt Sistonie, by then an elderly woman who walked with a cane, was privy to a body of knowledge about my mother that I'd never dreamed existed. It seemed never to have occurred to me that my mother had had an earlier existence as a child, or as an adolescent—I had never heard any stories about her childhood. In fact, I had never quite grasped that my mother had grown up with my great-aunt and not with her mother.

A couple of years later, Sistonie lay gravely ill in Harlem Hospital. She was eighty-three years old. As a doctor, she could have had a bed in almost any hospital, but she insisted on leaving the white hospital downtown she'd first been admitted to. "I feel more comfortable here," she told my mother. She was a difficult patient, as many doctors are reputed to be—this my mother added with a touch of pride.

In fact, Be-Be had had more success with Sistonie's treatment than any of the doctors. When Sistonie was sick with chills, Be-Be had gone down to Washington more than once to rub her old adversary with alcohol; and finally she had persuaded her to try her own favorite remedy, hot toddies with tea and lemon and whiskey. As she prepared the first drink for Sistonie, Be-Be couldn't help remembering the time at 511 Florida Avenue when she'd answered the door and found an obviously inebriated man seeking treatment. "Did you smell the liquor on that man's breath?" Be-Be had asked Sistonie after they had sent the man on to the male doctor down the street.

"I wouldn't know," Sistonie replied loftily. "I've never smelled it."

The hot toddy seemed to help my great-aunt, and when she came to New York to see doctors, Be-Be continued the same treatment and Sistonie rallied for long periods of time. "You shouldn't kick on it," Be-Be told her one day when she was feeling better. "It brought you around."

"You're right," Sistonie admitted, nodding her head gravely. She must have been mindful of the pledges of two generations of abstinent women in her family, and of the age-old connection between black churchwomen and abstinence. Her feelings about alcohol had been part of a tradition. In 1834, Sistonie's great-uncle, William Whipper, had addressed the Colored Temperance Society of Philadelphia to denounce intemperance as a scourge even worse than slavery. *The Liberator* printed his speech, in which he stated: "I do not wish to insinuate that we are more intemperate than whites, for I do not believe it, but that we must be more pure than they, before we can be duly respected, becomes self-evident from the situation we at present occupy in our country."

Her new outlook on life—and perhaps on death—led Sistonie to agree to travel up to Saratoga to visit Be-Be at the house on George Street. Be-Be went down to Washington to get her. She stayed the winter until March, then returned in the summer. I remember her making complicated fruit cakes in Be-Be's kitchen, and sitting contentedly in the crowded living room, crocheting lacy antimacassars and colorful afghans. She sent away for a loom so she could start hooking rugs, and as soon as it arrived, she worked at it daily.

On Sundays she would gather me up from wherever I was playing and call for a taxi to take us downtown to Bethesda Episcopal Church. I thought it very brave of Sistonie to have us join the all-white congregation there. The outside of the church looked much like St. Luke's, and the light inside shone through the deep purples and reds of an immense stained-glass window behind the altar, bathing us in an aura of holiness. In a sanctified mood, steeped in hymns and incense, we'd return to George Street, where we'd walk in the door to find that Be-Be had an early dinner of chicken or lamb roasting in the oven.

In the summer of 1951, the Spuyten Duyvil was in full swing, and Sistonie, being the sort of woman who didn't want to miss out on anything, moved one day from her usual post at the loom in the living room to the big round table in the restaurant and bar area. Be-Be had not yet received her liquor license, but there was some drinking going on, as some of the customers had brought their own bottles. After taking everything in without comment, Sistonie focused her attention on the bustling stables out back. One could see the general hubbub— horses paraded before prospective buyers, grooms rushing to and fro—from the large screen window at the back. Sistonie seemed to have been thinking about it for a while before she spoke. "Now, all these horses," she began, in measured cadence, "are they going to be *race* horses?"

Be-Be chuckled and replied that yes, indeed, that was what everyone—owners, trainers, jockeys, and on down—*hoped* they'd be.

From her new vantage point, Sistonie must have observed all the money going out of the Spuyten Duyvil as tradespeople trekked through the restaurant with their wares. Giant containers of salt, pepper, sugar, flour, and gelatin arrived. Spices and flavorings like cinnamon and curry, celery salt and vanilla, came in boxes larger than I'd ever imagined. The bin of the big refrigerator was filled with peaches and melons, strawberries and parsley. To pay the bills, Be-Be would fish for money in the pocket of her apron, or in her pocketbook—which was more than likely lost, which would mean I had to find it—or in a basket under the bed. One day Sistonie could hold her tongue no longer and offered to do the books for Be-Be.

"Books?" my gambling grandmother replied. "What do I need that for? What I've got I've got. What I haven't got I haven't got."

"Well," Sistonie said quietly, eyes downcast as her fingers worked the crochet hook, "you might want to refer to them sometime."

Be-Be thought about it and after a few days decided it might not be such a bad idea after all. She let Sistonie do the books for the Spuyten Duyvil, but soon Sistonie started trying to get her to economize. "Now, Virginia, you can't afford this," my great-aunt would say, but Be-Be resisted any restrictions, telling her, "Listen, I may be down, but I'm not *out!*"

The business continued at its usual frenetic pace, and one day Sistonie grew bolder and observed to my grandmother, "I notice you're drinking a lot of beer."

Be-Be recalled their earlier confrontations on the subject, but now the tables were turned. She was in her own house this time, and Sistonie was visiting *her*. "Listen," Be-Be replied calmly. "It's hot in that kitchen. Beer is just like a drink of water to me. Just like a drink of water."

At that, Sistonie must have realized she had reached the limits of her influence, for afterward the two women would sit together peaceably, Sistonie doing the books or crocheting, Be-Be with her bottle of beer.

Later, when Sistonie was in the hospital, she told her brother Leigh, "I want to go up to Saratoga. Virginia knows how to take care of me."

"Now, Onie," Be-Be heard my grandfather reply, "you know you can't go up there now."

And Be-Be always wished that Sistonie could have come to Saratoga one more time.

*   *   *

Sometimes I would walk over to Snookie's soda fountain on Seventh Avenue for the music and the noise, the cherry Cokes, the ice cream sodas, and the boys. From there it was a short walk to Harlem Hospital. I would find Sistonie lying quietly, in a small private room, her brown face smooth and moist, her skin almost translucent; and I would stand awkwardly beside her bed, or sit in one of the hard chairs, while she dozed.

My child self still remembered our trips to "the country," the feel of sitting beside her in her car. There were also a few dim but precious details of a long-ago bus trip to Capahoosic, Virginia, made for some reason I never knew. I remembered the two of us beside the bus at a roadside stand, where a small red bracelet and matching bead necklace were displayed. Then, wondrously, she was giving them to me, putting the bracelet on my arm, clasping the necklace around my neck. Later, as the bus rocked and bounced its way over country roads, we held on to our seats, feeling the cool sea air washing past us.

But the child I had been, the one who had loved Sistonie, was not in communication with the adolescent I had become, and at the hospital I stood by awkwardly, not knowing what to say or do. Sistonie's room, and the crowded corridors of Harlem Hospital, were depressing, and I didn't like going there. I was always glad to leave. Once Sistonie looked over at me and, understanding my dilemma, wisely waved me away. "Go on, go outside and play. This is no place for you."

At these words, the last she spoke to me, I kissed her soft cheek and fled through the grim hospital corridors. One afternoon about two weeks later I came home from school to find one of Sistonie's dresses hanging on the closet door. At first I thought she was well again and would need her dress to leave the hospital. But the expression on my mother's face told me that Sistonie had died and that the dress was for her funeral.

The funeral was at a Harlem Episcopal church. There were distant relatives from Washington who were dimly familiar to me, and other adults I didn't recognize, and I had little connection to anyone. When I saw my aunt in her open casket, I wanted to feel something—to cry—but I only felt more distant from everyone. I looked at Sistonie's face one last time but could not see her there.

About a month later, I was in Be-Be's bedroom in Saratoga,

listening to my mother and my grandmother talking in the adjoining dining room. It was summer, and the leaves were a rich dark green outside the windows. I picked up Sistonie's round ivory-backed mirror, the same one she often sent me looking for in Washington. Feeling the cool handle in my fingers, I looked in the glass and suddenly remembered that I'd dreamed of my aunt the night before. In the dream, Sistonie was talking to me much as she used to when I lived with her as a child. I wasn't sure what to make of it but was amazed that I could feel her again, that she was still alive to me. I called in to my mother and grandmother: "I dreamed of Sistonie last night. She was asking me to fetch her stockings."

There was a long silence. While I waited for their response in the other room, I could imagine my mother and grandmother looking at each other. They had recently given Sistonie's clothes to a friend of Be-Be's. I heard them discuss something about that, and then my mother said, "I made sure she had her stockings on. She definitely had them on."

7

An Exotic Flower

I HAD LONGED FOR WORLDLY experience, and as soon as I could, I journeyed far from Saratoga and Riverton—far from the women in my family—to find it. At the age of nineteen, I married a man who, I realize now, resembled "The Continental," the television character I'd loved as a teenager. André was a Frenchman who claimed to be a millionaire—albeit in French francs—and to be descended from European nobility. Not everyone believed this, and my first serious boyfriend, Ben, was among the disbelievers.

Ben was a handsome and savvy young black man, a pre-med student at Columbia, whom I'd met in my junior year at Music and Art High School. I wrote to him and told him I'd fallen in love with André and that I planned to be married and live in France. Ben, with uncharacteristic concern, called me at my dorm at Bennington College, where I was a scholarship student, and told me he was worried about me, that he was calling as a friend. He hoped I wasn't marrying a Fake Frenchman from Paducah.

I met André in the summer of 1955 at a party near the campus of

Atlanta University, where my father was teaching. I had just turned eighteen, and André's European clothing and smooth manner—and the fact that he was white—set him apart from the other men at the party. His presence on the all-black campus seemed daring; these were days when interracial groups and especially interracial couples were often singled out for harassment by the police.

André and I gravitated to a secluded room away from the others and stood together at a picture window, gazing at the lights of Atlanta below. He was a man of medium height, with straight dark hair and penetrating eyes similar, I thought, to Napoleon's in certain portraits. I learned that André was a trilingual translator from Alsace, fluent in French, German, and English, and about ten years older than I. I had been studying French for seven years by then, since the eighth grade. There was no denying I was already a Francophile. But I had not yet been to France, the place I had for some time considered my soul's homeland. My mother had once or twice spoken of a distant French ancestor, and in a way that made me feel that our family's salvation surely lay in that direction. And I remembered my mother's letters from Paris. I remembered her descriptions of the mirrors and the gold, the flowers, the paintings, and the velvet, on the *Île de France*.

André stood beside me at the window, his hands clasped behind his back. We remarked upon the view. "One night long ago," he murmured deeply, in his almost too perfect, mellifluous English, "I stood on a high hill in Lisbon looking out at the tiny lights and the water far below."

I imagined him there in a slouch hat and trench coat, smoking a cigarette. That night, back at my father's house, I thrilled to the thought of it. Some time after we were married—we were in our apartment in Alsace, and he was sitting on the couch as he had been for days, reading science fiction novels one after the other—I asked him: "When were you in Lisbon?" and he said: "I was four years old; my grandmother had taken me with her on vacation."

But that revelation was at least two years away. A few weeks after the party André and I were in my father's study, listening to the triumphant strains of the Marseillaise in Tchaikovsky's *1812 Overture*. During the lyrical, swelling section of music that follows, André began to speak of his château and of the stream that ran on the sylvan grounds of his home. This was where we would live once we were

married. His father, he said, was a millionaire—in francs, he carefully added, but I understood only the connotations of excitement and
luxury and lack of worry about money. His mother, André told me,
loved to travel. She would welcome me into their home with open
arms—an image that appealed to me more than anything André had
said thus far.

I lay on the floor of my father's study in Atlanta dreaming of lying
beside the flowing river behind the château, with turrets rising in the
distance. I imagined feeling peaceful and fulfilled at last, in the home
of a woman who would accept me completely.

I said, "Yes."

On my return trip north, a telegram was delivered on board my
plane during a short layover. It was in French: I was a *petit chou*, I
was *aimée*, I was *adorée*. Back at Riverton, André's special delivery
letters arrived every few hours, each letter bearing his initials in
sealing wax. When he called, his deep and throaty *"Bon soir, c'est
moi"* resonated over the phone receiver and vibrated through my
body. Then came a package of European perfume, which André said
his mother had sent by special courier to Atlanta, to welcome me into
the family. She was prone to do such things, he said. He had told her
all about me, and she loved me already. "What shall I call her?" I
asked.

"You'll call her Maman!" he'd replied.

My own mother, when she met André, seemed taken by his manners
but frostily resisted the idea of my marrying him. At nineteen, I was
far too young, she thought. I was to finish my schooling no matter
what. A few weeks later, André came up to visit me at Bennington
and stayed at a nearby inn. In anticipation of meeting my grandmother, who was coming for a visit, he decided to iron his shirt in my
dorm ironing room. Be-Be arrived just as he was changing his shirt
and throwing the old one in my closet. It must have looked as if we
were living together, and my grandmother was shocked and disapproving. Soon word reached me that she thought I should stop seeing
André.

But a month later, in New York, André heard from his father
that his mother had died suddenly. Forlorn, he came by our Riverton
apartment and cried and cried. Sitting at our dining room table, he

wrote letters to relatives. It seems to me that my mother and grand-mother's opinion of him changed as of then.

Not long after, we became officially engaged. The distance between my mother and me seemed to grow wider as our separation loomed. When I was home from college, we spent days barely speaking. One day I broke down and began to sob on the living room couch. Suddenly I knew there was no turning back; and for all my rushing away from my childhood, I was suddenly terrified of leaving it behind, of leaving my mother behind. After a few moments she tentatively approached and sat beside me on the sofa. She began to comfort me. "It will be all right," she said. "It will be all right." But I felt she wasn't really sure of that, and I wasn't, either.

Nonetheless, in June, André and I were married in the garden of the Spuyten Duyvil. "The bride wore a waltz-length gown of white organdy eyelet embroidery over pink taffeta, a bolero jacket topping the fitted bodice and the full skirt trimmed with rows of ruffles. Her French illusion veil was attached to a seed pearl coronet," read the notice in *The Saratogian* under the headline NEW YORK GIRL, FRENCH-MAN MARRY IN SARATOGA CEREMONY. The photographs show me beaming in anticipation of wedded life, excited about the trousseau my mother had helped me gather, including a traveling outfit and many crinolines, hats, gloves, shoes, and suitable pocketbooks. My mother is serious and frowning, her arms crossed in front of her; and my father is listing to the side a bit, somehow defeated-looking and sad.

A few weeks later, André and I sailed to Europe on the Italian liner *Giulio Cesare*. After nine days at sea, we spotted the first land— an exquisite moment. As I stood on deck, the shores of Africa lay misty and green to my right, and Spain, reddish brown with bits of green, extended to my left. Each continent seemed to pull me toward it, but the boat continued straight between. I watched mesmerized as we approached the Rock of Gilbraltar, growing steadily bigger. When we moored at Naples, vendors rushed out in small boats, bringing jewelry and baskets, perfumes and clothing to sell. André and I got off and walked a bit. I wore one of my full skirts with three crinolines under it. We passed a group of Neapolitan women, and after we'd gone a few feet, one of them suddenly ran up behind me and lifted my skirt to see what was holding it out. Laughing and chattering, she rushed back to report to her friends.

When I got my wish and stood at last on French soil, I was

uneasy. Oddly, the feel of land after ten days at sea was not reassuring. Suddenly I wanted to get back on the boat. *Don't tell me I'm missing the boat—don't tell me to sink or float,* lines from one of the calypsos my mother sang, came back to me as we turned away from the harbor.

We took a train almost immediately, but instead of finding myself in the France of my imagination, I arrived in a textile manufacturing town in the Haut-Rhin. I sensed immediately that I had landed in the middle of wounded territory. The Alsatians were still recovering from being pulled between France and Germany in two world wars. A new language had been imposed on them each time the territory changed hands, but the people continued to speak their own dialect, a melodic Germanic parlance called Elsaesser-Ditsch.

It was 1956. These were, I realized later, the last days of the old Europe, prior to television and the steady inroads of Americanization. Hardly anyone in the town we lived in had ever seen a black person. Everyone stared at me in the streets. Those who had some point of reference assumed I must be from a tropical French territory like Martinique. Inwardly, I laughed, remembering my child self bundled in snowsuits in Saratoga.

"A *negala, a schöne negala!*" people exclaimed, pointing me out wherever I went. I was told that people thought me beautiful, that this was why they stared, but I was still uncomfortable.

It was early morning when we arrived at André's father's apartment in town. The château was not yet habitable; Pappi was still doing repairs on the place, and everything had been delayed by his wife's death. For the meantime, we would live in the apartment in town, where Pappi also had his dentist's office.

Pappi, clad in white and holding a dental instrument, rushed from his office into the parlor, where we were waiting. He was a big, gruff man, with florid cheeks and sparse gray mustache and whiskers. "Uh, Carole," he grunted. *"Bien venue."* His French was thickly accented and came with difficulty. He kissed me on both cheeks and then turned to André and began spouting Alsatian. I had never quite realized they'd be speaking a great deal of a language I didn't understand. Later André translated some of their exchange for me:

"She is an exotic flower," my husband had told his father in his usual dramatic manner. And his father had replied with his own kind of drama: "Ah yes, but sometimes exotic flowers do not transplant well."

Pappi rushed back to his patients, and his mother, a frail white-haired woman dressed completely in black, arrived to greet me. She removed her veil and, pressing her dry little cheek to mine on each side, made a small, sharp kissing noise. *"Bon jou',"* she said, and then continued in Alsatian. André translated her welcome into French and explained that Mammi's second husband had just died the night before and we were required to go view the body.

The château was actually a handsome French manor house, with a tower and beautiful grounds. But the first floor was rented out, and my father-in-law, to his everlasting amusement, had placed a toilet in the tower.

Telephones were rare in Alsace, and women still sent notes of invitation to tea a week ahead. Similarly, the custom of having your own *jour de visite*—a day when others knew you would be at home and available to visitors—was still common. I made these *visites* once a week or every two weeks with three women who were wives of André's old school buddies. Or we'd rendezvous at a *salon de thé* for delicious *mille-feuilles, pâtés à choux,* and *éclairs.* After we had met a few times, making polite talk, they began to reveal how unhappy they were with their young marriages—marriages that they nonetheless saw stretching out before them into old age. Their husbands had clerical jobs or positions with manufacturing firms. They would have to save for years for the smallest material improvements in their lives. They were already disillusioned with their husbands and angry at the stereotyped roles they, as women, were required to fulfill—but they saw no way out. How, they asked me, were things in America, where they had heard women were so much freer? They hoped to visit there one day, but it probably wouldn't happen until their husbands were retired. They wondered what life would have been like if they'd married American men. How could I stand it in Alsace?

Gradually I developed the same sardonic tone about Alsace that the Alsatians had. I had recognized it almost immediately; many black people in America talked about themselves in much the same way. I realize now that it was exactly that depressing feeling of being thought inferior to the society I lived in that I had hoped to escape by marrying

André. The vague sense of peace I'd imagined back in my father's study when I'd said "Yes" to André had much to do with my longing to assuage the painful and confusing aspects of blackness. Ironically, I found myself instead having to deal with the same problem in a new form. To the rest of France (the *intérieur*), Alsace was known as the *extérieur*. Many Alsatians mocked themselves, and some, affecting Parisian accents, aspired to be "more French than the French." It was all too familiar. There was no peace for me in Alsace, and although there was, for a while, a certain camaraderie, there was no love from my new husband.

I mentioned nothing of my sense of isolation to my mother and grandmother, or to my father. My letters to them were filled with details of my discoveries in Europe. I loved my new stationery, with *Madame* engraved on it. I wrote about the vacation we took on the Adriatic coast of Italy, and our trips to Freiburg and to Basel, where I could get milk shakes, Nescafé, and a semblance of city life. I told them about our black-and-white kitten, Paolo, and passed on things I'd learned from the latest *Elle*. I loved the gossip about the doings of European nobility in *Paris Match*. I passed on the tip that red wine was fortifying and good for the blood. I told Be-Be I'd been introduced to more different kinds of salads than I'd ever known could be made and that I'd discovered (easily enough, as we lived over a butcher shop) that the production of cold cuts and sausages could be elevated to a high art.

Our lives in Alsace, André always said—by way of explanation for the discrepancies between reality and the stories he had told me during our courtship—would have been completely different had his mother lived. And I clung to the memory of this woman I had never met, listening to relatives' accounts of her sunny nature, examining smiling photographs. Only long after I had left Alsace and André, long after I had ceased being *Madame*, did it occur to me that perhaps his mother had never loved me sight unseen, as André had said—as I had been so eager to believe she could. Yet it seems to me that had she lived, she might have protected me in some way. I discovered with André that I could be a victim or I could be a survivor.

The abortionist arrived night after night in his leather jacket, parking his motorcycle in the dark alley behind our apartment. We would close the old wartime shutters of the room in which we had our daily lunch; and then the two of them, the cyclist and André, would begin the "safe" operation, with hot water and soap and a syringe, that was supposed to terminate my pregnancy. André had felt it was too soon to have children and had persuaded me to take some pills that were supposed simply to bring on my period the next day. After that, I felt trapped, not knowing how much damage had already been done to the baby inside me.

Yet I resisted night after night, holding on to the baby, submerging the cramps they said would come "anytime now." Days I spent in the tub, the only place I felt warm and safe. A house was being gutted across the way, and in the mornings and afternoons, as I watched the wreckers at their work, I would fantasize about entering the house at night, when no one was there, and finding something I needed. I had no idea what it might be, something tangible, solid perhaps, in the midst of the destruction to which I was being subjected. It was on the evening of the last day of the wreckers' work, when the last board was thrown down, that I heard them talking in the kitchen as, once again, they boiled the hot, soapy water. "She is strong," they whispered. "Yes, she is strong."

That night I waited as usual in my skirt with nothing beneath it, in the darkened parlor between the kitchen and the dining room. But for the first time since this hideous process had begun, I admitted to myself what I had been too terrified to acknowledge before—that the two men, one of them the man I had married, were in collusion. They had formed a bond. My "strength" was a challenge to their manhood, and they were determined as a point of male pride to succeed in aborting me on the dining room table.

For the first time I allowed myself to understand that my very life was in danger. If I continued to resist by remaining numb, I could die.

That night, instead of feeling nothing, I felt nauseous. I knew that the cramps were coming. I was sick through and through. I knew that I could not give birth to a living child, not then, but I also knew that I could save myself.

In the hours after the abortionist left, I let go of the baby I had been holding on to, and gradually I felt life arriving from someplace very far off. It was coming to me in the form of pain. But it was life again.

In the old cupboard in the kitchen, there were ten jars of preserved deep-red Algerian "blood" peaches, which André's mother had put up many years before. During the days after the abortion, I ate nothing else. I lay in bed and ate them all, one by one, letting the rich, sweet flavor, the vibrant color, seep through me until they were gone and, miraculously, I was well again.

Before the abortion I had spent long, lonely days writing to friends, doing some painting, and writing short stories. Sometimes I would go up to the railway station to buy literary magazines. It was there that I found a magazine called *Arcadie: Revue Littéraire et Scientifique*. An article caught my attention, and I wrote to the author, who turned out to be one of the few women writing for the magazine. Her nom de plume was Claude Brunegarde. She spoke and wrote English as well as French, and she lived in the north of France with an architect and writer named Simone Marigny. They invited me to visit them, and I longed to go, but André had always said no.

Now, after the abortion, I told him in no uncertain terms that I was going, and he put me on the train. At the end of a cold, nine-hour trip, the two women greeted me and, though I was painfully shy, treated me to music and fine wines, a roaring fireplace, South American flute recordings, and literary talk. It seemed like the real world at last. It was Simone who drove me to Paris, as she had to go there on business and neither she nor Claude could bear the thought of my returning to Alsace without having set foot in the capital. Not since I was a child riding with Sistonie in her Chevrolet coupe had I felt such a sense of well-being.

Shortly after I got back to Alsace, André and I returned to the United States, and soon after that I left him.

I made one more trip to the château for my trunks. Pappi had stored them beside his wife's, which were still filled with her clothes and mementos of her trips to the United States. Opening one of my own trunks, I recalled the excitement that had gone into packing it and was suddenly overwhelmed by the scent of my mother's perfume. I sat in a chair by the sunlit window, watching the life of the tiny Alsatian village below, marveling at the power of my mother's essence to reach me over such a long distance, over time.

8

The Dead Are Still Alive

ON OUR RETURN TO NEW York, André and I settled on the top floor of a town house on upper Lexington Avenue, where we occupied separate bedrooms. André went to work as a translator for a bank, and I enrolled at NYU and later at the New School, studying French literature, philosophy, and writing.

Encouraged by André's philosophy of free love, I was soon involved in an affair with a brilliant, heavy-drinking married man, a bohemian twenty years older than I. Eventually we began sharing an apartment downtown, though for appearance sake I had my own place nearby. My mother didn't approve.

After my marriage my mother had started spending winters in Mexico, but she came up to Saratoga each summer to help run the Spuyten Duyvil. I resumed my summertime work there, and once, in the kitchen—where most important discussions took place—I mentioned the name of my new lover. To my surprise, my mother was livid. "I'll kill him!" she said.

Perhaps if I'd been able to tell her the truth about the failure of

my storybook marriage to André, she would have been more support-
ive. But that kind of revelation was not part of our relationship. None
of the women in my family, neither my mother, my grandmother, nor
my great-aunt, had ever talked about private things—sex, childbear-
ing, abortion. All along I'd felt alone in dealing with these issues.

From the older married man I moved on to another unconven-
tional relationship, with a woman painter who lived in a loft on Canal
Street. I had begun to understand that I was—like most people, I
thought—not simply heterosexual but sexual, and from then on I
would resist any labels on my sexuality.

The area that would become SoHo was desolate then; the nearest
supermarket was blocks away, and taking clothes to the laundromat
involved a time-consuming expedition on the subway. I spent my days
painting and, putting away all my dresses, started wearing jeans and
T-shirts. We were so poor that there were nights we barely scraped
up enough money for peanuts, a Hershey bar, or some potato chips.
During one particularly bad spell, I descended the five long flights to
the mailbox, to find that it had been stolen. On my birthday that year,
Be-Be baked me my favorite chocolate cake, wrapped it, and sent it
through the mail. We lived for two days on the thick chunks of cake
that survived the trip.

The relationships among my companion's friends were intricately
intertwined, and status in the group shifted from day to day. There
was an almost religious fervor and seriousness of purpose among us as
we tried to figure out the world. A poet whom I'll call Nan was
considered by most of us to be a prophet. She was awaiting a revolution. Two of the women were junkies, who would periodically try
to kick the habit. A young woman I'll give the name of Jessica tried
to pay homage to the young Dalai Lama, who was visiting New York
for the first time, and unable to get beyond the door of his hotel room,
she left all her ID there. She was admired by us for that but lost
status when it was discovered that she was an heiress.

One day early on I'd overheard several of the women talking
candidly about themselves and realized that most were or had been
call girls. I soon discovered that there was more than one way of
viewing prostitution. For some, angrily selling their beautiful bodies
to undeserving men was a tragic form of protest against early abuse in
their lives. They were tough and proud of it, but they hurt themselves more than they hurt others. I learned from one of Nan's poems

that policemen who pretended they were johns always turned the trick before they busted the hooker.

Just being around these women constantly tested my limits. My friend, however, tested her own limits in some very frightening ways. During the two years we were living on Canal Street, I would go up to Saratoga in the summer to work so that I could help pay the rent and continue to paint. By the time I returned to New York, I'd find that my friend had taken some new drug and was a completely different person from the one I'd left.

In Saratoga, there was a frosty politeness during these years. My mother and grandmother never talked about my relationship with a woman; though my mother must have felt that I'd gone from bad—a relationship with a married man—to worse, she confined herself to pregnant silences and piercing looks. My grandmother hinted that I should go back to André, or at least try to make myself more attractive to men.

At the Spuyten Duyvil now, a bevy of nervous waitresses, hand-picked and primed by my mother, had names like Gayle, Abby, and Paisley. Most of them were blondes, and in their white skirts with aprons that tied in big bows at the back, they looked like Alice in Wonderland. Sometimes they chatted with my mother about dating and men, and about which of our customers were eligible bachelor millionaires. I would listen, oddly jealous, while I buried my head in a book of poetry or my journal. I felt that my mother, on some level, wanted daughters like that—daughters who were neat and perky, privileged and white.

For Be-Be the waitresses were "that one with the funny teeth," or "the little fuzzy-headed one," or "the one who looks like a school marm." Often I'd have to shush her so the girl wouldn't hear. And if Be-Be was discussing a waitress at all, it was most likely because she was suspected of doing something wrong, usually having to do with money.

Be-Be was still turning out a dazzling array of food from the kitchen: In one day we might serve hot roast turkey with stuffing, steaks to order, fifteen broiled chickens, baked Virginia ham, broiled pork chops with a rich tomato sauce, rice, potatoes, string beans, garden tomatoes, corn, and, for dessert, fresh peaches, strawberries, cobblers, puddings, and cakes. As each plate went out, she'd survey it suspiciously. It was the waitresses' job to garnish the food before it left the kitchen. There had to be plenty of butter on the biscuits, a sprig of parsley on every plate.

There was an edge in the air at the Spuyten Duyvil, a feeling that often bordered on hysteria. Anything could happen. One night Be-Be's old friend Cab Calloway came in and got the whole joint jumping, everyone singing chorus after chorus of "Minnie the Moocher," while Fred Astaire stood gracefully in the garden. Cab returned, and Be-Be could be seen doing some of her old dance steps with him. The composer Luckey Roberts (Mr. Luckey to us) sat in at the piano one night when the regular piano player failed to show. And Noble Sissle, the songwriter, performer, and orchestra leader, who collaborated with Eubie Blake on the shows *Shuffle Along* and *Chocolate Dandies,* would come in every afternoon and night he was in town. One evening he went through all the songs of *Shuffle Along* for the customers in the bar.

Illustrious customers could cause problems too. One night a famous jockey sat at the bar way past closing time. "Mr. B., it's time to go," my grandmother said finally.

"I'll go when I damn well please," he replied.

Be-Be, who kept a meat mallet behind the bar for just such occasions (there was a baseball bat beside her bed for intruders), brandished it, then grabbed the tiny jockey by the collar and lifted him bodily from the barstool. "You're going *now!*" she said. He went.

Yearly, my grandmother threatened to "set the bucket down." The work was hard, and the money the restaurant brought in never seemed to be enough to make it all worth while. But no one ever took her seriously. Saratoga was a vital part of our lives and seemed it always would be, even for me, focused on my painting and my relationships.

When the relationship with my artist friend ended, I left Canal Street and got a job with an airline. The job was boring, but the travel benefits were fantastic: California for weekends, Paris on a "four day." When I wasn't traveling I lived by myself in a sublet in Chelsea. I was twenty-eight years old and lonely. What I had really been wanting for some time now was to have a baby. From the beginning, with André, I had gravitated to relationships in which that was impossible.

It was at the airline that I met Salvatore Joseph Bovoso, known then as "Joe," sitting across from me at the computer terminal. It was 1967 and he was an aspiring actor, younger than I was by seven years, and I discovered that he had had relationships only with men before me. Salvatore had an irrepressible personality and could talk his way into or out of anything. He made everyone around him laugh. As 1968's Summer of Love approached, I suggested he use his first name, and bought him a Mao jacket. He started to let his hair grow and to wear white kurtas. We found a Canal Street loft together not far from the one I'd lived in a few years before, and when August rolled around and it was time for me to go to work in Saratoga, I suggested that he tend bar there for the month.

My mother and grandmother were clearly disapproving of Salvatore. He was not suave and cultured, as André had appeared to be. For this I was grateful. He also had muttonchop whiskers and hair that made him look suspiciously like the hippies whose shocking doings were daily reported on television. The tension escalated when Be-Be, who was wont to distrust any bartender, accused him of stealing from the cash register.

One day, as Salvatore and I sat talking in my old room with the red-rose wallpaper, my mother, thinking it was improper, confronted him: "I think you need to leave. Carole is already married!" At first there was the stunned silence of disbelief. As Salvatore knew, I had been separated from André for eight years. Was she still hoping I would reconcile with him? Besides, I was almost thirty years old. Salvatore began cursing, and I chose that moment to announce that I was pregnant. My mother rushed to her own room and closed the door.

We headed for New York immediately, and then made arrangements to move to California, where, after a shaky start, some friends eventually loaned us their house in Marin County, overlooking Mount Tamalpais. "We want you to have your baby here," they'd said, handing me the keys. One day as I sat painting at the window, my belly big with my first baby, I counted seven rainbows crossing and crisscrossing each other over the sacred Indian mountain.

Content in colorful beads and caftans, I tried to put the estrangement from my mother out of my mind. I was looking forward to a future with my own family—a family I'd created, in which the men and women would be together, not separate as they had been while I was growing up. Salvatore was very devoted, and I felt needed, wanted. I would lie in bed listening to the owls hooting at night, as

I tried to find a comfortable position for sleeping. It was during one of these restless nights that the dreams began.

An older woman is leading me through a forest. She is Sistonie. Finally, we reach a clearing at the edge of the trees, and there, stretched out before us, are many, many dead bodies. Sistonie guides me past the gray and lifeless forms, and as we pass each one, she bids me look closely. And I look, and I see that eyelids begin to flutter, limbs begin to stir. I wake up in distress.

"Your aunt is looking after you," Be-Be explained to me on the phone when I told her about the dreams. "She is taking care of you." I didn't understand; how could I interpret these gruesome dreams as my being taken care of? But I believed Be-Be, anyway, and began taking a closer look at the dreams. As I considered them, a message came clear: *The dead are still alive.*

A few days later, we headed across the Golden Gate Bridge at dawn toward the U.C. Medical Institute, where Alessandro, who began crying even before he had fully emerged, was born by cesarean. The exhilarating feeling I'd had while pregnant—of *life* moving inside me—continued as I began to feed my baby with my own body, my own milk.

But it took me four more years to understand Sistonie's message fully. Then, in the days after my first discovery of her mother's diary, I would read that a certain tribe of northeastern woodland Native Americans, the Fox or Muskaki Indians, have a special ritual. When a woman is pregnant with her first child, a special woman in her family comes to her and she is taken aside, away from the tribe. At this time she is initiated into the mysteries of all the women in her family and gains entrance into their circle.

9

Exile

"A LITTLE LUMP OF GOLD," my grandmother called Alessandro as she had once been called. "Just a little lump of gold come down from heaven."

We had come east because of the prediction that a big earthquake would take California in 1969. We decided to stop in Saratoga long enough to prepare for a trip to Spain. The island of Ibiza had been very much in the news, as a kind of mecca for hippies. In sleepy Saratoga, we began to daydream about what it would be like to live in a community in which we would feel more comfortable than in the United States.

The arrival of the baby had soothed my grandmother's feelings, and she now accepted Salvatore wholeheartedly. He certainly couldn't be all bad, having helped produce the miracle of her first great-grandson. Soon my mother arrived from Mexico, and she, too, was delighted with the baby. I was contented, feeling that I had somehow redeemed myself. I had managed to create a wonderful addition to our family. Alessandro as a boy child in our family of women provided a new experience for everyone.

I was loving all the hard lessons of motherhood, which Alan Watts's books had led me to consider the finest Buddhist training. New mothers must come to terms with the concept of impermanence or perish. I learned immediately that a fresh diaper and a clean baby are only fleeting illusions. Watching my baby grow and change brought home both the precariousness of life and its amazing potency.

I had also begun the long process of coming to terms with myself as an artist. Once I had the urge to draw while Alessandro was sitting quietly in his bassinet. I gathered my drawing materials but was distracted by my baby, who at the moment wasn't even demanding attention. Starting to draw anyway, I found that parts of me had changed since I gave birth. My concentration was not the same. Was the change merely temporary, I wondered, or was it permanent? Was my artist self different from my mother self? Were they at odds? It was something women all over the world were thinking about in new ways, and the next six years of having babies provided me with my own testing ground.

Racial issues were also coming to the fore in society and the media. Black people were letting their hair look the way it really looked and thinking that it was beautiful. I had not yet mustered the courage to let my own hair go into an Afro, but I only straightened it once in a very long while and wrapped it up most of the time.

Alessandro was a creamy brown, with straight black hair. My grandmother's Saratoga friends began dropping by to see him, but I grew sensitive about all the compliments. I suspected that many times Alessandro's straight black hair, his non-"blackness," were being touted; that I was being congratulated for "whitening up" the family. What if I had had a little black baby? What if my baby had had "bad" hair like mine? Would he have been less loved?

I was embarrassed one afternoon when one of Be-Be's friends chucked Alessandro under the chin and said, "I'm going to be your chauffeur, boy, when you grow up!" Salvatore heard, too, and told me that it had made him sad. A joke, it had a serious underlay, like my grandmother's "Come on in, this is a colored place." That, too, was meant as a joke, but it was a *true* joke, serious. Even as a child I had felt that there was pride in being *colored*, and yet something else went along with it, a self-denigration that seemed to give over too much power to whites, to take too much away from us. I hadn't understood why we couldn't all get along like the interracial characters I created in my coloring books. Why did so much have to be made of our differences?

If you're white, you're all right. If you're brown, stick around. If you're black, get back. I may have wanted the famous old expression to be otherwise, but I was finding more and more that it was true. It was only my own anger and pride that kept me from acknowledging that it was. I had always wanted my life to be so much larger than black and white, just as my allegiances to and feelings for country were larger than the United States. I did not want to be limited by color or by nationality or by gender.

But I was finding that it was not that simple. Every time I headed toward the concept of "freedom," I was brought up short, brought back to another reality. In Europe I had already learned, despite the finger-pointing in Alsace, that my color was not always the main issue. Instead, I was often looked upon with curiosity and sometimes with anger as an "American." To my surprise, I found myself defending the United States against vicious Frenchmen, bombastic Italians, and flippant Spaniards. Ironically, by leaving the country I had become more American. Nonetheless, as we dreamed of Ibiza, I was still drawn to the possibility of being freer and safer, more at home, in Europe than in the United States.

We passed that winter in Saratoga with Be-Be, and Alessandro had his first Christmas there. But we were gearing up for departure, saving money and making plans. We found an ad in *The Village Voice*: a painter wanted to exchange his Ibiza house for a New York loft. We answered it, and despite several complicated setbacks, before too long we were on a plane to Spain.

Ibiza was filled with Europeans and Americans living another version of our old San Francisco life-style. People were traveling all over the world—India, Afghanistan, Morocco—and Ibiza seemed to be the place to return to before heading off again. The women wore colorful long skirts and Spanish sandals, straw hats and white pants, gold bangles and the requisite "Ibiza bag." Before we left Saratoga, Salvatore had bought inexpensive material at the five-and-ten and made us lots of wide-legged drawstring pants, tops, and caftans. We fit right in; tourists photographed us, and the others often nodded their approval as we passed.

My second child, Santiago Hylan Lewis y Bovoso (we had purposely inverted the family names to avoid separating my father's name), arrived by an unexpected natural birth, despite my prior cesarean, in the winter of 1971 in Barcelona. Salvatore and I were not yet married. It hadn't seemed necessary, and we found to our surprise that the Spanish, who had no divorce laws, were used to such circumstances and understood completely. The American Consulate, on the other hand, insulted us, and made us wait a month for Santiago's passport because we were not married. A few months later, we packed up all our things and returned to Saratoga so that the family could see the new baby. There, to simplify matters, we were married one day by a Justice of the Peace. We were also regrouping, having finally realized that Spain was not the place we wanted to settle in. Despite the illusion of freedom there, Franco had a strong grip on Spain, and his Guardia Civile was omnipresent.

In Saratoga, we gathered money through my writing and Salvatore's cooking and wrote to various realtors in France, and after several months, with the help of a loan, we bought an old stone farmhouse outside a little town in Haut-Provence. It had cherry trees lining the driveway, a garden and a stream out back. Mont-Saint-Euphamie rose up behind it. I spent my days drawing the view from the driveway, looking across wheat fields to the pre-Alps in the distance. Lavender fields bordered our land, giant cypresses grew beside the stream. The children played with their toy trucks and cars and tractors in the front yard. We planted hybrid corn from Be-Be's favorite vegetable man in Saratoga.

All this would have been idyllic, but for the fact that it was difficult to make a living there. We were so poor that we spent one whole rainy winter running up a tab at the *épicerie* in town. We had exhausted the sparse items on the shelves, and our goal was to try to make something exciting out of the same old ingredients. Over the next few years, Salvatore and I tried to live in the house, sometimes succeeding, sometimes not. We kept having to come back to America to get free-lance writing assignments, or other work, to save up enough to go back to France. As soon as things got intolerable in the U.S., for one reason or another—and they always did—we would figure out a way to get back to Europe.

New York friends envied us our exotic life. We loved the feel of France and Spain. We loved the Mediterranean. Whenever I returned to Ibiza, or to France, I felt that this was where I really belonged, and wondered how I could imagine ever wanting to live in the United States. We liked being expatriates, but things didn't quite work *there,* and they didn't quite work *here,* either. We had not yet created a home together, not really.

In 1973, we were in New York City, having rented out our house in France. I was pregnant again, but I was not at all reconciled to giving birth in the States. At the last moment—in my eighth month—my father loaned us money for tickets, and with an enormous sense of relief and gratitude, we got back to Ibiza, where we stayed at our friend Tim Pickering's house, Es Puas.

My mother, who loved the *corridas,* wrote to say she would come visit us in Barcelona. She had become enthralled with bullfighting in Mexico, where she was known as La Perla by the other aficionados. The bullfighters all loved her and had taken her into their confidence as a kind of godmother, and she had begun her own club, which would periodically sponsor young bullfighters of talent.

In the same luxurious yet inexpensive *clínica* in Barcelona where I gave birth to Santiago, my third child, Antonio Leigh Rollin Bovoso, was born. I had taken his middle names from my grandfather, Leigh Whipper, and my great-aunt, Ionia Rollin Whipper. The name Rollin, I seemed to remember hearing, had something to do with our French ancestry.

With the new baby in my arms, and the other boys playing in the back, we set out from Barcelona in our old VW van, heading for our little house in Haut-Provence. I felt triumphant. I now had all the babies I needed to have. With Antonio's birth, something important had been completed, something lost regained. The feeling was so strong that I wondered if Antonio could be the baby I had given up in Alsace, finally returned to me. My father's secretary, "Miss Bea," came to visit a few days later and photographed me holding Antonio. As I posed, I knew it was a moment I'd long remember.

My father came to visit that autumn and, as we sat in our vaulted, cavelike dining room, for the first time confided something of his childhood. He told me about how, as a boy of twelve, he heard his father get up and go into the kitchen to boil water for tea. He followed him there and saw his father fall to the floor, taken by a stroke. He ran to get a mirror to see if his father was breathing, and then ran to get the doctor. He told me of how he had been sent to live with the Bassette family in Virginia not long after his father had died, and how surprised the family had been at his bright and studious nature. His foster father, Dr. Edward E. Bassette, took him under his wing and saw him through college. "I owe everything to him," he told me.

I had never even thought about what my father's life as a young boy might have been, and walking along the road one day after he'd left, with Antonio in a sling at my breast, I found myself suddenly moved to tears about this new connection to him, my knowledge of his time spent in Virginia, his presence at his own father's last breath. At last I understood something I'd heard my mother say to him once, "We were both orphans, really, you and I."

After my father had gone, things got harder for Salvatore and me. There was still the problem of never having a steady income. But mostly things were hard because of Salvatore's unhappiness. Salvatore cooked whenever we had company, which was often—we only had to mention to the most casual stranger where we lived to find him or her ambling up the driveway before another season had passed. Salvatore cooked so much, in fact, that I began to think that it was his way of separating himself from everyone. As long as he was there behind the counter, he was not really a part of things.

Salvatore also took care of the children and did some writing and painting. But there was a secret, his secret, and because I was keeping it too, it was ours. He was a gay man living a heterosexual life. I had told him at the very beginning that it didn't matter to me. He didn't have to pretend anything. But I was naive to think it was that simple. There were friends, important to us, who, Salvatore was certain, would never understand.

He often had bad dreams. A man would be chasing him, and though he might look different in each dream, it was always the same man. In one of these dreams, Salvatore and I were dancing, when the man came and interrupted our dance. There had been different versions of the dream since Salvatore was a little boy. It awakened him one night on the Costa Brava. We walked together down by the Mediterranean beside the cliffs, overlooking the coves where the children played in the daytime, and we talked it out. The moon shone creamy yellow, high over our heads, as I walked with him over the rocks and we talked until he wasn't frightened anymore.

Sometimes I'd ask him if he wouldn't rather be with a man than with me. But his answer was always no. No, he did not really want that. He wanted to be with me. He would try valiantly to make our marriage work, and then, frequently, he would give up and stop trying at all. And I found myself trying too hard all the time. I tried not to take his depression personally, but one day I realized I *wanted* it to be personal, to have something to do with me. Much as we hated to admit it to ourselves, our search for a new kind of life, free of sexual stereotypes, was failing.

10

An Illuminated Diary

ONCE MORE, IN THE HOPES that moving would solve everything, we rented out our house and came back to New York. We found a cavernous loft in Brooklyn, under the Manhattan Bridge, behind which were slums worse than anything I had seen in Harlem. Salvatore began cooking at a halfway house in Queens, and I sought out free-lance writing work.

I had returned to New York after four years to find that I was no longer a Negro girl but a black woman. I was a little taken aback the first time someone called me that, because only moments before, it seemed, the word "black" had been derogatory (as in *If you're black, get back*), and "woman" implied not dignity but age.

Black people's Afros were growing immense, but I remained on the line in terms of making a political statement with my hair. I kept to my own eclectic look: I usually wrapped my head—in rags, Be-Be said—and draped myself in capes and long skirts. For years I wore an indestructible pair of authentic antique lace-up shoes bought brand new. Beneath the wrappings, my hair was returning to natural from periodic straightenings, pulled up and tied in a rubber band.

Women in general looked completely different from the way they had when I left. Combat boots, sneakers, and khakis had replaced the bangles and beads and frills of the sixties. I became part of a group of women writers and editors who were beginning to meet at each other's apartments for what were laughingly called Ladies' Literary Luncheons. The feeling at the meetings was one of great excitement, of empowerment. As I recall, I was the only black woman there. I was also an anomaly, with my three children running all around me as I wrote at home, at a time when most of my women acquaintances were choosing not to have children.

As I looked for ideas for articles, I decided to write about the women in my family. I remembered that my mother had once mentioned a diary written by Sistonie's mother, and thought I might include that in a story about my mother, my grandmother, and my great-aunt. On the phone from Saratoga, my mother told me that a historian named Dorothy Sterling had been studying the diary, and she arranged to have her send it to me.

The little package arrived at the loft by mail, landing in the middle of my strained marriage, in the middle of my life of mothering and writing. The diary was covered by a small piece of protective cardboard, and I left it intact on my desk all that day, waiting for undisturbed time to look at it. That night, once the children were asleep, I took the diary to a comfortable corner of the loft and knelt on the creaky floorboards. I could hear the dull drone of cars whizzing past in a mechanical ocean of sound overhead, as the children slept peacefully.

The diary's fine brown leather binding was worn by age, and the light of my small lamp played on pages that were covered with a faint, elegant script. I couldn't make out the handwriting at first. On the title page, the words *Illuminated Diary for 1868* were printed in an ornate scroll, and underneath, a delicately drawn schooner, sails full, traveled neatly circumscribed waves.

I quickly scanned the information at the beginning of the book: *Rates of Postage: Letters to any part of the United States, 3 cents for each ½ ounces or part thereof. Difference of Time: When it is 12 o'clock noon*

at New York City, it will be morning at all places west of New York, and afternoon at all places east. Moon phases and Eclipses, Morning and Evening Stars: Venus will be Evening Star until July 16th; then Morning Star the rest of the year. Schedule of Movable Fasts and Feasts . . .
Already I could feel myself sinking into the time of the diary. I took a deep breath and turned to the first page of faded writing.

January 1 Boston Mass. A rainy, gloomy day. Speeches tonight at the Tremont Temple, but so terribly rainy that there is no possibility of reaching there. I sent a letter to mother today which I wrote last night . . . the latest hour nearly of the old year.

The year renews its birth today with all of its hopes and sorrows. Uncertainty and doubt are in its wake. To me and mine I know not, but may God enable me, whatever may be my lot, to murmur not, but patiently bear and wait and labor.

My reaction to this melancholy first entry was visceral. I could *feel* the presence of my great-grandmother as I yearned to follow that letter to "mother" to its destination. Who was my great-great-grandmother? I couldn't even imagine her. I came back to the diary. Frances Rollin was closer. I turned the page and, miraculously, there she was again.

January 2. Clearing up today somewhat. In the evening went to the Fair at Horticultural Hall. Imogene Howard and I met. We had been to see "John Brown" at Child's Gallery. I do not like the painter's license. He is blessing instead of kissing the Negro child. "The bold blue eyes grew tender and the stern harsh face grew mild, as he stepped around the jeering ranks to kiss the Negro child."

My great-grandmother was a woman who went to art galleries and quoted poetry. I recognized John Brown's name, but little else; later I found out that the fair was one of many antislavery meetings in Boston around the time of the Civil War. A *New York Tribune* reporter had made up the story that John Brown, on his way to the gallows for having led an insurrection of slaves in Virginia, kissed a black child. John Greenleaf Whittier then incorporated the story into his poem "Brown of Osawatomie," which my great-grandmother was quoting nearly verbatim.

January 3. Writing as hard as ever. I know not with what success I shall meet, but I feel there is a strength in the endeavor which will be of service to me hereafter. Mr. Richard T. Greener has gone over some of it with me, but he is cynical and apt to discourage instead of acting otherwise.

He lives in a grand intellectual sphere and is accustomed to only perfection.

She was writing, I would soon learn, a biography of Martin Delany, a man of whom I knew nothing. In her words about the effort being "of service to me hereafter," I sensed a lifetime sustained by that work and by the lessons learned that Boston winter. I felt a shiver as I realized that "hereafter" had included a future which now extended to me.

January 5. I attended on last Sunday the M.E. Church and heard a fine sermon. This afternoon I went to Mr. Gomes' Church—the sermon was humble. After, Emily and I went to Mrs. Hayden's and we took tea there. Mr. Chas Lennox came there for me and we went to the Church at the Boston Theatre. Rev Ed Everett Hale. "The good that I would I do not, but the evil that I would not, that I do." I was instructed and thought of the grand intellectual development for generations through his family and compared.

January 7. I spent an impatient day waiting for evening. I sat and listened to Dickens. He acted as only Dickens can. He knows his characters so thoroughly that he and they are inseparable. "Mr. Peggotty" was grand—his genius never emitted a purer ray than when it conceived the old rough sailor. It was so naturally told that we all saw him.

Dickens? The following morning I looked up the dates of Charles Dickens's visits to the United States and discovered that he had been here in 1867–68, reading from his books. I learned, too, that Lewis Hayden was a runaway slave who in 1868 was a messenger to the Massachusetts secretary of state. Staunch members of Boston's black community, the Haydens had turned their home into a busy station on the Underground Railroad.

I wondered about those generations of intellectual development, and thinking of the little I knew of our family, I, too, compared. I remembered my grandfather's pronouncements about the Whippers—all those great men of worth. But Frances Rollin's diary seemed to be about a different world, and it was begun before she was even married to a Whipper.

January 20. Writing as usual. In the afternoon went to Mr. Phillips. How his grand prophet face lighted up when I inadvertently saw I had succeeded. And how generously he offered to hear me read my ms. though it would take up his time. He gave me an invitation for the Anti-Slavery Festival and gave me Emerson to read. How it cheers me to spend an hour with such a masterpiece of humanity. It reconciles me to Americans.

In the 1960s and '70s, Wendell Phillips and the other Boston abolitionists in Frances Rollin's circle were just beginning to be taught in high school and college history classes. But my own education in the '50s had been sorely lacking in black history.

Later I looked at pictures of Wendell Phillips and tried to imagine him face-to-face with my great-grandmother. He had a strong face, a large, bold, balding forehead, stern features. One writer called him "the scion of one of Boston's wealthiest and most influential families." Phillips had abandoned the practice of law, which he considered boring, to become one of the outstanding orators of the antislavery movement. My father had memorized his speeches for his "declamations."

Phillips had an extraordinary magnetism, but no doubt so did Frances Rollin. I tried to imagine her standing, tall and serious, in conversation with the great man. But I had only half the picture. I had no idea what Frank—as Frances Rollin's friends and family called her—looked like.

January 22nd. Writing in the morning. In the afternoon dressed for the Anti-Slavery Festival. Mr. Phillips gave a generous clasp of the hand. The Redpaths were there. I had a miscegentic conversation with Mr. Pierce, editor of The Watchman and Reflector. *Mr. Pierce gave me a history of a colored young lady and a young white gentleman who had loved and prejudices kept from marrying. They feared ostracism. America is not the world.*

My great-grandmother had written this ninety-seven years to the day before my son Santiago's birth in Barcelona. I thought of my own misgivings about life in America, of my constant traveling. Unlike Be-Be, who despite her youthful wanderlust kept wondering why I couldn't settle in Saratoga, my great-grandmother would have understood. She had given thought to issues I had been struggling with for years. She, too, had grappled with racism and the difficulties of daily writing. And perhaps most important, through her diary she was willing to share her troubles and experiences with me—more openly than my mother, Be-Be, or Sistonie had ever been willing to do.

I soon discovered that when Frances Rollin spoke of "Americans," she was using a parlance current among people of color, who were acutely aware that they were not yet "American" in the eyes of the law. She was not implying that she was French or of any other nationality; she was simply acknowledging that she was counted out of the body politic, as both a black person and a woman. In 1868, neither blacks nor women had the right to vote.

I read on, beginning to get better at deciphering the fine, sometimes hasty script. The importance of this discovery was slowly dawning on me. I had always felt that there was something missing in the way my family had presented itself to me. Frances Rollin, her whole life, her guidance, had been lacking. I wondered why my mother had never shared her knowledge of Frank with me. Why had it taken me so long to find her? But somehow I couldn't help feeling that it was *she* who had found *me*.

March 1. Worked on my book in the morning. Later, there was a sitting for spiritual purposes. The table was clearly lifted and twisted about and the spirit answered to C.L. Felt as though it meant Grandma. I left the room. I am no sceptic. "I thank God," as Goethe said, "that I do not doubt the possibility of anything."

I felt a chill as I read these lines. The initials of my maiden name were C.L. (Carole Lewis). Who was whose ancestor? Was Frances Rollin mine, or was I hers? I wondered about the concept of timelessness current in physics. Had our two spirits been allowed to connect? My great-grandmother was no skeptic. She did not doubt the possibility of anything. Nor did I.

Turning the pages slowly and carefully, I read as long as I could. Finally, I closed the book and put it back in its protective cover. It was late when I got into bed. Salvatore was asleep, and I could hear the children's soft breathing nearby. They would be up at the crack of dawn, so I had to sleep. But my mind was spinning. I didn't know what I had expected from the diary; some pleasant woman with a simple story, perhaps. Certainly not this strong personality, this philosophical woman who was so passionate about ideas and dedicated to her work. Not the complex, relevant story the diary seemed to be telling.

Already I felt as if I knew Frank. She was opinionated, witty, and intelligent. She was both angry and determined. Yet I didn't know when she was born or when she died. Nor did I know anything about the book she was writing. I would have to find it and read it. She said in her diary that she wanted to "make her mark in Literature," and she clearly loved Literature, with a capital *L*, as I did. *I am reading MacCauley's* History of England *and La Martine's* L'histoire des Girondistes, she wrote. Later in the winter, she added that she was reading Whittier's prose, De Quincey's *Life of Mohamet*, Lamartine's *La Restauration*, Emerson's poetry and essays, Carlisle's *On Heroes*, Dante, Shakespeare, and Dickens.

Frank obviously read French, and so did I, but there were Latin phrases I would have to look up. The diary was filled with references to people and places I knew nothing about. What I did know, I reminded myself, was that my great-grandmother had had three living children, and I knew from firsthand experience what that was like. Her children were my great-aunt Sistonie; Winifred, a teacher and nurse, who died long before I was born; and Leigh, my grandfather, still living in New York.

Dorothy Sterling was researching some of the diary references and told me she would gladly share her information with me. But there were myriad details of my great-grandmother's life that I would have to get on my own.

As I forced myself to go to sleep, I already felt less alone.

That night I dreamed of Sistonie again. I hadn't dreamed of her since the time before Alessandro was born. "Anne is an important family name," she said.

In the morning I called my grandfather. "Uncle Billy, what was your mother's middle name?" I asked.

"Anne," he replied. "I think it was Anne."

11

The Magnificent Whippers

"UNCLE BILLY" WAS THE name I chose for my grandfather when I was a child in Washington, one night when Sistonie and I sat in her office listening to the radio. She was very excited, and I noticed that her eyes were shining. Her spirits seemed light in a way I wasn't used to. On the radio, Shirley Temple was calling someone "Uncle Billy," and a man's voice responded. We leaned in closer to the radio. Sistonie smiled at me. "That's your grandfather," she said, and the excitement in her voice made me pay attention.

When I began my search for Frank, I made several visits to the grandfather I hardly knew. I was nervous and excited. I was thinking about my great-grandmother; I was thinking about *family*.

I had made an appointment to see my grandfather at his place in the Dunbar Apartments at West 150th Street. I brought a small yellow notebook and a tape recorder. Antonio was with me, and I had unwrapped him from his sling carrier and placed him on the sofa in my grandfather's small, dimly lighted living room. I tried not to show my impatience as my grandfather finished talking with a professor who had come down from Yale to interview him about his career in theater.

My grandfather would be ninety-eight in November, or so he said—my mother told me she sometimes suspected him of upping his age toward the end, to achieve more cachet. Like everyone else in the family, he had apparently given himself any age he wanted, depending on the circumstances; but with my grandfather there was evidence to support his claim. Still, Uncle Billy looked to me as if he could go on forever. Only his sight had diminished, despite an operation several months before. Afterward, he had told me proudly on the phone, "They say I'm the oldest man ever operated on for cataracts. It's a new operation!" And I'd heard of a miraculous moment of remission during a Christian Science service, when Uncle Billy had risen from his pew and exclaimed to the congregation, "I can see! I can see!" But now his sight was all but gone.

Nonetheless, the strong profile, the thundering thespian's voice—these were still intact. He was Leigh Whipper, the actor, and a very fine one indeed, the inspiration for more than a generation of black actors. Both Ossie Davis and Honi Coles told me later that he was their mentor. He had cofounded the Negro Actors Guild in 1937 and was its president for many years. At a time when blacks were unwelcome in Actors' Equity, the Guild sustained not only black actors—one didn't have to be in the theater to join—but people of color generally.

In 1920, my grandfather had been the first black actor allowed to join Actors' Equity when he played in *Those Who Walked in Darkness*, the first of his twenty-one Broadway shows. Now he was the oldest actor on their rosters and had just been awarded a lifetime union card. He had also played in some forty-three films, including *The Harder They Fall*, *Marjorie Morningstar*, and *Of Mice and Men*. In 1943, the Ethiopian government awarded him the Star of Ethiopia for his portrayal of Emperor Haile Selassie in *Mission to Moscow*, in which he somehow managed to look more like the emperor than did Selassie himself.

But Uncle Billy's demeanor was always imperial. He was royal even in the smallest role. Of all his features, he was most proud of his aquiline nose, which he called "the Whipper nose," since it—along with his deep mahogany color and his oratorical flair—had apparently been inherited from his father, William James Whipper. On the few occasions when I saw my grandfather, he always asserted that I had "the Whipper nose" as well. And when he had held my infant son Alessandro in his arms, Uncle Billy called him "Alexander the Great" and pronounced that he, too, had "the Whipper nose."

Leigh Whipper had always been, in his own words, "a human toothpick." He was six feet one and lanky. I watched him now as he sat in his chair in his bathrobe, talking about the play *The Emperor Jones,* and my mind wandered to my favorite film role of his, Sparks the preacher in *The Ox-Bow Incident.* I was remembering the moment in the film when self-appointed vigilantes take the law into their own hands and prepare to hang the innocent Dana Andrews and Anthony Quinn. After the hanging my grandfather begins to sing, his voice rising into the night. *You got to go to the lonesome valley / You got to go there by yourself / Nobody here can go for you / You got to go there by yourself.*

They are powerful words, and there is an odd break, a tremolo of emotion, in the voice itself—a haunting, solitary quality—that is transcendent. My grandfather's voice, rising deep and rich, contains within it all there is to know about the injustice being perpetrated by self-righteous, bigoted men.

I'd heard the same emotional quality in Sistonie's speaking voice, and in her voice beside me in church as she sang the old familiar Episcopal hymns. I wondered now if Frank's voice had had it too—if both of them might have inherited it from their mother. I sat there quietly, absorbing the strange reality that this would be as close as I could ever come to hearing my great-grandmother's voice.

Finally, it was my turn. The professor was getting up to leave. At last Uncle Billy and I sat facing each other. I got out my notebook. "Tell me about your mother," I asked him. "What did she look like?"

I imagined that she was beautiful. A few weeks before, I'd sat with my mother as she told me what she must have heard from Sistonie: "She had large, prominent eyes—you know, the Creole eyes that run in the family."

And now my grandfather was telling me, "Good-looking—yes, Mama was a good-looking woman."

How I envied him calling her Mama!

"She was fair," Uncle Billy continued. Then he paused. His head was tilted upward at an angle, as if he were seeing that long-ago face.

I leaned in close, straining with him, trying to follow his inner vision. "Very light-skinned," he went on.

Impatiently I rushed in, coaxing. "Yes? And her hair? What kind of hair did she have?"

Uncle Billy relaxed. Suddenly all the tension was gone from his face. He smiled. "Oh, it was straight," he said. "She had good hair."

I could feel the hair on my head without touching it. It was covered, wrapped in colorful scarves. But though my appearance, this exotic way of dressing, certainly comforted some ancient African longings in me, I was also hiding my hair. I felt protected in my scarf, secure. No one knew exactly what my hair looked like. A white acquaintance had recently remarked, "No one's seen Carole's hair in years." And this was pretty much true. I preferred living with my head in a scarf to being seen in New York City with an Afro; only much later, when others were again straightening their hair, did I allow mine to be "natural." This was partly because I hated following the *fashion* of blackness—or any other fashion, for that matter. I resented having to pitch myself as a "black writer," now that writing by blacks was suddenly in demand. I just wanted to be a writer; but I also wanted to be me, and that very definitely included being black.

Now, confronted again with the hair issue, I made a quick mental search. Both my mother and my grandmother had "good" hair, my mother's long and straight, my grandmother's fine and naturally curly. Mine was fuzzy, woolly, nappy—everything I didn't want it to be. I had inherited my father's hair, or so my mother had told me. But as I gazed at the thinning fuzz on Uncle Billy's head, it struck me that his was not so "good," either. None of the men in the immediate family had "good" hair, not counting my three half-Italian sons, whose sleek curls were so admired by my mother and my grandmother. Like mine, my father's and my grandfather's hair was "bad." Oh, not in the worst *degrees* of "bad"—for there are degrees, and by certain standards it was comparatively good—but "bad" nonetheless. Did this make my mother and grandmother love me less, did it create a subtle distance between us?

To this moment with my grandfather I brought years of memories of my grandmother struggling with my hair, trying to make it manageable, combing and tugging and braiding. In my mind, I was running out the door as she called me for this daily grooming in the living room; and I was sitting in a hundred beauty parlors, enduring the hot smoking irons, smelling the acrid odor of frying hair. I was enduring this torture to make myself more acceptable, and I was wondering: to whom?

Suddenly I wondered what Frank would have thought of me—of me and my hair. My anxiety was growing, and I began to feel an urgent need to *see* Frank. If I could see her, I would know from looking at her face who she was. Perhaps Uncle Billy had a photograph of her somewhere.

"There's a picture of my dad over there, I think." Uncle Billy gestured toward a corner of the living room, and I took in an array of awards and theater memorabilia there. A life-size bust of my grandfather stood nearby. I looked in all the corners, on shelves and dressertops, and tried to modulate my voice. I had to speak loud enough so that Uncle Billy would remember, and yet not so loud that my sleeping baby would awaken and begin to cry.

"Where is a picture of Frances Anne Rollin? Where is a picture of your mother?" I pleaded. But Uncle Billy didn't know. He promised to try and locate one. There used to be one, a really big one, he remembered; he felt it ought to be around the apartment somewhere. The baby stirred and began to cry, and something within me sank. My interview with my grandfather continued, but my confidence was shaken. I was less sure than ever what questions to ask.

"Where," I asked, "is your mother buried?" Uncle Billy didn't quite remember. "Where is Ma buried?" he repeated, searching his memory. "Down there in Beaufort . . ." His voice trailed off.

It was time for me to leave. I made another appointment with Uncle Billy and packed up my notebooks and tape recorder and baby.

A few weeks later I returned, worried because I had somehow become entangled in Uncle Billy's life in a way I hadn't expected. I had visited him two times since our previous meeting. Since I was his nearest kin in the city, two Social Services nurses who seemed to be vying to take care of him had begun to call me at my Brooklyn loft. My grandfather had also been calling. From what I could understand, one of the nurses was accusing the other of leaving Uncle Billy unattended.

As I climbed the dark stairway to his apartment, I remembered my mother saying that when she moved to New York, she thought her father was an old man. He was already in his seventies by then. She was prepared to be the dutiful daughter. Calling to see how he was, she would be shocked to discover that he had women friends who resented her calling, and that he would use her to deflect unwanted attention by telling women that his daughter disapproved. My mother felt that a great deal of bad will was directed toward her.

I rang the doorbell, but there was no answer. Inside, however, I could hear faint sounds. Fearing that something was wrong, that he had fallen and was lying helpless on the floor, I bent down to peer into the keyhole.

Within the narrow parameters of the opening, a clear view of the living room appeared. I was stunned by what I saw. Uncle Billy, alone in the apartment, was rising from his chair to his full height. Stark naked, he was making his way very slowly to the door. He was a tall, thin, black Giacometti man, an Ethiopian king, a Native American medicine man. He was every part he'd ever played. He was my grandfather, my great-aunt Sistonie's brother, and—I had to remind myself because it was still so difficult to grasp—he was Frank's son.

I recalled at the end of my first interview with Uncle Billy, when I stood at the door, beginning to undo the heavy locks. He had called out to me from his chair, "It would make a good book, this story." His face was in shadow, but I could see the tilt of his head, his strong chin jutting forward. I knew that his unseeing eyes were closed as he added, "It should be called *The Magnificent Whippers*."

12

Dear, Dear Boston

SOMETIMES I WONDER WHAT it would have been like if I had grown up with Frank as a role model. Instead, it took many years for me to find out about her life and to come to terms with mine—years of asking questions and sifting through archives. Like the pictures on my Morton's Salt box, the search for Frank seemed to stretch on into an indeterminate future.

Always, though, I kept coming back to the first glimpse I had of her, sitting at her desk on New Year's night, with her new diary in front of her. Through the long years of research, I often lay in bed imagining Frank looking out her window at the rain. I would envision a passing carriage splashing mud onto the cobblestone walk below as it turned the corner. Frank would see her own reflection and her room mirrored in the glass, and I'd imagine that she might almost see me, looking in on her.

I saw Frank pulling her shawl tighter around her shoulders and glancing at a few of the pages of her diary for 1867, the year that had just passed; one of the many diaries she must have kept that did not make it through time to me. She wasn't ready to put it away, not yet. Much had happened since her arrival in Boston in November. There had been, since the end of the war, a long, protracted battle waged by the Radical Republicans (led by Senator Charles Sumner, Thaddeus Stevens, and abolitionist Wendell Phillips) against the racist policies of President Andrew Johnson. Johnson had in 1866 vetoed both the Freedmen's Bureau bill and the Civil Rights bill. In March of 1867, Congress had mandated black suffrage for the Confederate South. In the local elections in October and November the northern states had shown their reluctance to give the vote to blacks, and President Johnson had thoroughly denounced the concept of black suffrage, comparing it to the debacle of the recently ended Civil War: "Of all the dangers which our nation has yet encountered, none are equal to those which must result from the success of the effort [the Radicals are] now making to Africanize the half of our country."

Frank's new diary lay beside the old one, similar but as yet untried, like the new year. It had cost fifty cents of her tightly budgeted funds. But it was well worth it. She could confide to her diary things she wouldn't tell even her sisters. Looking at the new diary, she had a sudden feeling of apprehension, and she prayed silently that the worst she feared, whatever that might be, would not happen within the year's space of those blank pages.

She listened to the reassuring sounds of Mrs. Bailey in the kitchen, making tea. There were visitors in the parlor. The Baileys, friends of her father and mother, had rented a room in their house to Frank. Mr. Bailey was a fencing instructor, who taught near the Harvard campus. The Baileys' daughter, Emily, was a hairdresser and, like Frank, was in her early twenties. The youngest member of the household was Peter, a mischievous boy who, in April, would rush up to Frank's room to announce the arrival of a package, only to cry "April fool!"

In her small room—she described it as "minuscule" in letters to her sisters—there was the familiar hiss of the gas lamp, the sizzle of the coals in the grate, and over all the sound of the windswept rain against the glass panes. Over on the dresser, near the washstand, her letters were piled in neat bundles and wrapped with ends of ribbons left over from her sewing. The floor beside the bed held books, manuscripts, and notes. On the night table, on a plain white linen doily she'd brought from home, were a candle with a brass holder and her Bible. Her crocheted bookmark, a white cross with a purple border, lay at verses of Saint Paul: "Faith is the substance of things hoped for—the evidence of things not seen."

I imagined Frank's bundles of letters looking like those my mother said Sistonie kept tied with ribbon in her room in Washington. They were letters from a suitor killed in the First World War, my mother thought; but perhaps there had also been letters from Sistonie's mother, Frances Rollin. Frank might have written to encourage Sistonie in her studies at Howard Medical School, or to tell her of her illness in 1901. But those letters were long gone.

The Bailey home, a two-story brick house on Blossom Grove, was poised at the edge of the city's black neighborhood, known pejoratively as "Nigger Hill." The houses on Blossom Grove were torn down by the time I got there, but the golden-domed State House was so close that I knew Frank would have seen it gleaming in the sun as she made her way to the center of town. The sight of it must have lifted her spirits no matter how discouraged she might be.

And she was frequently discouraged. She often felt alone and homesick in Boston, despite the genuine warmth of the Baileys, the companionship of friends and acquaintances, and the attentions of various gentlemen callers. Her parents and her four younger sisters were all home in Charleston. Her work was hard, and the pay from Delany came infrequently.

Frank first met Martin Delany when he was an agent of the Freedmen's Bureau in South Carolina immediately after the Civil War. Charleston was then under martial law, which forbade discrimination on public transportation; nevertheless, on her way to the Sea Islands on a steamer, Frank had been refused a first-class seat by the captain, W.F. McNelty. She sued, with the help of the Freedmen's Bureau, and won one of the earliest civil rights cases in the country. There was quite a stir among the Charleston old guard when McNelty was fined $250.

After the proceedings, Frank confided to Delany—who was a novelist and essayist himself—her desire to become a writer. She showed him some of her work, and Delany decided she would be the perfect person to write his biography.

Born free in the North, Delany's family had moved to Virginia, where his mother had to outwit local whites in order to obtain an illegal education for her son. Her efforts paid off so well that he later became a medical student at Harvard. A generation before meeting Frank, Delany had shocked whites *and* blacks by suggesting that being black was not merely equal but in many ways superior to being white. Among the country's most outspoken and eloquent spokesmen for his people, he edited one of the first circulating black newspapers, *The Mystery,* in Pittsburgh. He also founded *North Star* with Frederick Douglass in 1847; the paper's masthead read "Right is of no Sex—Truth is of no Color."

Midway through his career, Delany came to feel that blacks would never be accepted by Americans, and he considered the possibilities of emigration to Canada, Guatemala, and Africa. He was one of the few nineteenth-century blacks to travel to Africa to meet with tribal leaders. In England, he was both acclaimed and vilified following his announcing before Parliament, "I am a man!" Later he would be called the father of black nationalism. His choice of Frank as his biographer was not surprising, for he was also a feminist and believed wholeheartedly in the superiority of black women.

Delany had been told that certain Boston publishers might be interested in his life story. He also knew personally many in the abolitionist community there, who would support such a project; he would arrange introductions for Frank. And Boston was, at the time, a mecca for intellectuals, particularly aspiring writers. If she was going to make her mark anywhere in the United States, she must have felt, it would be in Boston.

The lectures that winter in Boston were enough to prove the point. Emerson spoke in January, and in preparation Frank added his lectures and poetry to her other reading. She also managed to see Dickens in January, on his first night in Boston, despite the fabulous prices demanded by ticket scalpers; the whole country was in the grip of Dickens fever. She was amused at the fact that she, the only one of her race in the audience, created almost as much of a stir as Dickens himself. On the night of Dickens's February reading of *A Christmas Carol,* Frank leaned a bit forward in her seat and noted *the genial and grand face of Longfellow, the kingly publisher Fields*—James T. Fields was a junior partner with Ticknor and Fields, publishers of *The Atlantic Monthly—in the same line as us—brilliant authors and handsome women. Upperdom was there in full blast.*

At the Emerson lecture, she was accompanied by two young men: Ludie Mathews, a son of the socially prominent Mathews family of

Philadelphia; and Richard T. Greener, soon to be the first black graduate of Harvard. Both were frequent escorts, but she found the overly intellectual Greener too cold and the ardent Mathews too immature to consider them as serious suitors.

At twenty-two, Frank had definite opinions about men. She made some telling diary entries about Ludie: *He is ambitious and is appreciative of talents, hence he persists, but he does not exert himself to originate, is yet to search out for himself enough. He is malleable in an intellectual sense and in [an intellectual] atmosphere might expand. I think he will yet make his mark. His faults are those belonging to youth and are only such.*

She also wrote: *I am not sure that he understands the highest female character,* and in February related the following: *L. came and wanted to impress me with the belief that he loves me. He might see that it would be advantageous to have me near to direct him. Further than that I do not know. I read after he left.*

There was another suitor, back in Charleston: *Received a long burning letter from W. E. J. today, but I feel that he acted so selfishly when my means were out that it would only mar our union if we were married.* William E. Johnston was a cabinetmaker who would become a member of the South Carolina legislature. But Frank's feminism and common sense precluded what she considered an ordinary romanticism. She wrote of an evening of dancing—mirabile dictu *I actually danced, even waltzed, with Mr. Rob Howard! He escorted me home and played the gallant to perfection. If I intended waltzing through life, I might fancy him for a partner*—but she clearly did not intend to waltz through life. The man she had in mind was one of action and courage, someone who would appreciate her intellect and her desire for a career in literature.

In February, she saw a list of those present at a Philadelphia meeting and hurriedly scanned it for a name. *Then I saw the subscription list and the name among them that stirs a thousand memories. Is ——— but a shadow of hope or is ——— a tangible reality yet for me?*

Because she fondly recalled a sermon that he preached, I surmised that the man later identified as P. or Phil was a minister. Someone with a flair for language and a talent for stirring an audience or a congregation—this was the kind of man who interested her. She was still thinking of this man of spiritual and political dedication in March.

Today my dream of P is stronger than ever upon me. . . . Perhaps it will all come alright some day. "Gods are to each other not unknown" and hearts gravitate to each other by the same desire necessarily.

Because she was not entirely certain of his feelings for her, my great-grandmother tried—without success—to keep him out of mind. There were many other things to occupy her thoughts. On Washington's birthday, Frank established herself in the downstairs living room and wrote: *If things continue as they are, there will be but little country to celebrate it. For myself I am no enthusiast over patriotic celebrations as I am counted out of the body politic. I wrote very satisfactorily today.*

Her work on Delany was coming along well. *Next to his pride of birth and almost inseparable from it, is his pride of race, which even distinguishes him from the noted colored men of the present time,* she wrote. Later on she quoted the black abolitionist Frederick Douglass: *"Delany stands so straight, he leans a little backward,"* and later still, *"I thank God for making me a man. Delany thanks him for making him a black man."*

Frank traced Delany's pride in his African ancestry to his Mandingo grandmother, who described their heritage *with all the gorgeous imagery of the tropics, as the story of a lost and regal inheritance.*

On February 8, 1865, Delany, who had used persistence and luck to obtain a meeting with Lincoln, succeeded where many other black leaders had failed.

At the time of Delany's interview, there had been a rumor that Lee planned to arm the slaves and use them as Confederate troops. Delany wanted to assure the President of the loyalty of Southern blacks to the Union, and also to propose an army of black soldiers commanded solely by blacks to assist the Union.

"The President claimed to have been contemplating such a move," Frank wrote, "since the moment of his Emancipation Proclamation, and to have only been lacking the means of implementing it. Impressed with the Major's presence and credentials he asked him then and there to take command of a regiment of black soldiers loyal to the Union." He handed Delany a card to take to the war secretary, which read: "Do not fail to have an interview with this most extraordinary and intelligent black man. A. Lincoln."

On Sundays, Frank took time off from writing to visit churches of various denominations, where there were often thought-provoking sermons. Yet she was rarely certain of her welcome in the white churches of Boston. A sexton at one church attempted to assign her to a segregated pew in the upper gallery, and Frank declined, heading to another church, where she was too furious to pay attention to the sermon. Once she returned to Blossom Grove, the words fairly crackled from her pen. *We are compelled and tenacious of our rights or else we will be sunken by these Americans.*

On reading these words, I recognized Frank's anger as my parents' anger and my own. My mother had often told me of poor treatment in clubs in New York City, on trains in the South, in segregated stores and movies in Washington, in trying to get apartments or jobs. And my father had shown me the parking lots, bowling alleys, and shopping areas, like the one in Saratoga, that have decimated black neighborhoods all over the country in the name of urban renewal. He had pointed out black couples sitting in dark corners or behind plants in restaurants, politely steered out of the way by imperious maître d's. He had commented on things I myself might have overlooked, though I, like all of us who are not white, was wary enough on my own. My parents' experience had been harsher than mine, and they walked and breathed ever conscious of our color; but we had all experienced the rage of being turned away or treated badly because we were black. Not so much had changed for us since my great-grandmother's time.

In the first pages of her book Frank wrote *While the war between sections has erased slavery from the statutes of the country, it has in no wise obliterated the inconsistent prejudice against color.*

While Frank was in Boston, a fierce debate broke out between Wendell Phillips and William Lloyd Garrison, who, after being in the forefront of the abolitionist movement for many years, decided not to continue the fight for black suffrage after freedom from slavery had been won. Phillips criticized Garrison, and Garrison responded by accusing Phillips of "great self-inflation" and "a pitiable hallucination of the mind." During the height of the furor, Frank thought it wise not to take sides. She admired both men, and both men seem to have admired her. Still, Garrison's position pained her. *Mr. William Lloyd Garrison spent the morning with me. I think him a grand noble soul. A singularly perfect development of God's highest humanity. A great intellect consecrated to one idea—but is he a humanitarian? How can his practised pen and ready heart remain uninterested while the same wrong exists under another form?*

Frank read Garrison portions of her manuscript, and impressed by what he heard, he sent a letter to Ticknor and Fields, praising her work, and later arranged a meeting for her with both Howard M. Ticknor and James Fields. She was also encouraged by the dedicated feminist and abolitionist Thomas Wentworth Higginson, who would shortly begin an encouraging correspondence with Emily Dickinson. There was always a friendly welcome and moral support at Higginson's home, where he enjoyed reminiscing about his military days in South Carolina and giving Frank pointers on her writing. *Very cold snow. Went to Higginson's for fried oysters and coffee.*

By March, a draft of the book was completed. *Late in the afternoon I completed it. It has been no easy task to me writing under so many difficulties and uncertain of my prospects while it is in the hands of the publishers. I am not feeling very well about my scant pay while writing. I think I have not been dealt with according to the letter of the contract [with Delany]. I would gladly have written otherwise if my circumstances were different, but as it is, it is more* con amore *than for cash.*

Among the difficulties was the winter cold, which brought with it chills and fever that no medicine seemed to help. Frank made periodic visits to the doctor, who prescribed quinine among other remedies. And at one point, after no word from Delany for two months, she was forced to take a job sewing for a Frenchwoman. *Went out to sew today,* she wrote ruefully. *Thought when I began Literature that that was ended.* By April 10, with what Frank called *the forty-second snow storm of the year,* she was feeling very discouraged. She had received word from Ticknor and Fields that they did not want her book, though Lee and Shepard was interested. And she was worried about her mother's health; Margarette Rollin had been diagnosed as having dropsy, now known as edema.

Frank's friend Lewis Hayden found her a job copying legislative documents and other official papers at the State House, and Frank divided her time between writing, sewing, and clerical work up on the hill. She managed to bring in enough money to keep afloat, even though by June, Delany's payments had stopped altogether.

As summer came on, Frank's chills and fever worsened. Visitors arrived at Blossom Grove with flowers and ice cream. She visited the doctor almost daily and began to dream of Phil. *Cloudy day. Dreaming of seeing Phil last night. I wonder if he is here! . . . Returned home about half past ten and retired.* No letters. Not a sign of P's being here.

Frank's book was finally accepted by Lee and Shepard, but her joy was hollow. She began to think seriously of returning home. In Charleston, Reconstruction was gathering momentum, and blacks and whites had participated together in the first state constitutional convention of its kind. (Ironically, though the Reconstruction Acts required that blacks be allowed to vote in new elections in the Confederate states, it would be another two years before the Fifteenth Amendment would guarantee black male suffrage in the rest of the country.) All eyes were turned toward South Carolina, and blacks from all over the country were gravitating there. Her sisters had been keeping her abreast of the news, and more and more it seemed as if Frank could be part of the political scene back home. In Boston, there was discussion, but the action was in the South.

Knowing that Frank needed a job, E. J. Adams, an old friend who was now a minister in Charleston, recommended her to William J. Whipper, a lawyer who was looking for someone to write for him. Like many of the members of the constitutional convention, Whipper must have known of the beautiful and political Rollin sisters. He lost no time in writing to Frank from his newly purchased home on Hilton Head Island, telling her that he would be honored if she would take on the job. When she sent back her acceptance, he wrote her again, explaining that she would be working in his new law office in Columbia, where he would be a newly elected member of the state legislature from Beaufort County.

I am very pleased with my Hilton Head letters, she confided to her diary.

Frank packed her bags and picked up several copies of her book at Lee and Shepard. The day before her departure, she went up to the top of the State House and looked out over the city. Leaving Boston behind, with its exciting literary scene, was like leaving behind a part of herself. On July 28 she wrote: *Boston,* Vale—*Up very early—my last day in Boston, dear, dear Boston.* Then she put the diary in her handbag, where it would be close within reach. She was going home.

13

Being Be-Be

I LEARNED OF UNCLE BILLY'S death when I was in France late in the summer of 1975—less than a year after our interviews. I was told that he had fallen while alone in his apartment and had been taken to the hospital, where he died shortly afterward. The night I received the news, I had a dream:

Uncle Billy comes to me and shows me two outlines on a sheet of paper. He says, "Here is a footprint of your great-grandmother. And here is a footprint of your great-grandfather." I begin to color them in with beautiful colors.

Over the next few years, Salvatore and the children and I tried to settle in Saratoga so that I could pursue my research and continue writing. We found a big white house to live in, and Salvatore began a cooking job that seemed more promising than the others had been. Alessandro attended P.S. 4, my old school. At first it felt as if there was finally a foundation for us, some continuity to our lives. It seemed as if we could build a life in Saratoga.

But as usual, once we'd stayed in one place too long, Salvatore began to grow sad and pensive. I wrote in my journal:

So sad yesterday evening—to the point of tears as I lay reading Tao Te Ching *in bed. Buffeted by his depressions—it is most disturbing to realize that they don't have anything to do with me at all. That is the problem. Like most women, I want to be adored, to be loved, to be cherished. I miss that a lot, although it is only sometimes that it becomes acute—as when he withdraws so completely or becomes suddenly, unexpectedly hostile.*

The effect is that today I am listless—unwell—must force myself to the desk and typewriter, must stir up the embers of my interest in the writing— which is nonetheless, I am always surprised to find, still there.

The week before, I had written: *Cocteau says, "Without resistance you can do nothing."*

My mother and grandmother, embroiled in their own spats, were reticent with me. I was beginning to realize, as I had with Salvatore, that their problems did not have anything to do with me, either. They were caught up in their own story, and I felt like an intruder in their lives. My relationship with my mother did not seem to be mellowing now that I had the children; if anything, our differences seemed to be worsening. After our arguments, my mother would not speak to me for days.

She is making me wait, I confided to the journal. *Before the reconciliation I must suffer. . . . But is my strength greater than hers? Is my trying to be the wiser, the older, the more understanding, the less petty, the best thing to do? I long to be petty too and get away with it. But my one outburst the other day has caused these days of pain and confusion. Sometimes I want only to be away from it, in another town, another country, and I knew that that is a large part of why I have lived so long abroad.*

Life at the Spuyten Duyvil, too, was becoming more and more stressful. Modern living and increasing popularity were clearly a strain on the "old shack." My grandmother's place remained one of the few restaurants for real home cooking left in the country, and it continued to operate as it had in the past; we had no new system for handling the greater volume of business. Be-Be refused to buy another cash register, and during the hectic "Sales Week" when the yearlings were sold directly next door to us, money piled up in little straw baskets in my bar shed in the garden. When the ice machine broke, we'd have to run to the Grand Union supermarket for ice. Our air conditioner couldn't make a dent in the thick smoke that hung over an indoor crowd. Be-Be kept the lights out in the house in order to confuse anyone who wanted to rob us; we'd have to locate the key in various hiding places and then grope along in the dark. Since the key was always getting lost or misplaced, Be-Be pinned one to her dress, and soon I began to pin one to me too.

Some things did change, though. I knew we were entering a new era when I looked up from my service bar in the garden one night to see Andy Warhol sitting bleakly at a nearby table. During Sales Week, Fasig-Tipton, who owned the yearling sales company, installed a closed-circuit TV at the inside bar and one in the garden to alert our customers as to which hip number—the horse's identification—was up for auction. The amounts of money at stake caused otherwise sanguine men and women to order double vodka tonics as they examined their catalogues and dabbed at the perspiration on their upper lips. Hard drinkers who used to be partial to stiff bourbon on the rocks switched to pale white wines and watered-down Scotches. Some customers' doctors had forbidden them to drink at all, and they began to bring their own stashes of nonalcoholic beer and diet soda, asking if we'd put them on ice. Husbands returned with new wives. Wives sat at the piano bar with new husbands, while Ida, or Bob, or Rudy, or Bubbles, smiled and sang, winked and pounded out tune after tune. The photographs lining the walls of the bar, snapped in the fifties and the sixties, remained as mute testimony to the fact that many who continued to come year after year had once been young and handsome, or young and beautiful, had once had gorgeous wives with beehive hairdos, or thin husbands with hair, had once had more fun, somehow, than people were having in the seventies and eighties.

Some black people in town complained that in August my grandmother catered to whites, shunning the colored people who hung out on Congress Street. In her desire to keep the Spuyten Duyvil a "high-class joint," Be-Be hung an old mislaid jacket behind the door and thrust it upon any man who showed up without a coat. Some white locals complained that she catered to millionaires and snubbed *them*. Though they may have comported themselves with dignity elsewhere, the wealthiest of men used the Spuyten Duyvil for long songfests, vying with each other for high notes or low notes and competing long into the night to see who could remember the most lyrics to old favorites like "Danny Boy."

It was true that in August the townspeople, both black and white, had a hard time getting into the place, not because my grandmother discouraged them from coming but simply because there wasn't enough room. "You can't please everyone," Be-Be would say, and shrug her shoulders.

One night during Sales Week, I watched as my mother stood under the green-and-white-striped tent on the far side of the garden, attending to the flowers on the tables where Sonny Werblin, high-powered realtor and owner of the New York Jets football team, would sit with his retinue later in the evening. The colored lanterns had just been turned on, and a waitress held up Liz Whitney Tippett's floral arrangement for my mother's approval. I watched her nod and touch the bouquet; the flowers had been sprayed to duplicate Mrs. Tippett's racing colors.

Clay Camp, an imposing figure of a man who also loomed large on the horse scene, was selling that night. He came quietly into the garden through "Camp's Gate," which led to his customary stables to the left of our house. Dubonnet on the rocks was his drink until he changed to white wine. His voice, reflecting his presales jitters, was a soft Southern drawl. "Do me a Dubby, would you please, C'al?"

The first drink orders came in to the service bar, and I prepared to pour liquor and take money from the waitresses. A party of four was being seated at one of the far tables, and more customers started to arrive. Sleek women in summer silks vied for attention with the even sleeker and perhaps inherently sexier horses. A famous jockey arrived with his tall wife on one arm and an equally tall girlfriend on the other. Suddenly it was so crowded I couldn't see beyond the bar. The waitresses' eyes began to glaze over as they looked at me pleadingly. "What's a Rob Roy?" "What's a Pink Squirrel?" "Have you ever heard of something called Old Fitz?" People began to get desperate for drinks as the crush got deeper and the waitresses had trouble making their way through the crowd.

Because the Spuyten Duyvil was open only a short summer season, procedures that had worked the year before were usually forgotten by the time August rolled around again, and by the time new ones were worked out, the season was over. Each year a new crew of waitresses tried to grasp the oddities of the place. No one, for example, would know where last year's butter dishes were kept. And Mr. Camp would come and sit at the big back table before anyone was ready, spreading out there for the day, looking very much like a Tennessee Williams character with his entourage. He'd want a big bowl of tomatoes from Mr. Zetterstrom's farm—Mrs. Camp liked them peeled—and plenty of extra corn on the cob. He'd want twelve steaks for potential buyers who would be arriving at different intervals throughout the afternoon: two well done, three medium, four medium rare, one very rare, and the rest simply rare. New waitresses would quake at the sound of Mr. Camp's deep drawl and would try to bear in mind his reputation as a big tipper. But there were always moments at the Spuyten Duyvil when you wondered if the money could possibly be worth it.

Be-Be herself had begun to look more and more like a wizened *patronne* in a Paris café as she sat at her usual spot at the inside bar, keeping a baleful eye on the bartender. She would also have a critical ear on the piano player for wrong notes or unsuitable tunes—she could wake up from a sound sleep inside to rush out to chastise a startled pianist for some minor musical faux pas.

Yet Be-Be was well loved, despite her nerves and a propensity to throw people out if they stayed too long. "Don't you people have a home?" she asked one surprised party of late-night revelers. "We want to go to bed." Everyone wanted to see Virginia, including Governor Carey. "Introduce me to Virginia," he said when he came to Saratoga one year.

"Why do you think he wanted to meet me?" Be-Be still asked years later. "Because you're the famous owner of the Spuyten Duyvil," I always replied. "Or maybe he knows you were almost district attorney of Saratoga Springs." Shortly after we moved to George Street, someone from the Labor party had persuaded Be-Be to let her name be put on the ballot, assuring her there was no chance she would win. But Be-Be had gotten two thousand votes, which startled her and impressed all the rest of us.

My mother was less popular than Be-Be and seemed unsurprised when various bartenders, waiters, and waitresses complained about her, either just before or after they were fired. Even though she would be insulted, she seemed almost proud of her difficult reputation. "You see," a disgruntled piano player who had had a few drinks too many told me in an oddly amiable tone, "I'm just here because of your grandmother. Your mother is a pain. But that's all right," he continued, "because you see, I'm a pain too."

Be-Be would defend my mother no matter what. She had spent a lifetime, I realized later, trying to make up for the past, trying to let her daughter know how much she truly loved her. The two of them were locked in their own battle against the world. No one but my grandmother and my mother, I realized sadly one year, would ever "own" or even contribute managerial advice to the Spuyten Duyvil, not even me.

Though the money flowed in August, somehow it hardly ever lasted the entire winter, and paying what Be-Be called "that old devil liquor bill" was always a push. People assumed we were wealthy when they saw all that money floating around in baskets; certainly someone should have been. Be-Be would pay me nominally for my week to ten days of family help—"You're the only one we can trust," she and my mother would say; "we can trust family"—and they would divvy up the rest of the money somehow. My mother would head for Mexico, and Be-Be would stay in Saratoga. By the end of the long Saratoga winter, Be-Be would usually be broke.

My grandmother was often disillusioned with the difficulties of managing the Spuyten Duyvil, yet she resisted the help of would-be saviors. Bartenders who tried to pitch in by assuming managerial duties would be fired as soon as they began to take their authority for granted. "Mmph, he thought he owned the place," Be-Be would say when asked what had happened to the person who had been such a help the year before. Waiters and waitresses were judged guilty until proven innocent where any money discrepancies were concerned. After a morning conference between my mother and my grandmother in the kitchen, the suspect would suddenly be replaced, usually with someone far less competent. Sometimes honest waiters and waitresses were fired, while dishonest ones were kept on simply because they had been around for years.

Gradually my grandmother curtailed food service, so that only certain special customers could eat. When Be-Be decided to cook during sales week only, Mr. and Mrs. Camp could eat. The Tuttles could eat. "Honey Chile" Snowden could eat. Anyone from Fasig-Tipton could eat. Most anyone else could not. The running joke was, you had to be a millionaire to eat at the Spuyten Duyvil.

Some years before, Be-Be had tried consigning the kitchen to other cooks, but the results were always disastrous. The customers complained that the food wasn't as good, and my grandmother couldn't bear to have the quality of her cooking compromised. Most other cooks' rolls or biscuits were not up to par, or they were not served hot, an unpardonable sin. "You've *got* to have hot bread," Be-Be said. There had always been a rivalry between my grandmother and those of her women friends who also made pie crusts and biscuits. Ultimately, it seemed, Be-Be's friends were judged on their pastry skills no matter what other good qualities they had. "Mmph, too heavy. She calls that a biscuit?" "Mmph, she's just making cobbler because she doesn't want to make two crusts," she would comment.

Sometime in the late seventies, Be-Be started "weakening in the stretch." Instead of staying up her usual twenty hours a day during the month of August, she could only work eighteen. It was harder for her to climb a ladder to retar the flat roof over the bar or to shovel snow from it in the winter. She often felt faint in the one-hundred-degree kitchen. Still, any member of the family arriving with a suitcase would have to fight to keep her from carrying it. "Are you hungry? Do you have enough covers? Don't lift that heavy bag!" were still her war cries. Yet I knew that the admission of any weakness at all had to be taken seriously.

Around this time, Be-Be told me not to tell anyone, but she was really about four years older than she let on. That meant she was eighty-nine.

That August, I took the bus up from New York and offered to do the cooking myself. I promised to do exactly as she told me, if only she would stay in the rocker on the comparatively cool front porch. The first year, I had a helper, a boy named Luke, who miraculously seemed to understand everything without explanation. We turned out the corn and the potatoes, the steaks and the rolls, the chickens and the roast beef, and the tomatoes, peeled and sliced, for the Camps. We made sure there was parsley on the plates.

Everyone knew it wasn't really Be-Be doing the cooking, but Mr. Camp was appeased. Someone in the family was in the kitchen, someone who cared. And I did, because through all the chaos at the Spuyten Duyvil, Mr. Camp was a mainstay, a comprehensible man I'd known so long he was kind of family. I resisted the thought that my feeling for the Camps bore a resemblance to the uneasy "kind of family" relationships between blacks and whites, slaves and their owners, in the South—but I couldn't help feeling that no matter who owned the place, we were still somehow at the mercy of our white customers.

It wasn't supposed to be like that, I thought. It was supposed to be the other way around. But I pushed these thoughts out of my mind and drank beer to cool myself off in the raging kitchen heat. Though I refrained from yelling at the waitresses, I insisted upon the parsley and the extra butter on everything—even when Be-Be stopped poking her head in to see if I was doing it right. My mother, who continued to oversee the waitresses and the prime tables out back, seemed to approve. I cooked at the Spuyten Duyvil for five years after that, each summer remembering my grandmother's old expression for the August frenzy in Saratoga. I was "standing on my eyebrows," being Be-Be.

14

An Album of the Heart

ON NOVEMBER 19, 1979, Frances Anne Rollin would have been 134 years old. In her honor I had oysters and coffee in Boston. But I saw hardly any black people downtown; Boston's reputation among blacks as a seat of freedom and enlightenment had faded long ago. The Blossom Grove house Frank had lived in had recently been torn down.

I had never been to Boston before and was traveling with my friend James, who knew it well. He and I had spent the summer of 1978 making a transcription of Frank's diary. Salvatore was in another relationship, and he and I were hardly speaking anymore. Thoughts of Frank eased my pain. It was wonderful to have someone to share Frank with, someone who seemed to respond to her. We relived her indignation and exasperation with Ludie, her earnest young suitor, and sympathized with her reaction to Boston's cold weather. I liked to think of the day she sewed herself a new calico dress, or leaned out the window and spoke with a passerby. I could feel the windowsill as if I were leaning on it too. And there were the dreams she had—mostly of Phil—which intrigued and touched me, as they were even more ephemeral than Frank herself.

That autumn, my father had agreed to help my research by treating me to train tickets to Washington. My grandfather had mentioned a scrapbook that I might find there; perhaps a picture of Frank would turn up. I took Alessandro, ten years old by then, with me to meet his Washington cousins, whom I hadn't seen in more than fifteen years, ever since my father's brother, Uncle Harry, died.

We stayed with my father's sister, Aunt Elsie, who began to tell me about the Lewis family. I learned about her mother's mother, Louisa Smith, who had developed a hair pomade in Philadelphia that she cooked in a big iron pot and sold from door to door. And there was Sarah (nicknamed Muff), the mysterious part Native American woman who was my paternal great-grandmother. But though I took notes, it was hard to focus on these other stories. I was trying to get closer to Frank.

Aunt Elsie dropped me off at Howard University, where I found Frank's book in the library, *The Life and Times of Martin Robeson Delany,* first published in 1868 by Lee and Shepard. It was listed in the card catalogue under Frank A. Rollin, with no mention that Frances Anne Rollin was the true name of the author. Among the papers that Uncle Billy had bequeathed to the library were several items relating to his father's law practice and several family photographs, but there was no photograph of his mother.

The librarian directed me to another special collection, where a notebook of some sort had been left by my grandfather. She said she thought there was a family Bible. I sat in a small room by myself and thought: Perhaps this is it. Perhaps I'll find the Rollin sisters, all five of them, for even though my grandfather had told me that there were three sisters and two boys in his mother's family, I had discovered that all five were girls.

First the librarian brought out the Bible. I touched its surface reverently and hurriedly opened it to the frontispiece. But the large plain book was devoid of the genealogy chart usually found in old family Bibles. There was nothing more than the name of its owner: my great-great grandfather William Rollin. Then the librarian handed me a leather-bound autograph album. I felt a wrench of emotion when I saw its title: *An Album of the Heart.* The date below it was 1859. The book must have belonged to Frank when she was at school in Philadelphia. Someone—could the elegant script have belonged to my grandfather?—had written on a blank page near the front of the book:

> Autograph Album of
> Mrs. Frances Rollin Whipper
> Nee
> Frances Anne Rollin
> Wife of Judge William J. Whipper
> Mother of
> Alicia Whipper, Winifred Rollin Whipper, Ionia Rollin
> Whipper, Mary Elizabeth Whipper, Leigh Rollin Whipper
> Grandmother of Leighla Frances Whipper Ford,
> James Myles Whipper
> Leigh Whipper Jr.
> Great Grandmother
> of
> Carole Ione Lewis

I was astonished. It was a bit like going to the moon and finding my name inscribed there on a rock. Who would ever have known? I imagined the rare scholar examining this list of names, with mine at the bottom, without ever knowing who I was, who any of us were. If I myself knew so little about who we were, what could a stranger hope to know?

On the following page I found Frank's obituary attached with yellowing Scotch tape to the frontispiece. The headline read: DEATH OF A CULTURED COLORED WOMAN. I drew in a sharp breath and read on: "The wife of William Whipper the eloquent Negro lawyer died here yesterday afternoon."

No, I thought, not now. I wasn't ready for Frank to die yet; I had hardly found her. Dutifully, unwillingly, I read the obituary through, then skipped into the pages of the autograph book and found scores of poems and dedications, including one from Charlotte Rollin, my great-grandmother's sister:

> To Frank,
> Frank, thy departure from me seem
> As if first awakened from a dream
> Alas I find that thou art gone

And I am left here all alone.
I'll think by day and night of thee,
Can'st thou but do the same for me,
While sailing o'er the surging sea
Oh breathe one word of love for me
Charlotte M. Rollin
Charleston July 15th, 1859

If Frank had been born in November of 1847, and her sister was three years younger, as I had read, then Charlotte would have been only eight or nine years old when this poem was written. I thought of my own autograph books and how we revised popular poems or songs to suit our purposes—this might have been similar. Or had Charlotte written her poem herself? Later I found records indicating that Frank was actually born in 1845 and Charlotte in 1849 which would have made Charlotte ten at the time of the poem. Old records are notoriously faulty, but I couldn't help wondering if Frank had put her age back two years at some point—if even she was not immune from the family habit of revising one's age.

Inscriptions in autograph books, like tombstone engravings, often reflect on mortality and the passing of time, and some of the entries in Frank's book were chilling: *As o'er the cold sepulchral stone some name arrest the passer by / Thus when thou view'st this page alone / May mine attract thy pensive eye / And when that name is read / Perchance in some succeeding year / Reflect on me as on the dead / and think my heart buried here.*

I wanted to take the album with me; I didn't have enough time to study it. It seemed that it should belong to me, but it was the property of the library now, and I had to leave it there.

When I finally rushed outside, Aunt Elsie was waiting with my father and Alessandro in the car. The next stop was John and Carrie Robertson's house.

Dorothy Sterling had sent me an essay that Carrie's father, Demps Whipper Powell, had written about the family. It was titled "A Providential Relationship" and was written in 1940, just around the time when I used to visit him as a child. I remembered him as a sweet white-haired old man, but I was only now beginning to understand how he was related to me.

"In the life of my second adopted Mother, Mrs. Frances Anne Rollin Whipper," Demps had written, "there was something refreshing and stimulating, something more than ordinary. Yes, something worthy of remembrance and emulation. A woman of gifted philosophy, that of which is sorely needed in this our modern life. Her life's judgments and opinions were reflected by the events of each passing day. She was a woman of deep thought and vision, she endeavored to visualize the thought that every act and deed were as a seed sown today, which would be the harvest in the future."

Demps! How I'd loved him. Sistonie had often taken me to his house to play. Upstairs there'd been a pillow that spelled out the word M-O-T-H-E-R, with definitions of what a mother could mean. I remembered sitting alone on the window seat, admiring the bright embroidery on the pillow, thinking I was seeing the air itself as I watched dust particles lazily descending in a shaft of sunlight.

I remembered the man with whom I used to drink a little tea with milk while looking out on a garden, a shed. Now I knew that he was Frank's adopted son. Perhaps I was too young for him to tell me about her, or perhaps he *had* told me. He might have told me how much she would have loved me, and I might have held on to the subconscious knowledge of her ever since. But all I remember are conversations about Trixie, the dog, and about the garden, and about the hummingbirds we watched from the window one day.

The last time I'd seen Carrie, Demps's daughter, had been during Sistonie's illness. I stood by, awkwardly, in the hospital room. Sistonie's vision cleared enough for her to recognize her old friend— her niece—and she weakly motioned to her, raising her arms as Carrie rushed to embrace her. Her green hospital gown began to fall away from her naked breast, and, already in tears, Carrie moved deftly to protect this last bit of privacy, before she hugged my great-aunt to her.

As we approached Carrie's house, my fingers, touching the railing, knew it! My body recognized this place better than my adult mind did. So much time passed after we rang the bell that I feared the worst, that John and Carrie had died. But finally a very old man, John Robertson, answered the door. We all entered and found Carrie inside. She was frail and moved carefully; but I was looking at her through all the years I'd known her, with the eyes of my child self.

She had a lovely oval face and deep-brown eyes—her beauty shone through—but more important, for me, was her overwhelming familiarity. Carrie was family.

"It's good to see you, Carole. It brings back memories," Carrie said.

Later, when I asked her about Frances Anne Rollin, Carrie replied: "I remember meeting her when I was a little girl. We lived in Burton, South Carolina. It was about three miles to Beaufort. I used to go over to visit her when I was about seven years old. She was fair, with black hair and a medium build. . . . Papa was, yes, very fond of her."

Carrie was probably the only person I would ever talk to about Frank, besides my grandfather, who had actually laid eyes on her. When I closed my own eyes, I could almost see Frank through Carrie's. But Carrie had nothing more tangible from those days—no letters, for example, and no photos of Frances Anne Rollin.

When we returned to New York, I overheard Alessandro—who had met only his Italian cousins before this trip—excitedly telling his father, "And, Daddy, they're all black, all my cousins in Washington are black!" Alessandro had already shown signs of becoming the family historian. He had a prodigious memory and a proclivity for dates. And now he was making some discoveries about the family on his own. Caught up in my search for Frank, it had never occurred to me that the color of the Lewises would be so startling to him. As hard as I was trying to build a sense of family, my son was surprised he had so many brown-skinned relatives.

In 1980, my twelve-year marriage (counting all the years we'd been together) was finally over, despite my trying to keep it together against all odds. I had wanted so much to be the first one in the family to do it. But I had pitted myself against a centuries-old pattern of torn families, and it had proved impossible for me to break.

As so many women do, I took the failure personally. I was ashamed and frightened; a man had left me, and I was alone. Only now do I know that I was in good company, that each of my foremothers had known this—something in the bones beyond loneliness. Sitting in my Chambers Street loft with my children—now eleven, nine, and seven—I was as alone as my grandmother giving birth by herself in Georgia, as my mother and I, that night in the car in Alabama. At the birth of my first child I had been brought into a part of the circle that rejoiced in new life. Now I was introduced to another female mystery—the one of separation and sadness.

Yet, oddly, just as I was beginning to understand something of what the women in my family had all been through, my separation from Salvatore caused more bad feelings between my mother and my grandmother and me. My grandmother, probably remembering how Uncle Billy had left her and my mother to fend for themselves, seemed impressed that Salvatore did not completely disappear after our separation. By comparison to the men she'd known, Salvatore was a saint. My mother, who still had a great deal of bitterness about raising me without my father, seemed to feel the same way, and continued to bring Salvatore Christmas presents from Mexico. Meanwhile, my mothering became suspect. Salvatore was an excellent cook, and both my grandmother and my children expressed doubts about my own cooking. My cooking in Saratoga didn't seem to count. There, I was "being Be-Be." On my own, I lacked self-confidence. I felt betrayed and, faltering, began to have difficulty making money and feeding us all.

I needed Frank more than ever. My fingers placed lightly on a Ouija board, I held my breath, wondering who would come through. Clearly and simply, from the pointer, came words that brought welcome tears: "Frank cares."

Through the years, I always had to squeeze my research and writing into a hectic daily life of raising children, writing for magazines, and teaching poetry. Now that I was no longer trying to hold my marriage together, I was free to dedicate myself to Frank in a more focused way. Historians had been sending me scraps of information, and bit by bit more of the pieces of her life were fitting together, but there were still maddening holes.

I had discovered that Frank's father was a mulatto, so fair-skinned that there was nothing about his appearance to distinguish him from being white. This was true of many free people of color in Charleston. Frank described her father as "a descendant of one of the proudest and most honored families of Santo Domingo," but I had so far been unable to find out how exactly this was so. While Frank and her sisters were children, William Rollin ran a profitable lumberyard and had numerous city contracts; his sloops transported lumber between the plantations and Charleston.

Frank described the 1840s as a time when the free colored people of Charleston were at the "zenith of their prosperity." They were tradesmen and merchants and, with few exceptions, preferred workmen. They lived in a world of contradictions and ironies, in a social stratum layered between slaves and whites. They were privileged, and many, like the Rollins, were kin of prestigious white families who recognized them as such and provided various kinds of protection and business advantages. Yet they were subject at any time to arbitrary restrictions. They were denied the vote and could not testify against whites in court; and if they traveled out of the state of South Carolina in the years right before the Civil War, it was against the law for them to return. Frank described this complex state of affairs in her book on Delany:

> They were an intermediate class in all the slave states, standing between the whites and the bondmen, known as the free colored; debarred from enjoying the privileges of the one, but superior in condition to the other, more, however, by sufferance than by actual law. They were subject to the machinations and jealousies of the non-slaveholders, whom they rival in mechanical skill and trade. Prior to the rebellion these represented a fair proportion of wealth and culture, both attributable to their own thrift and energy. Unlike the same class in the North, they had but little, if any, foreign competition in the various departments of labor or trade against which to contend. . . . [Yet] they were excluded from the more liberal and learned professions. . . . [And] there were influences always at work to deprive them of the fruits of their labor, either openly or covertly. On the one side were exorbitant taxes for various public charities, from the benefits of which the indigent of their race were deprived, and for the public schools, to which their children were denied admittance. Business men found it in many instances impolitic to refuse requests for loans coming from influential white men, under whose protection they exercised their meager privileges, and the payment of which it was equally impolitic to press, nor were they allowed to sue for debts. Thus their position in the midst of a slave community was altogether precarious, as they were looked upon as a dangerous element by the slaveholders. Their lives and material prosperity standing in direct contrast to the repeated assertions of the

My great-aunt Sistonie, whose name was Ionia, liked to call me "Little Ione" as she held me in her arms outside her office at 511 Florida Avenue.

My grandmother Be-Be, in alliance with my mother, called me "Little Carole" as we posed under Sistonie's plaque.

My mother in the early thirties around the time she and my father met.

My father and his foster father, Dr. Edward Bassette, in Hampton, Virginia, 1928.

My mother and Sistonie may have been returning from church on a sunny Sunday in Washington, in the thirties.

My mother and Be-Be enjoying themselves at Belmont racetrack, in the forties.

I think this was the lucky day at the track when I helped Be-Be win big money by picking the great Whirlaway as the winner.

At our first house in Saratoga, Be-Be and I played with my first puppy and the first of a long series of kittens in our lives.

My mother, always the most glamorous of them all for me, is shown deckside during one of her transatlantic crossings, in the fifties.

This portrait, in which Sistonie is wearing her favorite crystal beads, manages to capture both her strength and her compassion.

I was fourteen when my mother and I posed in Saratoga by our garden gate near the clover patch, with the Fasig Tipton's stables behind us.

I could always recognize my mother from a great distance by her wide "picture hats." This is the only photograph I've ever found of my grandfather, my mother, and me.

I was blissful and nine months pregnant for the first time in Mill Valley, wearing the dress that served for three babies. (Victor Atkins)

The Spanish love babies, and during a stopover in Valencia en route to Ibiza, Alessandro and I were well attended. Santiago would soon be born in Barcelona.

Frances Anne Rollin, "my" Frank, as she looked during the time she was writing her 1868 diary. (Schomburg Center for Research in Black Culture, New York Public Library, Astor, Lenox and Tilden Foundations)

My great grandfather, William James Whipper, a lawyer and a member of the South Carolina State Legislature, looked very distinguished in this portrait taken around the time of his marriage to Frank. (South Caroliniana Library, University of South Carolina)

This picture, taken in Washington, D.C., at the turn of the century, shows a concerned Frank, her high collar reflecting the seriousness of the times. The tragic failure of Reconstruction in the South and a series of other sobering events had impacted strongly upon her life. (Schomburg Center for Research in Black Culture, The New York Public Library, Astor, Lenox and Tilden Foundations)

Frank and Whipper's daughter, my great-aunt Winifred Whipper, was a teacher in Washington when this picture was taken.

My grandfather Leigh Whipper, at his charismatic best, sent this photo to Onie, his sister, sometime in the fifties.

I recall the sweetness of Demps Whipper Powell, my great grandfather's adopted son, during our tea parties when I was a child in Washington. (Goldcraft Portraits, Washington, D.C.)

(*Inset*) *Be-Be is a young girl of sixteen or seventeen in this picture, one of her favorites which she kept near her all her life.*

My grandmother appears to be a lily in this costume from an unidentified show.

Be-Be loved this photograph of the Whitney-Tutt show, The Smarter Set. *My young mother is sitting next to my grandmother on the right and at the feet of Be-Be's great friend Homer Tutt.*

Be-Be, who was always proud of her legs, is third from the right in the 1929 Hot Chocolates *chorus line. When the women turned around they appeared to be wearing a completely different costume.*

It seems to me that my father's father, Harry Lewis, well known in Washington as a golden tenor, shows his Native American/black heritage in this pose.

Ella Wells Lewis, my other great-grandmother, who was said to have gray eyes, was even more elusive to me than Frank.

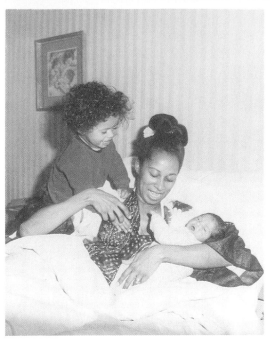

At the Clinica DeXeus in Barcelona, I was feeling a sense of euphoria after Santiago's natural birth. My first son, Alessandro, was also delighted.

My sons, Alessandro, Santiago, and Antonio, now distinguished young men, cringe at the way they look in this eighties' photo taken with my father and me at my father's apartment. (Françoise Burgess)

In the seventies, my antique lace-up boots, much like those that Be-Be wore and no doubt Frank before her, were a regular part of my life, and lasted through a decade of steady use. (Jonathan Umbach)

One day in 1988, Be-Be and I went to Hattie's Chicken Shack in Saratoga to have soup, and I photographed her beneath a picture of Miss Hattie as a young girl.

advocates and apologists of slavery, that they would, if free, relapse into barbarism, or would burden the states in which they were found, for support.

William Rollin and Margarette, a mulatto woman also from the islands, were married in 1844, and were living on America Street in Charleston when their first daughter, Frances, was born on November 19, 1845. Frank's father was Catholic, like most of those whose ancestors came from Saint-Domingue. He employed and did business with a number of Irish Catholics and wielded considerable political influence in Charleston before the war—despite the fact that he himself was denied the vote. He sent Frank at a very early age to a parish school, to be taught by an old French family, and she learned to speak French before she was entirely fluent in English. At the time, there were a number of excellent private schools for free colored people in Charleston, and well-off families in other Southern cities often sent their children to be educated there.

In 1857 and 1859, Frank accompanied her father on his annual business trip north, and visited Boston, Philadelphia, Providence, Newport, Portland, and New York. Rollin's business interests were so interwoven with influential people of both races that they were able to travel and return home in safety despite the laws forbidding their crossing and recrossing the South Carolina border. On the eve of the Civil War, when there was talk of reenslaving free blacks in South Carolina, Frank's parents engaged private tutors for her in preparation for sending her to Paris. But Frank was unwilling to travel so far from home, and instead chose to go to school in Philadelphia, where she boarded with a family of former Charlestonians.

Many other free colored people in Charleston were selling their property and heading north, but William Rollin had no intention of leaving Charleston. Her sisters Charlotte and Louisa and Kate followed Frank to Philadelphia. (Charlotte and Kate also spent some time in Boston, enrolled at Dr. Dio Lewis's Family School for Young Ladies, where prospective students were instructed to bring "rubber boots, umbrella, and napkin ring, one trunk and two or three long dresses, a single short dress for constant wear.") The fifth sister, Florence, was still too young to leave home.

Philadelphia, like Boston, became a second home to Frank. She lived there for almost six years, between 1859 and 1865, and attended church—St. Thomas's Episcopal Church, known simply as the "African Church," the first black church in the United States—and meetings, and read back issues of William Lloyd Garrison's paper, *The Liberator,* and the many other newspapers and pamphlets circulating among the black community. She was in good company: her idols Sarah M. Douglass and Grace A. Mapps, pioneers of higher education and culture for women, lived in Philadelphia; she became friends with Charlotte Forten—whose diary of her experiences teaching Freedman on St. Helena Island between 1862 and 1864 would become well known.

Both St. Thomas and the African Methodist Episcopal Church were centers of black culture and activism, and it was no doubt for this reason that Frank began to prefer Episcopalianism to her father's Catholicism. She also formed friendships with some of the members of the Banneker Society, one of Philadelphia's many early black literary organizations. Several leaders of the Underground Railroad dipped their pens in ink and signed her leather-bound autograph book, along with the black historian William Henry Dorsey and the poet and activist O. V. Catto.

In addition to intellectual stimulation, there was the companionship of sewing meetings. In 1860, a young man named A. Y. Bruce extolled the virtues of the "Ladies' Sewing Circle" in a long and witty poem; the lines intended for Frank were particularly sweet: "And many sparkled from a gem of far off Southern clime / A lady of superior mind, aye talent too and grace / of very keen perception and a highly polished taste / Her gay and social qualities are sung by every mouth / Miss Rollin is the 'Pretty' brilliant Star of sunny South."

At the Quaker Institute for Colored Youth, Frank studied Latin, trigonometry, physiology, algebra, geometry, and, of course, literature. Founded in 1837, the ICY was funded by Quakers but always taught by blacks. It was here that Frank became a politically conscious young woman, for the curriculum at the school was, to quote one historian, "steeped in Black Nationalism." While they were growing up, the Rollin girls had been spared the worst manifestations of slavery; nonetheless, while they had been learning their lessons and studying the piano, the slave trade was flourishing all around them. The busy block of the slave market was only a short walk away from their home. The girls were antislavery, as their parents had taught them to be, but they were still the products of sheltered lives. The mulatto families of substance in Charleston were a fairly close-knit society: there were about 120 families in all, most of them well educated and politically articulate.

According to the records, the girls' father owned three slaves himself. This in itself is disturbing. But I like to believe that unlike those free blacks who owned slaves in earnest and for status, Rollin, like so many others, bought human beings, relatives perhaps, with the intention of freeing them, then found himself unable to do so when South Carolina laws against manumission were passed. The only hint I have of Rollin's stand on slavery is an 1871 newspaper account that mentions his involvement with the Underground Railroad.

The Rollins belonged to a generation that had learned how to survive in the midst of injustice through compromise and a system of favoritism that hinged upon family ties to the white world. Frank, well coached by her father, was proud of her heritage, which included blood ties to French nobility. She would never forget that they were the *Rollin* family, without the Irish *s* that Americans always insisted upon adding to their name.

During her stay in Philadelphia, living and studying among some of the most outspoken activists of the time, Frank began to understand her unique position in the South, to see herself from a new perspective. Her studies were interrupted only months before her graduation by the blockage of communications from the South. The war had all but ruined William Rollin, and he was forced to rely on his farmlands for revenue, selling vegetables to the Confederate troops. Stranded in Philadelphia, Frank and her sisters were aided by friends and acquaintances; and Frank used her skills as a seamstress to help support them.

Finally, the end of the fighting came, and Frank left Philadelphia to teach under the auspices of the Freedmen's Bureau on the Sea Islands, not far from Charleston. At the war's end, William Rollin's land had been sacked by the Union Army, and he had been shot and wounded, though not seriously, defending it. Frank's own memories of the chaos and devastation of her home would be useful when she wrote of Delany's arrival in Charleston after the war:

The city was in ruins—the population consisting of only a few regiments of Union soldiers on duty, the former free people of color and the newly freed slaves who had descended upon the city, having been driven from the plantations and the upper portions of the state. A few white families remained in the city, representing the defeated South. An air of mournful desolation seemed to brood over the city. There existed no signs of traffic except in the stores of the regiments. Confederate bonds and scrip were most plenteous, and but a small amount of currency was in circulation with which to purchase the common necessaries of life.

Soon Frank left the Freedmen's Bureau to take a job at an increased salary (fifteen dollars a month) with the American Missionary Association, an organization that sent thousands of teachers— including many other daughters of Charleston's mulatto elite— throughout the South to set up schools for newly freed slaves. These former slaves were anxious to learn, and many crowded into small classrooms to receive the education that had been denied them. This must have been particularly rewarding for Frank, who had been educated illegally in Charleston, along with other free mulatto children, at a clandestine school.

Then Frank had gone to Boston to write her biography of Major Delany.

I knew very little of what had happened to Frank after she returned from Boston. Her diary entries trailed off after she married William J. Whipper, who had something of a checkered political career in the South Carolina state legislature. And I didn't know any more about the mysterious C.L. of Frank's spiritual sitting, nor had I found the French ancestor my mother and grandmother spoke of. Worst of all, I had still never seen Frank's picture.

One day I took a bus uptown from my father's Central Park West apartment and found myself winding through the territory of my youth. At each stop the bus filled with more loud and exuberant black children, heading home from school. Several older black ladies in hats shook their heads disapprovingly, and I remembered my own rowdy days on the bus coming home from the High School of Music and Art.

The bus passed the Loews 116th Street Theater, where my mother had cornered me when I was a teenager, and I noticed that the theater—once a prime spot for features like *No Way Out,* a story about racial injustice—was now closed and seedy-looking. It had been turned into a Baptist church and had a neon cross outside. People stood on cold street corners, looking angry and displaced. Metal grates covered the windows and doorways of empty shells of buildings. Deserted lots were filled with ripped plastic garbage bags. The streets were dirty and ugly under a darkening winter sky.

Nothing has changed, I wrote on a yellow pad as the bus careened around another corner. *Harlem is even worse now than it was when I was a child—No Way Out.*

I got off at 135th Street and Lenox Avenue and entered the Schomburg Collection of the New York Public Library. I was looking through a card catalogue when a librarian suggested that I might want to see some scrapbooks that had been left to the library after my grandfather's death in 1975. They were upstairs, she told me, in the manuscripts department.

I rushed upstairs and applied to see the scrapbooks. Standing at the counter, filling out the necessary forms, I could feel my excitement growing. Two large envelopes were handed to me, and I took them to the nearest table.

When the scrapbooks finally lay before me, I was almost afraid to turn the first page. I could feel what was about to happen. I pulled back the first leaf tentatively, then all the way. And there she was. There was not only one picture of her, but two. In one she looked like the Frank I knew—and had known, it seemed, forever—the Frank of the diary years. Wearing crystal earrings, she looked out with eyes that were, as my mother had said they were, Creole. Island eyes.

In the other picture she was older; time had passed, many things had happened: things she could not have suspected at the time of the first photograph, things I wished I could have warned her about. She was more difficult to recognize. I returned my gaze to the Frank of the diary years. I wanted to shout—to dance wildly around the silent, carpeted room. There had been too much silence. But of course, I couldn't. I tried to signal my enormous pleasure to the librarian, who came over to look. She was pleased for me, and we talked for a moment in hushed tones.

Afterward, I settled as quietly as I could into my seat, the book open on the table in front of me. Following on the heels of my elation came another emotion. I felt a terrible pang of envy. The photograph, and the album and all of its contents, were the legal property of the library. I was grateful that the book had been preserved and that at last I had found its precious contents, but I felt it belonged to me. And I was furious that my grandfather, by intention or by oversight, had in essence given his mother away to strangers. I had by now come to understand much of my mother's anger about her father. I knew that during the years when she was trying to make it as an actress in New York, she and my grandmother both felt there were things Leigh Whipper could have done to help her. There were things she would have expected a father to do that he never did.

Relatively late in his life, my grandfather and his wife had adopted two boys, Jim and Richard. Jim was tragically killed in Korea, and Richard became an aspiring actor, changing his name to Leigh Whipper, Jr. Uncle Billy tried to foster his career. Whatever parental urges my grandfather had were apparently spent on these two children—boy children, my mother would have been quick to point out.

From the very beginning, both my mother and Be-Be had resented Uncle Billy's distance, his lack of help where it counted, and although they had maintained tentative and sometimes cordial relations through the years, that resentment had endured. Even though he was gone, they were still angry. Now I was faced with my own version of that anger. I was outraged that Uncle Billy had chosen to give family papers and memorabilia to the special collections at Howard and the Schomburg—as though it all had only to do with him. I longed to take Frank home with me, where she belonged.

As I continued to examine the scrapbook before me, I found that Uncle Billy had titled it "Debts I Failed To Pay—To you without a struggle." What an odd thing to call his scrapbook, I thought. I had the uncanny feeling that he was speaking directly to me. The words seemed apologetic, as if he thoroughly understood the anger and resentment he had caused in his life. As if now, by finally offering this book up to me, he had redeemed himself.

There was also a clipping written by a man named Edward Orleans: "To begin with I know that in proportion to what there is to know, what I know is insignificant. Therefore, I have learned not to be hasty in opinion. . . ." These words, too, struck home. Clearly my grandfather had had an introspective side that I had never known.

Turning yet another page, I found a torn and yellowing clipping glued to one of the soft black pages of the book. I recognized Frank's handwriting immediately. She had written: *Charleston, January 14 '95* above the headline JAMES ACHILLE DE CARADEUC. Underneath, she had added, *Nephew of Wm. A. Rollin.* The clipping was an 1895 obituary in the *Charleston News and Courier.* The subheading read: "The Death of an Estimable and Accomplished Citizen—A Grandson of a Lieutenant of the Marshals of France—A refugee from San Domingo—The early Life of Mr. De Caradeuc—Civil Engineer, Botanist, Horticulturist and Artist." The article that followed detailed de Caradeuc's ancestry and told of his life in Charleston. At one point, the writer was moved to add: "A man of strong prejudices, he ever cherished the traditions of the old South as productive of a finer civilization than that of today, and to the Confederacy, he gave the lives of two sons, who distinguished themselves on many a battlefield of Virginia." After clipping the article, Frank must have sent it off directly to Leigh.

I had memorized my mother's words, her recent account, telling me practically all she knew of our ancestors: "They came from San Domingo. He [the head of the family] had two families—one white, one of color. They were Creoles. He recognized both families. He was the lieutenant governor or lieutenant general of the island. When the revolutions came, they were forced to flee the island. They went by boat to Charleston, where he provided for both families. They were very well-to-do."

Be-Be had said: "Sistonie told me that her grandfather's brother was French and was governor. There were two families, a white family and a colored family, and they were the colored family. Her mother's mother soaked tough meat in vinegar. They did West Indian cooking—ate okra and rice."

For years I had tried to puzzle out these stories, searching for French Rollins without ever being able to get a direct line of descent. Now I finally had the name of the missing French ancestor. And beyond the sensual islands in my mother's rhythmic songs, beyond the island of our Riverton living room, there was a real island in our past. I looked back at Frank and saw again that her eyes were indeed what I thought of as Creole, large and black and shining with intelligence, and that Sistonie was present in her lovely face. In the eyes and somewhere around the jaw, my mother was there too. And so was I.

15

Island Tales

CHARLESTON IS A BRIGHT, clean city with the storybook atmosphere of well-preserved Americana. I could feel the South Carolina heat rising around me. I had not been south since the days of segregation, and I felt a little outdated. This, I was being told, was the New South, old enough now that a whole generation seemed not to recall what came before it.

I was suspicious. It almost seemed as though it was all right to be black there. No one stared in the hotel. Black women sat weaving beautiful baskets on the streets, and the old slave mart had been turned into a cheery open-air market featuring trinkets. Everything seemed so mild and easy. But as in Boston, there were very few black people strolling downtown. A distance from my hotel, I found blacks living in the same areas they'd lived in a century before, beyond what used to be called "the line." Once just outside the city, these neighborhoods were now neatly incorporated within it.

I called cousins I'd never met before, including Reverend Benjamin Whipper, the head of a thriving Baptist ministry in Charleston and the grandson of my great-grandfather's brother, Samuel T. Parker Whipper, who had been a tenant farmer in Carl's Branch, not far from Beaufort. By coincidence, Reverend Whipper's wife, Lucille Whipper, was just leaving a job as director of the Avery Research Center, which evolved from the old Avery School, where Frank once taught. Sistonie and her sister Winifred both attended there.

Reverend Whipper was an imposing man. While I was with him I basked in the rich darkness of his color—a sense of my grandfather, of family, seemed to exude from him. Lucille had done her own research on her husband's family and was fascinated by it, and together we puzzled over the abolitionist William Whipper's relationship to the family. The Whippers told me that their Grandpa Samuel had loaned a lot of money to his brother William James Whipper, to help him with gambling debts. One day they drove me out to look at all that was left of Uncle Billy's childhood home. Someone in the family still remembered the large run-down house, statues of lions on the stoop. But the house was gone, and we had to content ourselves with looking at a street sign that read: "Whipper Barony."

Two friends were in Charleston, helping me research. In my journal I wrote:

I feel that everyone else's interest is more leisurely than mine. I feel a little crazy. . . . Wanting something, not just a photograph, not just records— something that may not even be possible.

There are archives and archivists, libraries and librarians. I am received with true Southern hospitality. These are experts—people who know the period in which Frank lived, know scores of other periods as well. I sit at wooden tables, poring over old manuscripts; at clumsy machines, looking at microfilm.

I dine on she-crab soup and eat delectable broiled oysters on toast.

When I call my grandmother on the phone from Charleston, she asks, "Are you staying in a colored place?" She is amazed that I can go everywhere, eat in white restaurants. She recalls stopping in Charleston with a show years ago, sometime in the '20s. She tells me her landlady made her a dinner she never forgot. The best thing she ever tasted, a spaghetti dish mixed with clams and crab and other sea fare. I feel as though I can taste it through her memory. I hang up the phone and I go out to eat shrimp, corn on the cob, beer.

In Charleston, I look at the carefully preserved buildings, trying to imagine my great-grandmother passing by, perhaps even entering . . . living in them. . . . I see houses, corners of streets that turn out to be places she must have walked, buildings she could have entered. I seek out her old family house, but it is no longer there.

I walk on East Bay and find the incredibly elegant homes that are there now, facing the sea. But they were built shortly after the Rollin family lived at number 27. The present number 27, a fabulous structure, makes my heart beat for a moment, but it is not the old one—the numbers have been changed. The old 27 no longer stands. . . .

Something is bothering me—the truth is that I realize that I had thought I'd come down here and find her, really find her. That one day I'd not exactly see her but somehow feel her turning a corner. But she is not here.

I am immersed in research, surrounded by elusive facts that should be making me happy. But these facts only seem to take me farther away from her. Friends who are with me are caring and helpful, but I find myself curiously angry, curiously removed from them and what is going on around me. Whenever I handle a piece of paper pertaining to my family, it touches some very deep personal part of me. I feel raw and exposed.

Beaufort, in the Sea Islands, is too quiet and calm. I find the most tangible evidence of my great-grandparents here on paper in the extensive real estate dealings that transpired when Frank was bailing Whipper out, putting properties in her name so that they would not be confiscated because of his gambling debts. I find some of Whipper's probate (property) transactions as well, but at the courthouse there is no record of his years in office. I am angry because William Whipper was probate judge in this town from 1882 to 1888 and there is hardly a trace of him, in life or in death.

A young black minister, Reverend Rumley, attempts to help me, driving me to various cemeteries and telling me of the steady inroads of whites attempting to buy blacks out of long-held property on nearby Daufuskie Island. He tells a story of a small black boy listening to whites talking about his home, looking up, and commenting, "But they don't know Daufuskie."

I know that Frank died here and was buried in the colored A.M.E. graveyard after an Episcopal ceremony at the Baptist church. Even her death escapes me. In all the graveyards that could be what was then the colored graveyard, I find not a trace of Frank or her husband. The old stones have worn away—some have sunk deep—some are covered with tangled vines. I step on marshy ground in old overgrown graveyards, where the salt air, the moisture, has destroyed many headstones. I find myself moving beneath trailing hanging moss, among the faded, too-sweet-smelling flowers. I sit in the dark beneath the live oaks, in the ruins of old praise houses, early places where blacks gathered to worship, on the Sea Islands, feeling spirits all around me but not inside me. They cannot come close enough, it seems. . . .

My friends are staying at the Sea Island Motel, in the room beside mine. They are here to help me, but I am feeling a need to be alone. Part of it is that I am mourning and cannot explain it. Part of it is that they are white and that I am feeling a need to be black in Beaufort. And that is something that I cannot tell them—something I cannot explain even to myself. I risk hurting them, and how to understand that I myself am hurt by it?

Visiting Hilton Head, a few miles away, where Whipper once owned land—where he wrote enthusiastic letters to Frank up in Boston—I find a frighteningly slick white resort town with gates and checkpoints for visitors. Everything in me cringes.

One day as I am walking to the Beaufort library, passing crisp clean houses, I hear the loud sound of funky black music pouring forth from one of the houses. It blasts for a few minutes and then fades out. It washes over me and momentarily fills me with life.

Back in Charleston, I decide one day in desperation to drive back out to Beaufort alone. I take a rented air-conditioned car, I circle round and round the Westley A.M.E. Church, which I feel may be the one where Frank is buried, though there is no marker that says so. A small red bird comes to land on a tombstone that says simply "Mother." It is Mother's Day. I must content myself with this. But I am not content. I circle back around after eating my lunch in the car, and I find a woman raking and cleaning the cemetery—Mrs. Adalee B. Roberts. She tells me that she and her husband do this as often as they can, in all the old black cemeteries around town. It is a long, tedious job, and so many of them are overrun with weeds. Because of the marshy land, the graves have sunk, and the headstones are no longer visible. She tells me she will keep looking for me.

Lying sleepless in my room that night, I felt vulnerable as a child. A memory surfaced of my first train ride south, in the early fifties. I was about thirteen years old, and I knew about the Mason-Dixon line, that imaginary but nonetheless real border, somewhere in Maryland, beyond which black train travelers had to continue in segregated cars. But I had been told that due to a relatively new regulation, since I had a reserved seat on the train, I would not have to change.

"It will be all right," my mother and my grandmother had assured me. "No one will bother you." But though I reminded myself of this as I sat in my reserved seat, I felt a curious kind of shame. It was the terrible shame of having them not want you there and of being there anyway. No matter how hard I tried to be invisible, I was still there.

That summer my father, then teaching at Atlanta University, arranged for me to stay with friends, because his own apartment was too small for him to put me up. The Hills had three daughters around my age, and with them I began to explore the intricacies of Southern life. As an only child, I had always viewed siblings with awe; among the Hills I began to learn a little about the politics among sisters.

Dr. Mozell Hill was a sociologist, like my father, and he and his wife, Marnesba, lived about a block away from where my father was living with his second wife, Audrey, and their new baby, my half-brother Guy. This was on campus, in the comparatively safe shelter of the university. There were several white faculty members, and white people came on campus for various reasons without harassment—but there were problems in the other direction, when black people wanted to go into the white world.

It was a strange island we lived on, one of black social mores, of polite and elegant gatherings, of card parties for bridge and whist, of Sunday-afternoon visits accompanied by cool lemonade and cookies. Beyond this island I sensed a vicious and unfathomable white world. Standing on the sidewalk out in front of the Hills'—in much the same way as I would stand in front of Be-Be's house in Saratoga, bouncing my golf ball, wishing on the pink-and-blue clouds—I saw an innocuous sky, yet I could breathe molecules of hatred that seemed to float over to me from beyond the campus.

From time to time we ventured downtown. Certain shops, I was told, like Rich's department store, had begun to serve black people, and we were even allowed to try on clothes in the dressing rooms. I rode in the back of the city buses with the Hills and observed the white and colored waiting rooms, the white and colored drinking fountains in public places. I saw the stretch of Woolworth counters designated for colored customers. "Negroes" were second-class all the way. The smaller, darker rooms, the cheaper materials, the no-frills product, the difficult, the demeaning, the depressing, the unpainted, the uncleaned—whenever we encountered any of those things, we knew they were intended for us.

One day the Hills and I decided to go downtown to the Fox Theater to see *Gone With the Wind*. When we got there, I looked up and saw a long line of black people climbing several stories on the fire escape to get to the doors of the upper balcony. It was there that we had to sit if we wanted to go to this theater, and we joined them.

A few days later we went on a church picnic. There were about twenty of us black children in a school bus, rented for the occasion. The bus broke down. We were stuck somewhere on a country road. It was almost noon, and the southern heat had already begun to beat down on us. I looked out the window at the alien landscape—a few trees, the red Georgia clay—and I felt the temperature rising. It was then that I discovered a trick I could do. By telling myself, "Cool, cool, be cool, stay safe and cool," I managed to will my temperature down.

The Hills invited me to extend my stay in the South to accompany them on their family vacation to Daytona Beach, Florida. We drove through town after town without incident, past the red dirt of Georgia. When we passed through St. Augustine, Florida, we saw that the town had been meticulously restored to look as it did in the old days, with its white buildings, palms, and wide avenues. Black men in colonial livery sat placidly in buggies, waiting for passengers—and as we passed them, Dr. Hill suddenly began to curse. He cursed loudly and fiercely as he drove slowly all the way through the town. I could see beads of sweat standing out on the back of his neck. We seemed to be going through the town in slow motion; it seemed as if we'd never put it behind us. Even Marnesba Hill's urgently whispered "Mozell, Mozell—now, Mozell!" could not hush her husband's anger.

Our chattering silenced, we girls exchanged embarrassed glances, then averted our eyes and stared silently out the windows. The moment stayed with us long after we'd left the town.

We traveled several miles farther south, toward the pale-cerulean waves of Daytona Beach and a motel owned by blacks, a way station in a hostile land. There, over the next few days, the Hill sisters and I raced across the sparkling sand to spend our days out in the water, riding the waves, allowing our skins to get darker and darker in the Florida sun.

If you are quiet enough, if you are polite enough, they will not kill you. The unspoken message that infuriated Mozell Hill en route to his vacation is an old one. For women of all colors, for blacks and other nonwhites of both sexes, it is an old trick to smile into their faces, pretending to acknowledge that you fall short of their perfection. They are so full of themselves, so blind to others, that they are appeased.

They consider you a good woman, or a good nigger, a good colored, a good Negro, a good black, a good child.

*   *   *

On my second trip to Charleston, I was armed with the name of the French relative Frank had referred to as William A. Rollin's nephew—James Achille de Caradeuc. I had begun to hope that it would unlock everything that had been missing so far in my under-standing of Frank and her family. I found the de Caradeucs without difficulty—they had left a trail of information that eventually took me not only to the many archives in Charleston but to archives in Sa-vannah, Durham, and Paris.

Document after document stressed the de Caradeucs' affection and admiration for each other. I read their many letters and diaries, with their accounts of day-to-day life; their words were often witty, elegant, and warm. Their wills called for the care and preservation of family mementos: James Achille de Caradeuc requested that his heirs "never mortgage the house" and that they attend to his "little bureau brought from St. Domingue a century ago." He asked that they do the same with "the family papers which I very highly prize. Keep them safely from moths and from fire: Your children will some day know their value and appreciate them."

His concern for the family history moved me. This was what I had wanted, I thought—a careful retelling of old stories to the chil-dren, an appreciation of the past.

A proud family of the French *haute noblesse*, the de Caradeucs had traced their line back to fourteenth-century Brittany and claimed to have had a relative in King Arthur's court, "Karadoc bref bras." Like most French colonials, their allegiance to the mother country was sacrosanct, and they were a clan who stuck together. After their arrival in Charleston from Saint-Domingue—the Caribbean island that later became Haiti and Santo Domingo—they stayed close, know-ing that their unity would protect them in this new country.

But these handsome and tall men and lovely, strong women were also fiercely "conservative," as they called it. They wrote quite elo-quently on behalf of slavery and took great care to pass their credos on to their children. I couldn't help but feel awed by the deadliness of the de Caradeucs' innocence. Born patrician masters within a vile system of slavery and abuse, they had remained loyal to that system, seemingly without regret.

I cried tears of bitterness that the French ancestors I'd finally found were not a family I could be proud of; whatever pride there was would have to be mixed with shame. No wonder there was so much confusion in my family. The problem of conflicting loyalties existed not only in this, the paternal side of my mother's family, but on the maternal side as well. I remembered how Be-Be would speak of her Uncle Vails, a black man who fought in the Confederate Army. "He was in there pitching," she would say, "but he was for the wrong side!"

The passion in Frank's words when she wrote of Delany's pride in his regal African heritage made me think that she, too, might have valued her African roots. Yet as far as I know, she wrote only of her French ancestry.

After finding Frank's newspaper clipping in the library, I uncovered our island heritage easily enough, but our African ancestry proved impossible to trace with any certainty. I spent two years trying to pin down the exact nature of the relationship between the mulatto Rollins and the white de Caradeucs. But there remained only the fragile clipping, with Frank's tantalizing clue. The de Caradeuc family, like most large white Sea Island families, had mulatto—or what was called on the islands *métisse*—lineages, but these were far less documented than the white ones. I also discovered that in Saint-Domingue, "no mulatto whatever his number of white parts," was allowed to assume the name of his white father.

As I combed through names and initials, searching the precarious limbs of scores of family trees, I often wondered: Why couldn't the Rollins have left me a clear understanding of who they were? Why, if Frank had been so proud of her lineage, wasn't there a single scrap of paper just setting the whole thing out for me? What if she had done so, only to have it lost in what Be-Be would call "the shuffle"? What if the information I needed was in the big trunk Sistonie brought up to Saratoga, which had long since been carted away to the dump?

Finally, I simplified my need for the truth, and out of dozens of possibilities, chose two reasonable scenarios: One, that James Achille's mother, a LaChicotte—herself from a large island clan—was William Rollin's half-sister, Rollin being the product of a mulatto liaison. This situation would bear out Frank's scribbled annotation that James Achille de Caradeuc was William Rollin's nephew. Or, two, if Frank meant grandnephew; a liaison between the family's proud African servant known as "Mama Monkee" or another female ancestor and General Jean Baptiste Laurent de Caradeuc could have occurred. Jean Baptiste Laurent had held the title Commanding General of the Patriotic Troops of the West (the western part of the island was and still is the French part) during the struggle between the French nobility and rebelling slaves. He was also a Lieutenant des Maréchaux de France, a high honor bequeathed by the king of France, a lieutenant governor or lieutenant general, my mother had said. She had not been far off.

"When the revolutions came, they were forced to flee the island. They went by boat to Charleston, where he provided for both families, one white, one of color. They were very well-to-do."

The island tale I put together was quite unlike the romantic tropical stories I imagined as a child in Riverton, listening to my mother's songs. . . .

> Les bon gens de Guadeloupe
> Les messieurs de Martinique
> Les seigneurs de Saint-Domingue
> —Old French saying

Cap François, Saint-Domingue, Autumn 1792

Under cover of dark, a small schooner hoisted sail and lifted anchor. As it drifted seaward, its passengers, General Jean-Baptiste de Caradeuc, his sister, Madame de Chateaublond, and the widower general's three young children, gathered at the ship's rail, watching the dark shoreline of their homeland as it receded into the night. In the distance, dotting the deep purple of the sky, smoke rose ash gray from the still-smoldering houses and plantations of the embattled colonialists. Over it all hung the scent of terror and blood; and the de Caradeucs could still smell it, even as they headed out over the Caribbean toward America, a country none of them had ever set foot in.

Left behind, guarding the one vast family sugar plantation still operable in Cayes, with those slaves who still remained faithful, was the general's younger brother, Laurent de Caradeuc de La Cayes. Laurent's chances for survival were infinitely better than his brother's; as Commanding General of the Patriotic Troops of the West, Jean-Baptiste was fiercely hated by the Republicans. There were many who wanted nothing better than to see his head perched atop a post, rotting in the heat of the day, as many a slave's head had done, by his orders.

The saying "The good folk of Guadeloupe, the gentlemen of Martinique, and the lords of Saint-Domingue" accurately reflected distinctions among the three French colonies. Each island had its own character, and that of Saint-Domingue was choice, not only because of the startling agricultural productivity of the island but because of the aristocrats who reigned there on vast sugar plantations, supported by thousands of slaves. In 1797, the de Caradeuc family alone owned 188 slaves. (Françoise, Marie Louise, Agathe, Marguerette, Olive, Magdeleine, Marie Terese, Henriette, Franchon, Genevieve, Zeline, Catherine—these were just a few of the women whose history is reduced to a few fading lines in a long-ago inventory.)

Since the mid-1780s, however, the island had been in turmoil, with bands of slaves revolting against barbarous treatment and the large class of those of *métisse* parentage agitating to be recognized as citizens. There was an African chant in the colonies:

> *Eh! Eh! Bomba! Heu! Heu!*
> *Canga, bafio té!*
> *Canga, mouné delé!*
> *Canga dokila!*
> *Canga, li!*

According to historian C. L. R. James, it translated as "We swear to destroy the whites and all that they possess! Let us die rather than fail to keep this vow!" The repercussions of the French Revolution created violent chaos on the islands. In 1792, three Republican commissioners arrived from France to ratify the National Assembly's decree that mulattoes be given citizenship and slaves be set free. It was not to be that simple—fierce fighting broke out once more as the French colonialists, led by General de Caradeuc, struggled to maintain control of their land and their fortunes.

De Caradeuc resigned his post rather than obey the new commands; and remembering the family motto emblazoned on their coat of arms, *Arreste Ton Coeur*, he "steeled his heart" to leave the island of his birth.

On board ship with the de Caradeucs was a retinue of loyal mulatto and black servants, some born free and the rest technically freed as a result of the French decree. Among them was a young man named Kyric, the son of an African king. There was also an old woman known simply as "Vieille Grannie" and a tall, powerfully built African woman of whom the family professed to be extraordinarily fond despite their pejorative nickname for her, "Mama Monkee." The name was a reference to what some members of the family considered the "extreme ugliness" of her first child.

Could Mama Monkee and her "ugly" child have been my ancestors? James Achille de Caradeuc recalled in his memoirs that the beloved Mama Monkee had nursed all of the general's children and had borne a number of mulatto children as well. Some of these, he took great care to note, "turned out well and good"; there is a strong possibility that they were the progeny of the general or of his brother Laurent. Presumably they were not considered ugly, like that first baby, who perhaps had African traits that offended the de Caradeuc sensibility.

After the surprise of coming across Mama Monkee's curious name and story, I began to imagine a beautiful black Angolan woman who still spoke her native tongue, still remembered her homeland. I conjured up a woman who still had night dreams of that dark continent, with its savannas and beaches, its palms and gemstones. Only in those dreams could she return home and be once more with her African family.

How shocked Sistonie would have been at the thought of having Mama Monkee as a foremother, I thought with a smile.

The route of the de Caradeuc boat was one that would become well traveled as more and more islanders, fleeing the escalating revolution, headed toward New York, Philadelphia, New Orleans, and—perhaps the most popular destination—Charleston. Charleston had a reputation as a city of patrician sensibilities, a place where "conservatives" like the de Caradeucs would be in like-minded company. And to free mulattoes, whose lives had been uprooted by the turmoil, had come word that there was a large society of others like them in Charleston.

In Charleston, as in Saint-Domingue, color lines were so blurred that it was often hard to tell which members of the same family were white, which "colored." There was no legal definition of the term "mulatto" by the state legislature. White Carolinians, perhaps afraid of pushing too many of their own over the color line, did not adopt the islands' elaborate system of labeling individuals according to the percentage of "black blood" in their ancestry. The courts of South Carolina, as confused as the populace, ruled at one point that the decision be left to "reputation" and "worth": you were considered white if you were known as white, or if you had money and obvious social stature.

Freedom was associated with fair skin color, as the majority of the "free colored" in Charleston, as on the islands, were mulattoes. Some were descended from indentured servants who had worked for their freedom. Others' ancestors had arrived before slavery had become firmly established. Many were the children of white slaveowners, who had given them their freedom. Still others had struggled for years to purchase their freedom and that of their loved ones.

By 1800, the brilliant black general Toussaint-Louverture, "the great Toussaint," as Frank called him in her diary, had gained control of both the Spanish and the French territories of Saint-Domingue. Large numbers of freed mulattoes and blacks continued to leave the island for Charleston. Baron de Montlezuns, a Frenchman visiting Charleston in 1817, remarked:

> Creole French is heard at every street corner; it seems that the white and black population of Santo Domingo has been poured out on all the continental beaches from New York to the mouth of the Mississippi. The white families from Santo Domingo are languishing and ill-starred here as everywhere else. There are three thousand French in Charleston. . . . Negroes and people of color, free or slave, are obliged by law to be in their houses by ten o'clock in the evening; those who disobey are arrested.
>
> He also wrote: "Slavery is here in all its severity."

Fearing that their own slaves would be emboldened by the success of the revolution on the islands, the legislature passed a law prohibiting the entry of free blacks "from any port in the Western Hemispheres." The fear of insurrection also led them to pass a law prohibiting free persons of color from leaving and then reentering the state.

Within a few months of their arrival, the de Caradeuc family settled on a plantation in St. Thomas Parish, just north of the city of Charleston. The slaves among their servants, though perhaps technically free, apparently remained in a state of slavery. Mama Monkee, always given special treatment, set up her own house on the grounds, where she ran a kind of commissary, selling to whites and blacks alike.

Within a few years, the family ventured into a small lumber and bricklaying business, which proved profitable. Some of Mama Monkee's mulatto children were probably involved in the business as well. Some thirty years later, one of the general's grandsons, James Achille de Caradeuc, returned to South Carolina from studying in France and married a young woman named Elizabeth de la Torre, whose family also lived in Charleston. In 1850, a French-speaking mulatto relative of the de Caradeucs moved in next door to the de la Torres; his name was William Rollin.

Rollin was tall and lanky, like the de Caradeucs, and he was apparently so fair that many considered him white. Like most mulattoes in Charleston who were "family" with prominent whites, he made good use of his connections. His lumber business, which he ran in collaboration with the original de Caradeuc family operation in St. Thomas Parish, was thriving, and he was moderately well off. He was already starting to purchase properties in and around Charleston. When he moved next door to the de la Torres, he and his wife, Margarette, a brown-skinned woman from the islands, already had a five-year-old child, whose name was Frances Anne.

16

Tough on Black Actors

I LOVE TO IMAGINE MY grandmother, Virginia Eva Wheeler, and my grandfather, Leigh Whipper, at the height of their relationship, arm in arm, stepping off their show train in unison to explore some new Southern town. Alongside this image, in my mind's eye, is that of Frances Anne Rollin and my great-grandfather, William J. Whipper, riding in a buggy through postwar Columbia, full of hopes for the future of Reconstruction.

My grandmother and grandfather traveled through the South on the TOBA (Theater Owners Booking Association) circuit, which was nicknamed "Tough on Black Actors" or, more candidly, "Tough on Black Asses." The circuit, extending from New York to Florida and from Chicago to New Orleans, was made up of black theaters like the Regal in Baltimore, the 81 in Atlanta, the Booker T. in St. Louis, and the Howard and the Lincoln in Washington. The Howard, long since darkened, still stands in the midst of a depressed neighborhood. It paid well for those stars who got top billing, like Bessie Smith and

Hamtree Harrington, Tom Fletcher and Ethel Waters (also known to many as Sweet Mama Stringbean).

My grandmother had come to Washington in 1910, and her first job was working for a florist, who sent her to graves and funeral parlors to gather flowers, which would then be resold to other mourners. The job was depressing and paid her barely enough to survive, but one day she returned to her boardinghouse and met S. H. Dudley, a big colored star of the time. And he introduced her to the stars of a popular black show, Salem Tutt Whitney and Homer Tutt, two brothers from Indiana who toured as Whitney and Tutt. Salem was the comedian, and Homer was the straight man, and they were pioneers in black theater in the South.

My grandmother had never been on a stage, but she told Salem and Homer, "Any step you can show me, I can do." She'd been to parties where she had outdanced every woman and man around. She invented her own dances, and had to be shown a step only once in order to be able to repeat it perfectly.

The brothers liked her. Her fair skin was a surefire crowd-pleaser on the black vaudeville circuit. The blond hair she'd had as a baby had turned a burnished brown and framed her face in loose ringlets. She was a lively eighteen-year-old country girl, and in addition to being good-looking, she had the spark of a natural.

Whitney and Tutt taught her a marching number that was in the finale of the show and urged her to join them when the show went out on tour. They appointed a tall, lanky, dark-skinned actor to "chaperon" Virginia and one other underaged girl in the show. His nickname was "College Bred," since he was usually the only college-educated performer in the show (his Howard Law School training came in handy in negotiating contracts for himself and the other actors). His real name was Leigh Whipper.

Both of Leigh's parents had been dead for several years when my grandmother met him. Frances Anne Rollin Whipper had died in 1901, and William James Whipper six years later. Leigh still spoke of his mother from time to time, with obvious pride. My grandmother retained mostly the things he said about his mother's aristocratic heritage: that she had come from a proud and accomplished family in Charleston and that the family was originally from "the islands." My grandfather stressed that he came from a family that believed in education, a politically active family that had tried to change things for blacks during Reconstruction. He mentioned his father, "the Judge," and his role in drafting the South Carolina state constitution. He also spoke affectionately of his older sister, who seemed to be single-handedly carrying the aristocratic family standard: Dr. Ionia Rollin Whipper, a physician in Washington, D.C.

"I couldn't stand him when I first met him," Be-Be said later, but she was impressed. I imagine her sitting backstage, or out in front of some empty colored theater between rehearsals, listening to Leigh, thinking of her own family. Her difficult, proud mother and her shoemaker grandfather were dead, and her beloved grandmother had gone off and gotten married to some "old codger"; she no longer knew if she was dead or alive. She kept silent about herself while Leigh talked and talked.

With his natural flair for drama, his deep speaking voice, and a riveting stage presence, Leigh had discovered that acting suited him well. At Howard, he had successfully completed his law studies but been refused a diploma after he publicly insulted a professor. He had gone through the motions of trying to live up to his mother's desire that he become a lawyer like his father, or that he distinguish himself in some other profession, but it wasn't really in him.

"Personally," he explained to me many years later, "I didn't want to do anything." His lengthy career was more or less an accident. In 1900, broke in Philadelphia and in debt to his landlady, he happened to pass the Stanton Theater on South Street and noticed some people standing in line. He fell in and before he knew it was wearing slouch hat and overalls, and singing "Old Black Joe" in *Uncle Tom's Cabin*. He got fifty cents a performance, or twelve dollars a week, and was allowed to draw on his salary so he could keep his room.

After his first taste of applause, Leigh decided to stick with the theater. In the Whitney and Tutt show, he got star billing and performed monologues and skits that he wrote himself. He was a natural leader and relished taking charge. When Virginia "graduated" from the chorus to doing numbers with Leigh, billing would always be a sore point between them.

"Leigh always had to be the whole cheese!" Be-Be told me. And my grandfather would say to me of her, "She was a chorus girl. *I* was a star."

The performers traveled in Pullman cars reserved for colored performers. Leigh and Virginia, despite their conflicts, were becoming inseparable, and one of their favorite activities was having picnics of cold cuts and beer on the train taking them from one Southern town to the next. As the locomotive pulled into the station of each new town, Virginia and Leigh would stand arm in arm, poised and waiting on the open platform of the railroad car, ready to step off the moment the train came to a halt. Then, with their steps perfectly synchronized—my grandmother, years later, could mimic it perfectly—they would hit the platform—"Boom!"—and rush forward to see what each new town had to offer.

There was a strong sense of camaraderie among the twenty actors and actresses in the troupe, but box office receipts did not always allow them to be paid adequately, and at some of the stops in the Deep South, in Texas particularly, the managers had to hire armed guards to protect the girls in the show from the attentions of white men who assumed they were prostitutes.

By 1912, times were worse than ever. Many of the small black theaters had closed, and the troupe, in deep financial trouble, was beginning to talk of disbanding. During this period, when they were performing in Atlanta, there was a comedian with them named Billy Higgins, who did an act with a chicken. He insisted that the chicken have its own dressing room. One evening, Virginia, tired of not having anything really good to eat, sneaked up on the chicken, killed it, plucked it, and baked it, just as she had done with many a bird back home. Then she served it to Leigh and a few other members of the cast. Though it was the toughest bird any of them had ever eaten, they were all glad to have it.

When Billy Higgins entered the room in the middle of the feast, there was a moment of stunned silence around the table. He stood in the doorway, his face beginning to contort in anger as he instantly grasped what was going on. Virginia began to quake with laughter. "Don't laugh, Virginia, don't *laugh!*" Billy cried, but that made her laugh all the harder. The others joined in, and finally Billy couldn't keep a straight face, either. Wiping away the few tears he had shed for his stage partner, he sat down and joined the dinner party.

Hard times did not solidify what was a passionate but stormy match between my twenty-year-old grandmother and my thirty-seven-year-old grandfather. In Atlanta, Virginia discovered that Leigh, who had been holding both their salaries, had spent all of her money. Enraged, she picked up one of his "big old shoes" and threw it at him. When he made the mistake of trying to hit her in return, she grabbed a frying pan and started waving it in the air over her head. "He flew out of the room!" she recalled later, laughing.

Virginia told Leigh not to come back and left the show, getting a job down the street at another colored theater. This time she managed to get star billing. She had a solo where she sang as well as danced; although her voice was never as good as her dancing, her great ambition was to be considered a singer, and she would fake it just for the chance to be on stage in that capacity.

Leigh revised his own act and returned to doing a solo. After a few weeks, unable to resist her curiosity, Virginia sneaked into Leigh's theater on a night when her own show was dark. In spite of herself, she had to admit that Leigh was a wonderful performer.

It was during this difficult year that my grandmother discovered she was pregnant. The show was in Augusta, Georgia, and many of the performers, pressed for money, moved on, looking for work in other cities. Leigh decided to leave too, making his way to Savannah, where he had aunts who might help him. Then he went to Washington, to his sister Onie's house.

"I told him to go ahead," Be-Be explained to me. "I always had confidence that I would be all right, even though I had no idea what I was going to do. I didn't blame him so much, because I knew how show business was. But I was down there with nothing. Only once he wrote and said, 'Here's five dollars that my sister gave me.' I never thought about anything much in those days. It certainly had never occurred to me that I could get pregnant. Me, pregnant? I was dumb."

In fact, it had been Leigh who first realized that Virginia was pregnant. He escorted her to a doctor before he left town. There, they had found themselves staring at a photograph, prominently displayed on the office wall, of the doctor's medical school class at Howard. Leigh proudly pointed out his sister among the graduates. Virginia, with a mixture of jealousy and awe, stood looking. Then all of that was swept away by fear when the doctor called her into the examining room.

Within weeks after that visit, Leigh was gone. Kindly neighbors supplied my grandmother with food and clothing during her pregnancy, and she took care of cows and horses in exchange for her lodgings. She also did clerical work for a man who wrote up insurance for poor people in the area; later he turned out to be a fraud, who had swindled hundreds out of their money.

Certain that she was about to die ignominiously in Georgia, far from family and friends, Virginia Eva Wheeler gave birth to my mother at about 7 P.M. on September 22, 1913. Virginia decided to name the baby Lelia, after her favorite aunt. The midwife charged five dollars for four days of her services.

A few days later, Virginia wrote Leigh about his daughter's birth, but she received no answer.

Aunt Lelia was living in Long Island at the time, working with her husband for a white family. Soon after she got the news, she took money from her savings and sent it to her niece, urging her to buy a ticket to New York. It was a long and hectic trip for Virginia, who was confused by mixed-up schedules and several train changes. A bunch of bananas was all she had to eat during the two-day journey. She changed and washed Lelia in segregated rest rooms along the way, missing several connections and literally spending down to her last dime to send a telegram with her new arrival time at each set-back. And following the midwife's suggestion, she rocked and rocked the distraught baby, but nothing seemed to help.

Finally, my grandmother arrived in New York. She was used to good treatment from porters and other male attendants because of her looks, but now, fatigued and carrying a baby, she was ignored. Then she recognized someone running toward her—little Aunt Lelia. Lelia bundled the baby safely in her arms and hugged and kissed them both. She had met every train coming in from the South since early in the day.

Four years later, when Leigh finally came to visit, he picked out his daughter from all the other little girls playing in the courtyard. "She looks just like my mother," he told Virginia. "She's got her eyes."

Unable to support herself or her baby on factory wages (twenty-five cents a week) and unsuited to paid housework, that year Virginia accepted an offer to rejoin the Whitney-Tutt show and took Lelia along with her. In fact, Homer Tutt had become her boyfriend, and where he was concerned, neither she nor little Lelia could do any wrong. "Homer was a good old top," even after they weren't going together anymore, Be-Be always said. Every Christmas Homer used to send a card, and even decades after his death, when Be-Be would sort through holiday things around Christmastime, a card from Homer would sometimes fall out. "He's still thinking of us," she'd say.

While on the road, Virginia was surprised to receive a letter from Dr. Ionia Rollin Whipper. The letter contained an offer: Dr. Whipper would legally adopt Lelia, and she would see her through college.

Perhaps the idea had come to Leigh when he was watching the child playing and noticed how much she resembled his mother. No one really knows. But it seems to me now that both Leigh and Ionia—raised to be proud of their family ancestry—must have been pleased that the family line was being continued through Lelia. Their sister Winifred had died in 1907, the same year as their father, and Ionia herself was in her forties and unmarried. She was a handsome woman, a woman of magnetism even, but this did not translate to sexuality; and in general her strong personality and her dedication to work had been discouraging factors in the arena of romance.

"She always felt she had missed something by not getting married," I was surprised to hear Be-Be say of my great-aunt years after her death. It had never occurred to me that Sistonie could have regrets about anything, certainly not about men—she had seemed so self-sufficient. "But she didn't miss anything by not having a man around. She didn't miss anything at all," Be-Be went on.

Certainly, Sistonie must have felt, her own mother would have wanted her granddaughter to have a good education and a good Christian upbringing. "She looks like Ma," Leigh had told her, and the words had stayed with her.

It was not an easy decision for Virginia, but she knew that on her own, she would never be able to provide the same kind of opportunity for her daughter. In spite of herself, she was touched at the idea that Leigh was trying to help her and her daughter in some way, and Dr. Whipper was *family* after all—it was not a question of giving up her daughter to a stranger.

And so in 1917, my mother—a charming four-year-old who was considered "smart as a whip," who knew all the lines in the show and was the darling of all the performers—went to live in the staid Victorian world of her aunt. It was an excruciating experience, leaving the warm, high-spirited show folk behind. There was Homer, the man my mother would always think of as her true father, and her mother's best friends, Ora and Grey, and a fellow named Mutt—they all had taken turns looking after her. "They were all my mothers and fathers," my mother explained. And suddenly they were gone.

When, as an adult, my mother asked Be-Be why she had given her up, Be-Be always gave the same answer: "She was real family. I thought it would be good for you. I had no idea she was going to prevent me from seeing you." But it could never satisfy my mother's question. In fact, as the years passed, the question seemed to work on her more, and her sorrow seemed to deepen.

Later I, too, wondered why Be-Be had accepted Sistonie's offer. Finally, it seems to me, the answer was this: she wanted her daughter to have an education. In the troupe—called the Whitney-Tutt Smarter Set—there had been an older child, the daughter of one of the other dancers, who hardly knew how to read or write. Virginia did not want that for her daughter. She was sensitive enough about her own lack of schooling. Despite her retrospective declaration that she was "dumb," my grandmother had been at the top of her high school freshman class in West Virginia. Then she was forced to stay home to care for her mother, who was sick with a series of illnesses my grandmother claimed were "mostly nerves." By the time she was able to return to school, months later, Eva Rhodes, as she was then called, had gotten too far behind to stay with her classmates (whose names she remembered all her life), and she was much too proud to return in a lower grade.

During one visit back home to West Virginia while she was on the road, my grandmother had been upset to find that some of her old school chums had become bank managers and businesspeople. Though many of these friends professed to be impressed with her glamorous life-style, there was no denying that Virginia felt distinctly inferior.

So Virginia brought Lelia to Washington and met with Dr. Whipper in her office. She gave her daughter a goodbye hug with an assurance that she would be back to visit soon. I picture Lelia, with her big eyes, looking up at my aunt. She saw a restrained, matronly woman who bore little resemblance to her real mother. My mother told me she didn't dislike her. She just wanted her mother.

Once Ionia knew that Lelia was coming, she promptly called the minister at St. Luke's Episcopal Church and made arrangements for my mother's baptism. She and Leigh had already figured out how my mother's name should be changed. It was recorded in the records at St. Luke's as Leighla Frances Whipper.

What my grandmother had not bargained for was that Dr. Whipper would soon forbid her to see her own child. She was "persona non grata," as my mother put it, and when she tried to visit, she was told that she was a "bad influence."

Devastated by the loss of her daughter, Virginia was plagued by bad dreams and worries. In the dreams, her child was always separated from her, and she was reaching for her hand, never quite grasping it. Or her daughter was in danger, and as she ran to save her, her legs would turn to jelly or she'd move in slow motion. She'd awaken in a panic and be unable to get back to sleep.

If only she could have her daughter again, she thought, things would be all right. But it was too late for that. She was powerless against the legal adoption. She should have known better than to trust Leigh and his sister; once more, she felt, she'd been dumb.

There was nothing more for my grandmother to do but continue her career, hoping that as time passed, things would improve and she would be able to see little Lelia—now "Leighla"—again. She pulled herself together and went out on auditions. She danced in the big chorus lines and in smaller acts on the Keith Orpheum Circuit, playing New York, Philadelphia, Washington, Chicago, and stops in between. She became so sought after that if she lost a job due to lateness—a not uncommon occurrence—she would just "go across the street to another show and get another job."

In New York, Be-Be played the Fourteenth Street Keith Theater on the same program with headliners like Martha Raye, Sophie Tucker, and the Marx Brothers. With other theaters, Be-Be said, black people were just lucky to get in the back door. On the sidewalk out in front of the Lafayette Theater on 125th Street was what they used to call the Tree of Hope. There was an actual tree, but gradually the general area was known by this name. "You used to see all the darkies standing, waiting out front for a job," Be-Be said.

From 1921 to 1923, Be-Be danced in the chorus of *Shuffle Along*, the Broadway hit by Noble Sissle and Eubie Blake. *Shuffle Along* drew on a vast pool of first-rate black talent, which had had little opportunity for expression elsewhere; it launched a long and impressive list of performers, including Paul Robeson, Florence Mills, and Josephine Baker. Baker was "the girl who was always cutting up at the end of the chorus line," Be-Be said. "She'd do any old crazy thing." Ethel Waters was also there; Be-Be claimed she had never known anyone with a cruder vocabulary.

Many members of the *Shuffle Along* orchestra were, or would soon become, prominent figures in the history of American music. Be-Be started going out with the oboist, William Grant Still—a man who would later be considered the dean of black American composers. His music made use of black themes, folk songs, and the rhythmic elements of spirituals, creating a unique combination of African and American influences; his *Afro-American Symphony* became a staple of many symphonic repertoires. In 1936, he was the first black person to conduct a major symphony orchestra.

"Have you ever heard of him?" Be-Be asked me. "He was a very-well-known composer. He wanted to marry me." There was a note of respect in her voice I'd never quite heard before. He wasn't just one of those "old boyfriends" or "old husbands" she mentioned from time to time. "I wonder why I didn't," she added. "I've never heard any music more marvelous."

The work of many talented black composers came to the attention of the public in the wake of the unprecedented success of *Shuffle Along*. Some of their names ring in my memory, for they were good friends of my grandmother's. There was Thomas W. "Fats" Waller, Andy Razaf, Maceo Pinkard, Luckey Roberts (Mr. Luckey), and Donald Heyward. Heyward often used to call at my grandmother's New York apartment in the early forties.

Shuffle Along started a trend, and in the years following, several colored musicals came to Broadway. White New York had "discovered" black New York, and white shows were hiring black dancers to teach their chorus girls the exciting new steps. The popular club Connie's Inn was entering its peak period. The Plantation, a restaurant at Fiftieth and Broadway, featured voguish musical shows starring Florence Mills. Bill "Bojangles" Robinson, Cab Calloway, and Duke Ellington and his band all played the segregated Cotton Club. The Savoy Ballroom was hopping.

Between 1924 and 1925, Be-Be performed in Sissle and Blake's new show, *Chocolate Dandies*, at the Colonial Theater.

The fast pace suited my grandmother. Often the performers would be hired to play at private events for wealthy whites after a show, and Virginia's energy always held up. In 1929, Andy Razaf and Fats Waller's *Hot Chocolates* opened at the Hudson Theater, with my grandmother on board. Several times she played the Lincoln Theater in Washington, and she and performer-producer Irving Miller did an act together at the Howard. Miller's 1927 show, *Dinah*, featured the "Black Bottom," the number Be-Be would later dance with such abandon in our Saratoga living room.

During these years, Virginia maintained her relationship with Homer Tutt, who was known for his soft heart and generosity. "All the broken-down actors came to him," Be-Be said later. Even the star of *The Emperor Jones*, Charles Gilpin, borrowed from Tutt when he hit hard times. Charles Gilpin had a voice like none Be-Be had never heard on a stage. She, like many others, felt he was the actor of all time, white or black. But "He let drink get the better of him" and, in my grandmother's racetrack parlance, "broke down in the stretch," to be replaced by Paul Robeson.

Throughout these years, my grandmother continued trying to reach her daughter, who stayed with relatives or close friends of her aunt's while Sistonie traveled through the South for the Department of Labor. One day when my mother was about eleven years old and in someone else's care while Sistonie was away, she was summoned from her play on Florida Avenue. She arrived at the house breathlessly, wondering what it was she could have done wrong. Once there, she was led into the front parlor, where she saw the shadowy figure of a man she didn't recognize. "Aren't you going to kiss your father?" her caretaker asked.

"Oh no, she's been trained by her mother not to," was the man's terse comment. Then he went into a long tirade about how bad she was and about how she should be good.

Afterward, my mother wrote to Sistonie telling her what had happened, and Sistonie, to her credit, wrote a scorching letter to Leigh. But three or four years later, he returned for a visit while Sistonie was in Washington. Leighla, upstairs, hung back, but her aunt commanded, "Now go down and kiss your father," and she obeyed.

When Leighla was in college, first at Spelman in Atlanta, then at Howard, Sistonie softened and allowed letters to pass between mother and daughter. My mother began to look forward to the rare occasions when she could see her mother. Several times Be-Be's show passed through Georgia, and she made a point of visiting her daughter. Once they spent Thanksgiving together in New York. When, in the late twenties, Sistonie needed financial help, Be-Be began to send regular sums of money, which my great-aunt grew to depend on to support her adopted daughter.

As my mother grew older, she began to dream of going into show business, even joining her mother on the stage, resuming the career she had begun as a child. She was talented. She played the piano every day and had started writing songs in college. She appeared in school plays, and writing gave her pleasure.

She would never forget how loved she had felt as a child among the theater people who had cared for her. Yet there was another world in her now—a comparatively colorless world in which my great-aunt dictated that she not dance or sing on Sundays and that a word like "damn" was never to be spoken. My mother always likened it to the staid environment that bid Alice in Wonderland to "put off jam until tomorrow." In this world her mother was considered bad—a bad woman, a bad mother. Even her mother's real name had been held against her—Sistonie had sometimes cruelly taunted my mother with it, drawing out the name "Eva" so it almost became "evil." The connotations of Eve and original sin could not help but come to mind.

"We know where that behavior is coming from, don't we?" Sistonie would ask my mother if she committed some minor infraction as a child. Then she would almost hiss it out: *"It's Eva!"*

Leighla could never understand how her mother, who was so kind, could be bad. In fact, as she grew older, her mother was more and more like a fairy godmother. Starved for the niceties and frills, for what she would later call "the necessary luxuries," my mother was thrilled when a special dress would happen to arrive the morning of the prom, or a little extra money would appear by mail just when she needed it.

Several times while my mother was living with Sistonie at 511 Florida Avenue, Be-Be's show played the Howard Theater, right down the street. Daringly, Leighla would sneak out of the house to see her perform. She would sit in the audience, overwhelmed by the glamour and the excitement. The dancing was liquid, the costumes were pure fantasy—feathers and sequins, satins and ruffles. Smiles flashed as the syncopated rhythms grew to a crescendo. Her mother was a dancer! The word itself must have danced in her heart. It implied a freedom she had never had with Sistonie, a freedom she still longed for. Sitting in the dark, watching her mother shine with her own inner glow in the spotlight, dancing so effortlessly, she must have known that despite Sistonie's messages to the contrary, there was no evil in her mother, none at all. Her mother was good. Later, I imagine, she would go back to the calm of Sistonie's, and wonder, if her mother was good, did that make Sistonie bad? How could she choose between them?

17

Return to the South

STANDING ON THE PLATFORM of the new Columbia railroad station in her stylish traveling clothes—including a parasol, no doubt—Frank must have been pleased to be back in South Carolina. She had gone to Boston hoping for "success" in literature and was returning with several copies of her book in her bag; it had received a favorable review from the *Christian Herald*. She planned to continue to write, to publish stories and articles, perhaps; to find a way to incorporate the best of Boston into this new phase of her life.

As my great-grandfather pulled up in a shiny new buggy, something must have stirred in Frank at the sight of him. William James Whipper was elegantly dressed, in bowler hat and Prince Albert–style frock coat, with a gold chain suspended between his watch in its side pocket and the second button of his vest. They had met before, in his adopted hometown of Beaufort, when she was teaching on the Sea Islands. But this morning, newly elected to the state legislature from predominantly black Beaufort County, he emanated the poise and self-assurance of a man who, in the flush of victory, was certain he was on the brink of a long and successful political career.

The last time she'd seen him he'd been a simple lawyer, working for Charleston's postwar Provost Court. And he'd been a married man. Since then, his wife, Mary, had died—in childbirth? none of the sparsely worded mentions of Mary Elizabeth Whipper bothered to say—leaving Whipper a widower with a young child, back in Beaufort being cared for by a nurse, and an adopted son as well. Whipper's loss must have added to Frank's immediate sympathy for him.

Whipper was charismatic and bold, able to charm and prone to antagonize. History would describe him as "dignified"; one white politician of his time would laud him as "the ablest colored man I've ever known." But the sensational Democratic press had already labeled him "a black, bestial, dissolute carpetbagger," and before ten years had passed there would be much, much more along this line.

The term "carpetbagger" would stick with him. "Dad was a carpetbagger," his son, my grandfather, would say, a smile playing about his lips. But beneath my grandfather's talk of family pride, another picture emerged: "Dad was a liquor head. He did the best he could, but he was out of his league with my mother." Later on he added, "He was a country lawyer. She was very proud of being from the broken-down aristocracy of South Carolina. She was from one of the first families of the town, a fashion plate, beautiful. She had straight dark hair that she wore pulled back. Her family was highfalutin society—members of the Brown Society. My father's side was more liberal than that." (Founded in the eighteenth century by free blacks, the elite Brown Society held regular meetings for decades and arranged insurance and burials for members.)

Whipper was dark-skinned, almost as dark as Delany, Frank must have noted as he approached. He had intense, piercing eyes; and although his expression was most pleasant this morning, it was clear that he could muster up a scowl that would be apt to prompt others to get things done his way.

My grandfather had alluded to his conflicts with a father who had wanted him to conform to his wishes—to be a lawyer, I presume. He complained that he'd never seen his father read a book, that all he ever read was newspapers. His mother, on the other hand, was an intellectual.

Whipper had the curious mixture of ambition and high ideals that often underlies a career in politics. He managed to incorporate pride and extravagance, bluster and brilliance. I had grown up hearing that he was the son of the renowned William Whipper of Philadelphia, only to find that on his application for a pension, my great-grandfather clearly stated that his father was Benjamin Whipper, a brother of the abolitionist. I have never been able to find out whether my grandfather deliberately misled everyone, in his zeal for good press, or whether the deception occurred earlier for reasons lost to history.

One late afternoon, my grandfather laughed as he recalled that Sistonie had once had the Whippers' genealogy traced for fifty dollars. "What good is it going to do us?" he'd asked her. She'd gone ahead anyway and said she found out that the original Whippers were all renegades and that William Penn had wanted them chased out of Pennsylvania. So Sistonie had let the matter drop, never mentioning another word about it.

I did find out some things about my great-grandfather that seem fairly straightforward. Originally from Glenville, Pennsylvania, William James Whipper took the bar once in Ohio, failed (according to my grandfather), then studied more and tried again in Michigan. After passing the bar there, he moved back to Ohio, but his practice was soon interrupted by the onset of the Civil War. Whipper immediately headed east with the intention of enlisting in the army, and found work recruiting other blacks into the service. He finally saw action at Petersburg, Virginia, and could hold forth for hours on the details of the battle. And he would always be proud of the fact that he and his regiment were present at Appomattox and witnessed the surrender of the Confederates.

After his release from his regiment, Whipper headed first for Charleston and then for Beaufort in the Sea Islands of South Carolina. Union troops had occupied the Sea Islands early in the war, and in January of '65, General Sherman, in response to a request from a delegation of black clergymen for land for freed slaves, ceded them most of the Sea Islands in Georgia and South Carolina and a belt of land along the adjacent coast. No whites apart from military officers and others in helpful capacities could reside there. For a time, until Andrew Johnson began his long list of pardons and allowed plantation owners to return, large numbers of freedmen lived on confiscated plantations, working the land for themselves.

Prior to the war, the extensive rice fields on the mainland and cotton fields in the islands had been tended by thousands of slaves, many of whom had had very little contact with whites other than their immediate overseers. This isolation meant that in the Sea Islands, Africans were able to maintain more traces of their heritage than elsewhere. They came from all along the West African coast, representing the Jaga, the Ibo, Yoruba, Kongo, and Madinka tribes, among others. Angola had been home for a large number of the slaves in the Sea Islands, and through the years, the Gullah dialect developed, combining English words with West Indian and African idiom and inflection. What to many whites seemed ignorant speech actually represented, and continues to represent, the remnants of a dispersed culture.

As Whipper arrived in Beaufort, numerous American Missionary Association schools dotted the area. Charlotte Forten, a friend to Frank throughout her years in Philadelphia and Boston, taught the freedmen at nearby St. Helena's Island. Learning was a priority for the newly freed men and women, and Northern visitors to the area sent back reports of the fervor with which the former slaves sought to educate themselves.

Whipper quickly set up a thriving law practice to represent the freedmen and the numerous formerly free blacks of Beaufort. He sent for his wife, Mary Elizabeth, who moved south from Ohio soon after.

A young camp follower from Georgia, the favored son of a white physician from Georgia and a house slave, had also made his way to Charleston after the war. Just turned fifteen, he was working as an office boy for the provost court when he met Whipper. One early morning Whipper found Demps Powell sitting in the doorway to his office. Demps had apparently been in the same regiment as Whipper and had recognized the older man; he may even have followed Whipper to Beaufort.

In any case, my great-grandfather, finding that the boy was all alone, with no mother and father and no place to live, wrote a note for him to take to his wife. Demps carried the note to Mary Elizabeth Whipper, who read it out loud for him. "This boy appears to be all alone, his name is Demps. Give him breakfast and send mine by him."

Demps played with seven-month-old Bud Whipper while Mary Elizabeth was getting breakfast ready. Before he left to carry Whipper's breakfast to him, she asked the boy, "How would you like to be my big son and take care of my little son, Bud?"

On his eighty-ninth birthday in 1940, Demps wrote of the moment, still remembering how his eyes had flooded with tears at "the idea, the thought of a home again, a little brother, a mother, a father."

"I know I would like it," he replied.

Demps became Mary Elizabeth and William J. Whipper's adopted son, and later he would be Frank's adopted son as well. Leigh Whipper often heard Demps correct his father's war stories. "I was there, I was in the battle with you," Demps would point out; and actually, my great-grandfather's military career had been less than brilliant. There were details of it that he reserved for himself, that he did not immediately impart to Frank. I wonder if he ever told her that he had had two courts-martial and rank reductions. The first incident was a gambling offense, for which he was transferred to another company. He then rose to the rank of sergeant, but managing to get into a fight with a lieutenant, he was again reduced to private.

These demotions could have been easily blamed on the vicissitudes of politics between black enlisted men and white officers in the army. On the floor of South Carolina's constitutional convention, Whipper had proved to be intelligent and eloquent, firm and persuasive. He had distinguished himself in any number of ways, not least of which, in Frank's eyes, was his daring advocacy of women's suffrage. He had spoken passionately in the moments preceding the vote for a new election law: "However frivolous you may think it, I think the time will come when every man and woman in this country will have the right to vote. I acknowledge the superiority of women. There are large numbers of the sex who have an intelligence more than equal to our own. Is it right or just to deprive these intelligent beings of the privileges which we enjoy? The time will come when you will have to answer this question. It will continue to be agitated until it must ultimately triumph. However derisively we may treat these noble women who are struggling for their sex, we shall yet see them successful in the assertion of their rights."

Whipper moved that the word "male" be stricken from the new election law, but though no other delegate replied to Whipper's speech, the motion was decided in the negative—South Carolina women's suffrage would have to wait fifty years.

As she arrived in Columbia, how could Frank have helped but remember that Whipper had spoken such thrilling words in a room full of men. He had also taken a stand for freedom of the press, insisting that even libelous and racist newspapermen be allowed entry to the proceedings. Even more controversially for some, he had insisted that the convention delegates were there "to serve all of the people," and he opposed the confiscation of land and its general distribution to the freedmen, stating: "The sooner every man knows that to acquire land he must earn it, the sooner he feels the Government has not lands to dispose of or to give him, the better. Do what is necessary to protect the laborer in his labor and you will effect the greatest possible good."

Whipper had reason to suspect that Congress would never do anything for the freedmen where land was concerned and that land reform proposals would only give false hopes to the people. Better, he felt, to stress the work ethic, the philosophy with which he and so many others, whites and (free) blacks alike, had been raised.

For landowners like Frank's father, confiscation had been catastrophic; thus Whipper's words and ideals had been well received by the Rollin sisters, who informed their father of Whipper's stand. Frank, too, was appreciative for her family's sake. But there were many who felt that Whipper was going too far out of his way to assist the former rebels.

There was hardly anyone among the politically savvy in Charleston or Columbia who did not know of the good-looking Rollin sisters. They were active in Columbia's social scene, where blacks and whites were mingling as they never had before. Charlotte and Kate had moved to Columbia to lobby for women's suffrage and raise money to found a progressive Rollin Family School. They were living on Senate Street near Jainey Hall (where all government business was conducted while the statehouse was under repair after the ravages of Sherman's march), in a house that could be reached by passing through the statehouse grounds and turning onto a side street. Many legislators stopped there before and after meetings, and the Rollin home was becoming a salon. Kate was engaged to marry a white Northerner, Senator George F. McIntyre, a member of the new government and their landlord on State Street. He planned to sell her the property for a nominal fee—the sale would be for appearance sake, since they were not yet married.

But that morning at the station, Whipper must have been impressed anew with the eldest of the sisters. Moving forward to clasp Frank's gloved hand, he bent to kiss it, managing to communicate the best of himself without actually touching the cloth of the glove with his lips. His grip was firm on my great-grandmother's elbow as he assisted her into his carriage. To the end of his life, even when both political and personal tides had turned irrevocably against him, Whipper would indulge a taste for the best buggies and wagons available.

To compensate for the sad appearance of a capital that was still recovering from war, Whipper must have described the excitement of the inauguration of South Carolina's first biracial government only a month before. City bells had rung out at noon, and cannons had roared in celebration. After the new governor, Robert Kingston Scott, a former Union general from Ohio, was sworn in, the mostly black onlookers had taken up the cry "God save the State of South Carolina." They made a rhythmic chant of it, shouting, waving hats and handkerchiefs, stomping feet and clapping hands, overjoyed at participating in their new government. Old-guard whites closed their shutters against the commotion, and many later made disparaging remarks about the noise.

In Columbia, as in Charleston, torchlight victory parades had wound their way through the narrow streets at night, climaxing in speeches as the Republicans celebrated their elections to the legislature. Whipper had proudly taken part in the procession into the chambers. Twenty whites, of whom only six were Democrats, and ten blacks had taken their seats in the Senate. In the House there were forty-six whites—including fourteen Democrats—to seventy-eight blacks, assuring a black majority in the General Assembly. Still, the top-ranking among the new leaders were white, as the Republican party had deemed it "impolitic" to put black men in high office.

As the procession entered the hall, none of the newly elected blacks, Whipper included, suspected that within ten years, the gains of their "Glory Year" of 1868 would have receded and that few of them would continue to hold positions of any real power. Yet the document they drafted at the constitutional convention would serve South Carolina for a quarter of a century and more; the revised constitution of 1895 would be little more than an amplification of the earlier document. In 1879, Frank's friend Wendell Phillips would be called upon to defend the work of the majority black convention and would declare: "Taking away the laws which white cunning and hate have foisted into the statute book, the legislation of the South since the rebellion may challenge comparison with that of any previous period. This is all due to the negro."

Soon my great-grandparents' radical revolution would fail, to be buried under a barrage of revisionist accusations, racial epithets, and violence. But for Whipper and Frank, riding through town that morning, it was a time to speculate about the great possibilities for action that lay before them. Whipper had declared publicly that if the Republican party could not afford to be led except by whites, many of them inferior, both intellectually and socially, to black candidates, then the party should "fall to the ground." Whipper must have spoken passionately to Frank of his feeling that colored men and women, working with sympathetic whites in the Republican party, could accomplish anything they set their minds to. He was thinking of running for Congress. He and Robert Brown Elliott and another partner, Macon Allen, were planning to open a law firm together in Charleston, perhaps the first black firm in the country.

By the time my great-grandfather helped her down from the buggy in front of a private boardinghouse with a neatly trimmed lawn out front, Frank's heart was won.

During the next few weeks, Frank was plunged headlong into the excitement and turmoil of Columbia. On the very day of her arrival, the town was in an uproar over news of a Ku Klux Klan "riot" the night before. A white man had been killed, and Joe Howard, a black man, was in hiding and suspected of murder. One of Frank's first duties was to assist Whipper in preparing the case. In addition to helping him with his private practice, Frank was clerk to the Judiciary Committee of the House of Representatives—of which Whipper was chairman—a position that put her in contact with the most prominent men of the state of both races.

Whipper called frequently at her boardinghouse and invited her out for buggy rides. On one occasion, he took her to the races, but she asked to be taken home, "as there were no ladies present." There were also old friends and even other suitors to see—one of them William Johnston, the man who had sent her burning letters while she was in Boston. (Johnston fiercely disapproved of her coming to Columbia under Whipper's auspices and raved that he felt like cutting his throat when he heard the news.) The Reverend E. J. Adams, one of Frank's mentors since her years in Philadelphia, was also in Columbia, one of many ministers from the North heading new congregations in South Carolina. As Frank began to feel more pressed by the charismatic Whipper, she often called upon Reverend Adams for advice and support.

There was also pressure from another direction, Frank's family. She had not yet gone to Charleston to see her parents; Whipper had paid her way only to Columbia, and she had yet to earn the fare for another ticket. But Frank knew from her sisters' reports that her father was less than pleased about her allegiance to Whipper and the new politics.

Frank had not been in Columbia a month before she received a hand-delivered letter from Whipper, asking her to consider doing him the honor of "going to church" with him as his bride. The request, though romantic in the extreme, seemed outrageous. While she'd been allowing herself to fall in love with Whipper, Frank hadn't given much thought to marriage. It was much too soon, and what would her parents say? How could she reply? Later that day, during the regular afternoon calling hours, Whipper arrived with flowers. When the opportunity came, for there were other callers present, my great-grandmother told him shyly that she would shortly reply to his letter.

Frank's diary entries become eloquently brief at this point. I imagine that she wanted to say yes but knew both that her father did not approve and that Lottie and Katie had feelings about Whipper that they were not communicating to her. It was complicated. Whipper had promised to find employment for Lottie and Katie in the government, and they had seemed quite pleased about the prospect. Yet Frank knew that underneath, they did not truly respect Whipper the way she did. He was a dark-skinned Northerner, a former Union soldier—he'd worn the same uniform as those who had shot their father in 1866—and a Radical Republican. No matter how conservative his views on confiscation of land and how generous his ideals, he was a carpetbagger, an older man (ten years her senior), and a very recent widower, with two children. And he was not exactly in their class.

True, the Rollins' elite class of free mulattoes had been abruptly abolished with the war, but the old views died hard. Of course, the sisters had all been taught to be open-minded and to accept people of all colors—as long as they were of good education and background. Yet the social pressures surrounding them had dictated otherwise. Of her family, Frank was the most flexible, perhaps the truest "Republican" in the most liberal sense. She bristled at the thought that Whipper's dark skin was a consideration in her family—yet my grandfather would say years later that Frank's family had found Whipper "too dark-complexioned" for their tastes.

Frank thought of her dearest friends in Boston, of the kindhearted and generous Lewis Hayden, the former slave who had painfully "grown himself up" after gaining freedom. Of William Wells Brown, who had walked with her the day before her departure from Boston, and of Martin Delany himself, with his philosophy of the blacker the better. She thought of her own dear Mr. Adams, whose philosophy spanned color and class. His Congregational church, to the outrage of some members, included uneducated blacks as well as fair-skinned and well-educated mulattoes.

In order to say yes to Whipper, Frank would have to challenge the Old World mores that still lingered in her family—and to some degree, though she could scarcely admit it, in herself.

She continued to stall for time. On August 14, she confided: *I wrote an answer to Mr. Whipper's letter asking a delay of the [matrimonial] decision. Mr. W. was at the office when I got there, also McIntyre, one of the committee. I watched my chances and placed it between the leaves of a book which he was reading. I saw him take it out.*

Whipper, displeased by Frank's response, grew colder, and Frank began to fear losing him altogether. The following days' diary entries told the story:

W. came while at Supper. He froze me up completely. Spent a most curious time which baffles all of my philosophy. What was It? What was it? Was it the waves of his departed wife—present, unseen, unwilling to give up her claim—or what? Both of us were unlike our real selves.

Thursday August 20: Woke up early. Wondering whether to throw up the sponge or accept a loveless life or not. Felt as though W. could not love anyone. A letter came from him today which restored and invigorated me, a real love letter.

Saturday, August 22: Promised Will.

*   *   *

One day in 1977, during one of those periods of comparative calm between us in Saratoga, my mother brought a small box out of her room. I had been talking about Frank, and she told me that she felt that I was meant to tell her life story; that she herself didn't have the heart to do it. But she wanted me to tell Frank's story without ever mentioning her, and I already sensed that Frank's story and my mother's were intertwined in ways neither one of us had fully understood.

"Have you ever seen this?" she said to me. "I want to give you this. You should have it."

I caught my breath. It was Frank's ring, handed down to my mother on Sistonie's death. On the inside, it was engraved: "FAR— WJW September 17, 1868."

I twisted the thick gold band around my finger, much as I had with my child's ring in Sistonie's tub. Wishing, wishing . . . Now I wished that I could go back in time to join Frances Anne Rollin Whipper, that I could instantly know everything I needed to know about who she was. I began to wear her wedding ring, almost as if my mother had married me to Frank.

The wedding took place, with Reverend Adams presiding, despite William Rollin's attempts to persuade both his daughter and Whipper to postpone it. *Married by Mr. Adams. Very nervous. Left for Columbia—Reached C. Elliott and Lee at the depot. A. O. James, Captain, Lottie and Katie.—Quite an ovation. In the evening a grand reception. All the State Officers nearly—ditto for the members of both Houses. A few outsiders. . . .*

A present from Governor Scott of a set of sterling silverware engraved with Frank's new initials, FRW, was unwrapped and much admired by all the guests—the thought that Whipper would soon be in the forefront of an effort to impeach the governor would have seemed very farfetched indeed. Over a hundred years later, when Alessandro was born, my grandfather gave me one of the thick silver forks as a gift for him.

While researching in Charleston, I came across newspaper accounts of a sudden temperature drop on September 17, 1868, the day of Frank's wedding. I imagined Frank and Whipper shivering with cold, reaching for shawls and topcoats—an omen of what was to come. Senator Benjamin F. Randolph, a member of their wedding party, was shot and killed in broad daylight as he stood on a railway platform only one month later. Randolph had been one of the few to argue for a ban on all racial discrimination in the state constitution. "The day is coming when we must decide whether the two races shall live together or not," he had said, and his provision was voted down.

The Ku Klux Klan's activities in the South grew bolder with each passing month, and fear of violence was an integral part of blacks' lives.

My great-grandparents' marriage was uniquely intertwined with the politics of Reconstruction, and over the course of the next decade as the revolution began to fail, it took a severe toll on them. But the brunt of that failure was still several years away. In the South Carolina legislature, blacks began to discover that many of their white friends were undependable. White administrators were bogging down the administration with corruption and mismanagement. Whipper and several of his black colleagues held a caucus and managed to make some changes; but it was clear that blacks, on the whole no more or less honest than their white counterparts, were also profiting from power.

Meanwhile, Frank's sisters continued their own political efforts. In 1869, Charlotte, about twenty years old, spoke eloquently on the floor of the state House of Representatives for women's rights. A *New York Times* reporter commented: "Her argument (so called) was to the effect that in as much as the Constitution did not define the voter as 'male' the intent and scope of that paper were that sex was unknown to the constitution, and that accordingly, women have as much right to vote as men have."

In 1870, Margarette Rollin came up to Columbia from Charleston to live with her daughters, probably fleeing her husband's ill humor; and in December 1872, Kate bought a house and land on Richardson Street, now called Main Street, and Charlotte bought a house on Barnwell Street.

"If you want a thorough posting upon political affairs in South Carolina, you must call on the Rollins," the *New York Sun* would say of the sisters in March 1871, likening them to behind-the-scenes heroines of the French Revolution. Readers in both the North and the South were intrigued and titillated by what they heard of the young women, and the newspapers pandered to this sensibility. The reporter from the New York *Tribune* described the Rollin home:

> A copy of Byron lay half open on the table, and a number of *The Atlantic,* with a volume of Gail Hamilton's works and another of Miss Louisa Alcott's, were in close and loving contiguity. . . . Thick carpets covered floors; handsome cabinets held costly bric-a-brac, a $1,000 piano stood in a corner; legislative documents bound in morocco reposed with big albums on expensive tables. In their salon, mingling white and dusky statesmen wove the destinies of the old Commonwealth.

Except for their ages—Charlotte, not Kate, was the eldest and would have been only about twenty-two—the reporter for the *Sun* was probably describing the sisters fairly accurately when he wrote:

> The eldest of the young ladies is a bright mulatto of about 25. She is tall, somewhat spare, and affable and agreeable in her manner. She was dressed in a black silk dress with a sweeping train, which followed her into the room like a wave on the beach. She talks very intelligently, although so rapidly as to be sometimes nearly unintelligible. This difficulty is somewhat increased also by a peculiar mode of pronouncing the letter "e" with a sound almost like "i" [a strong southern accent perhaps, or a Creole inflection learned from her father and mother?] and by a southern prolongation of the last word of every sentence.
>
> Miss Charlotte Corday is a darker young lady, but it is said is the most intellectual of the three. She is not so tall as her sister, and is more compactly formed. She is a good deal handsomer too. Miss Lottie, as she is called, was attired in a mauve tailored silk trimmed with heavypoint applique on body and skirt. An orange colored sash with heavy bow adorned her waist, and blue slippers encased her feet. Jewelry in great profusion was worn by all three. The youngest one, Miss Louisa Muhlbach, is almost white. She too, was handsomely attired in a short walking suit of black silk. She is quite young, and therefore did not take part in the conversation, although she was an attentive listener and nodded assent to everything her older sisters said.

Lottie worked for Robert Brown Elliott in his capacity as adjutant general of the state militia. Although I winced when I first read it—and while the reporter's attitude toward the sisters is clearly condescending and he seems all too likely to exaggerate for effect—I fear that Lottie's quote about Elliott and her brother-in-law was not his invention: " 'Our family never condescended to notice such small people as Elliott or Whipper, although Whipper married our sister Frances,' added Miss Lottie. 'They are both negroes, and our family is French.' "

In 1872, Lottie chaired the founding meeting of the South Carolina Womens' Rights Association in Columbia, with Katie as treasurer. Governor Scott sent a message of goodwill, as did several other members of the House and Senate, W. J. Whipper included, and the meeting was documented by Susan B. Anthony and Elizabeth Cady Stanton in their *History of Women's Suffrage*. Lottie's address before the meeting has been called the first published argument for black women's suffrage apart from Sojourner Truth's. She said:

> It had been so universally the custom to treat the idea of woman suffrage with ridicule and merriment that it becomes necessary in submitting the subject for earnest deliberation that we assure the gentlemen present that our claim is made honestly and seriously. We ask suffrage not as a favor, nor as a privilege, but as a right based on the ground that we are human beings and as such, entitled to all human rights.

By September 1873, the sisters had not yet succeeded in getting payment from the government for the teaching they'd done after the war. Their father's finances were stabilizing, but they needed money of their own. Lottie had already sold her Barnwell Street house, and Katie was behind on her mortgage payments. Whatever they earned in their clerical positions with the state was not enough to sustain their life-style or to help them start the Rollin Family School. Charlotte and Kate finally decided to journey to Philadelphia together to raise money. Lucretia Mott, the noted abolitionist and suffragist, wrote an account of their visit in one of the letters that she called her "scraps" to her sister:

> One thing I remember is the Rollin visit. Thou sd of course wonder why they sh'd call on you. I'm as sorry eno' for the infliction when thou was so tired. . . . We had known the girls in days past when Anna Massey and Abby Kimber and others were aiding them, their Father's property being in jeopardy; but we heard nothing of late till these two turned up,

their property recovered, they said, and they wanted to raise some money on good security. They called on Edwd. Davis who referred them to some brokers, could do nothing himself—tho't them bright young women, one quite a politician. Knowing them when childn, and finding they wanted to come here, I invited them to tea with E.S. Rachel Moore was interested to beg books for them as they sd they wanted to have schools for the Freedmens' childn. etc. After they left here for Auburn their landlady called on Edwd and sd. they hadn't paid board and she had to make them leave their jewelry, etc. Also some other complaints about them.

So now we hear that they were disappointed in Chas. Wood not keeping them with money, further than with tickets "back agin" here. That's all I know, for I make no enquiry of Emily, not meaning to enter into their case. There's no end to such dismal appeals. It happened when they were here that Joe Parrish had come out to tea with Maria H. and Isaac—Joe's only visit. As the company came in, they walked out, to the garden and around, and saw little eno' of them but eno' to have rather a poor opinion of them.

Such cruel words to come down through time to me, but it is the moment of their going out into the garden that makes them real to me. Their long dresses in the late September day, Kate wearing the good black silk described in the *Sun*. Their sisterly companionship, their solitude in the midst of the curious and the secretly snide. The moment reached me with all its emotional weight intact. Dorothy Sterling had chanced upon Lucretia Mott's account while researching some other life and had sent it on to me.

By 1875, Katie had defaulted on the Senate Street mortgage, and the land was sold at public auction via a Madison County, Florida, attorney. In 1876, the property on Richardson Street was sold in the same manner. Both properties had been in the name of Katie E. Rollin. It looked as if Katie and McIntyre had gone to Florida together, but I never found any sign of their having been married. As their story unfolded on paper, I found myself wishing them gone to Florida and safely living there, married or not. But one day in Charleston, I found a disturbing record of the death, on March 4, 1876, of a Katie E. Rollin, residing in Brunson, South Carolina, several miles from Charleston. I hoped it was some other Katie, for there were a number of Rollins in South Carolina. Then I read the cause of death, "consumption of the lungs," and remembered descriptions of Katie as the frail one who frequently suffered from fever and congestion. I remembered my mother warning me against smoking, and Sistonie shutting windows tight on cold nights, both of them saying that weak lungs ran in the family. Surely this twenty-five-year-old woman buried in the Brown Association Cemetery was my great-aunt. Two days later, on March 6, 1876, the sale of her property in Columbia was finalized by proxy from Madison, Florida—by McIntyre, I presume.

While her surviving sisters were struggling to sustain their hopes for South Carolina politics and for their progressive school, Frank was coping not only with politics but with motherhood. For eight years she was almost constantly pregnant. Her firstborn child, Alicia, died in infancy. Winifred was born in 1870, Ionia in 1872. Another child, Mary Elizabeth (named after Whipper's first wife), was born in 1874 and died shortly before my grandfather, Leigh, was born in 1876. It must have seemed a triumph to bring forth that boy child after eight years of pregnancies and births, eight years of celebrations and mourning. He was the first boy in the family after a generation of girls on her side of the family. Shortly after his birth, Frank wrote a letter to the papers suggesting that all babies born in the centennial year of the country receive a special medal.

As Whipper's political career waxed and waned, his drinking and gambling increased, and he began to indulge in long absences from home. Throughout, Frank supported her husband, edited the newspaper he published for his constituency, counseled him, and helped manage his debts. When his Beaufort property was in danger of confiscation, she had it put in her name. But there were limits to what Frank could do for her husband. During his first stint in the legislature, Whipper was chairman of the Judiciary Committee and later served on the Committee on Ways and Means. In 1871, he leveled charges of corruption against Governor Scott and led unsuccessful efforts to have him impeached. In the gubernatorial elections of 1872 and 1874, he ran on the "Bolters" ticket and was defeated. He had been trying for a number of years to procure a judgeship, and was particularly bitter about the fact that Jonathan J. Wright, another black Republican originally from the North, beat him out of a seat on the State Supreme Court in 1868, and again in 1872. (In the early 1980s, my friend Charles Wright, a descendant of the judge, and I enjoyed discussing our ancestors' old rivalry.)

Meanwhile, violence against blacks seemed to escalate daily. White rifle clubs sprang up throughout the state "for the purpose of picnics and dinners"; the weapon they adapted was not a sporting or a target rifle but a sixteen-shooter Winchester. The president of the South Carolina Rifle Club termed his membership "All South Carolina gentlemen of the older time." The Republicans managed to pass an anti-insurrection law and organized a state militia of ninety thousand men. President Grant declared a state of rebellion in nine South Carolina counties and dispatched additional troops, who arrested more than one thousand whites.

Against a background of increasing strife in the state and at home, Whipper ran for the circuit judgeship in Charleston in 1874, only to have Governor Chamberlain make a special trip to the Republican caucus to denounce him as incompetent and morally unfit. Chamberlain, though a Republican, had proved particularly vulnerable to the call of "society" in the form of the old Southern Democratic aristocracy. Although he had been elected with the help of his black Republican colleagues, beneath his political veneer lay a conviction that blacks were inferior and unworthy of being in government.

In the election of 1875, Elliott, in his capacity as speaker of the house, attempted to counteract a growing tide of hostility toward the radicals in the Republican party by arranging judicial elections during a period when Governor Chamberlain would be out of town. In Chamberlain's absence, Whipper, Moses, and Wiggins were elected circuit judges in Charleston. Whipper was elected to the first district, a particularly prestigious area. But when the news got out, the Democratic paper's headlines shouted "Black Thursday!" and Chamberlain, returning hastily to Columbia, claimed the election was an attempt to "Africanize the state."

"This calamity is infinitely greater, in my judgment, than any which has yet fallen on this state, or I might add upon any part of the South," Chamberlain declared.

Much was made of Whipper's being on the bill with a known fraud, Moses. Conservatives and independents seized upon the

Moses-Whipper affair to mobilize the Democratic party and run a Democratic candidate for governor. Chamberlain's histrionics and the term "Black Band," taken up by the press to describe the black Republicans, were clear indication of the racist character of the turning tide. Chamberlain, apologizing for his absence as guest of honor at a ceremonial dinner of the New England Society of Charleston, sent a telegram that read: "The civilization of the Puritan and the Cavalier, of the Roundhead and the Huguenot, is in peril. Courage, Determination, Union, Victory, must be our watchwords."

Frank and her husband could only look on in alarm as black Republicans were given sole blame for the hasty elections and white Republicans began to cast Whipper and Moses as a political evil as reprehensible as a coalition of white Democrats. Whipper's name was vilified throughout the state. Not one white Republican came to the defense of the vote. In an unprecedented move—for the group had been legally elected—Governor Chamberlain refused to sign the commissions of Whipper and Moses, claiming a technicality, which nonetheless did not prevent him from confirming the other nominees.

The Republican party was in a shambles all that spring, and when a rumor spread that Whipper planned to take his seat by force, Chamberlain issued an order stating that force would be met with force. In August, the Democratic state convention nominated a charismatic Southern aristocrat named Wade Hampton as their candidate for governor, along with a full slate of candidates for every office. Hampton had been the highest-ranking officer from South Carolina in the Confederate Army. He expressed a fondness for blacks and sincerely felt that their place was menial. He proved to be the perfect candidate for white supremacists.

Wild rallies and torchlight parades marked the nomination; and conspicuous among the throngs of the galvanized racists were the rifle clubs and the red shirts that would soon become the uniform of the "redeemers." A varied group throughout the South, according to historian Eric Foner, "shared the commitment to dismantling the Reconstruction states, reducing the political power of blacks, and reshaping the South's legal system in the interests of labor control and racial subordination." Dozens of organizations sprang up after Hampton's nomination; many referred to themselves euphemistically as "baseball clubs."

"The whites have wanted sufficient excuse to rise up and overthrow the African government under which they live; and now they have it. Before long you will hear of a 'great Democratic victory in South Carolina,' " a contemporary observer had written after the botched judicial election that spring.

"When they refused my dad a judgeship in Charleston, he got mad and moved to Beaufort," Uncle Billy had told me, and after Whipper's political downfall, the family did move from Whipper Barony to a big house not far from the water in Beaufort. Whipper went ahead, to secure the house and begin a new practice; Frank and the children followed him later. Although Frank must have been disheartened by her husband's weaknesses and the vicissitudes of his political career, she still believed in what he stood for. "She remained loyal to him," my grandfather said.

18

A Little Lump of Gold

BE-BE WOULD TELL ME BITS and pieces of her life from time to time, but it wasn't until she was ninety-three and, as she put it, "so much water had gone under the bridge" that she began to tell me the important stories about her past. Finally, it seemed as if we were, each of us, worn down to a smooth and essential place—a place that made telling everything all right. I would sit beside her bed or keep her company beside her rocker on the front porch in Saratoga, pouring a little bit more sherry when she asked. Wherever we were, I was listening.

Eva Wheeler was born to Ida Wheeler on March 17, 1892, in Covington, Virginia—the heart of the Alleghenies. Her grandfather, George Washington Wheeler, had built their big two-story house himself. Eva learned by listening to the talk around the fire at night that the original white Wheelers were from Virginia and had arrived in 1607 from England. Be-Be's grandfather and his brother, Tom, were born in Hot Springs, West Virginia, children of a white master and a half-white mother. George Washington Wheeler made his living as a shoemaker, but for most of his life he had been a slave—what was known as a "preferred houseman." Raised in the "big house," he was considered by the other blacks during slavery and after as "one of the big niggers in Hot Springs up in the country." Be-Be remembered him as a tall man with a refined manner. He had burnt-orange skin and fine straight hair much prized in the family—"Didn't have no bad hair," Be-Be emphatically declared.

It was someone in the big house who had taught George and Tom to play the violin. Every Saturday night the brothers would play at the Intermount Hotel up on the mountain; George's daughter Ida played the trumpet. "Don't you worry about those Wheelers up to The Hot," people used to say. Almost everybody in the family worked in Hot Springs, known simply as "The Hot." (Other places were called "The Healing," "The Warm," and "The Cold.") "Up to The Hot," they'd say, "you don't see nothing but Wheelers."

Ida also played the organ. Her sister Emma had healing hands and was often called upon by local doctors when they didn't know what to do. There was another sister, Mamie, and a fourth sister, Lelia, was a natural pianist. She did a German woman's housework in return for lessons that included pieces by Paderewski. There was a concert every night at the Wheeler home while Be-Be was growing up.

The Wheelers were a proud family. George Washington Wheeler wouldn't associate with his wife's brother, Uncle Vails, calling him a "damned issue free nigger." (Uncle Vails was apparently one of the hundreds of thousands of slaves who became free workers under federal auspices in 1865.) Uncle Vails used to sit around the fire at night and reminisce about the Civil War. He would talk about cannonballs landing at his feet and would do a little sidestepping dance to show just how close they came. And he would tell how if anyone was missing during the fighting, they'd say, "Oh, he's gone to the Yankees." Uncle Vails had fought for the Confederates.

Be-Be's mother, Ida, may have learned to cook from her mother, Ellen. Ida proved to be talented early on and went to work at a hotel up on the mountain, owned by a white man named Albert Kemper. Kemper was taken with this dignified, dark-skinned sixteen-year-old girl. Dignified or not, she was still a child, really, when he seduced her one night up at the hotel.

It was the task of the younger children to read to the family, and Ida was reading to her father one day when she said, "Papa, Papa, there's something inside me."

"Yes, child," her father answered wryly, "I've been thinking all along there was something inside you."

"That something was little me," Be-Be told me, and laughed as I listened incredulously, trying to imagine a time when a girl wouldn't know that she was pregnant.

Ida told Kemper, and he talked about marriage, but state laws against "miscegenation" forbade it. So Ida went through her pregnancy with a double sense of shame—and later betrayal, for the relationship with Kemper soon ended. Her older sisters had already found husbands and started families. She was the only one to have to endure the shame of being an unwed mother.

Ida stayed home for much of her pregnancy, cooking for the family and doing housework; there, in her father's house, she went into a long and difficult labor. She gave birth to a baby who was white, with hair that was almost golden, and named her Eva.

Ida's body felt abused. Her swollen breasts hurt and became infected. The baby's crying distressed her. Her sisters and her stepmother rallied around to help, but she must have felt that she was doing it all wrong, that she had no natural talent for motherhood. She hadn't intended to be a mother, had never even thought about it before. She longed to be free.

As soon as she could, Ida left town. She headed for Charleston, away from the gossip, and concentrated on getting work as a cook, both for white families and in restaurants. And soon she began to send money back home for Eva's care. It always seemed miraculous when it came. "Imagine," the Wheelers would say to themselves, "Ida so far away, and thinking of us, sending money every time you look around."

George and Ellen Wheeler were more than happy to raise Eva. She was a great joy to them now that the other children were grown, and they lavished affection on her. Her aunt Mamie was also fond of Eva and enjoyed taking her for rides in her buggy. One acquaintance asked, "And whose baby is this?" expecting to hear the name of some white family in town. "This is Ida's baby," Mamie answered, proudly.

"What? A nigger baby?" the woman exclaimed.

As she was growing up, Eva would often hear family members refer to her mother as "the backbone of the family," but she didn't see it that way. Periodically, Ida would visit from the city, bringing presents and money to pay the taxes. She'd bring nice coats, dresses, scarves—Ida was always dressed in the latest styles. She had a lot of what used to be called "oomph," Be-Be said. But when her mother made her dramatic appearances, Eva would cling to her grandmother's skirts or run out of the house to hide.

Be-Be told me she always had an adventurous streak. As a child, she used to sit in church, the wooden bench hard beneath her bottom, hearing the Baptist preacher's drone and imagining that she was far, far away.

Even though Eva was an only child, she never lacked company; she had plenty of cousins who lived not far from her grandfather's house. Weeknights could be lively at the Wheeler home. Often Uncle Tom's sons would come by, bringing their instruments; and every Friday there would be a young folks' prayer meeting, with ice cream and cake afterward. On weekends and holidays, visitors would stay all day and play cards.

Though Be-Be said that her grandfather always waited until his shoemaker's shop was closed, drinking was one of his favorite pastimes. There was a winepress out back. Sometimes at night Wheeler would get to drinking, and Be-Be would lie in bed and listen to him rummaging around the house. Finally, he would cry out: "Ellen Kent, you can take your two pillows and go!" (Ellen had brought her two favorite pillows with her from Richmond when she'd married him.) Then he'd shift gears. "I—am—a—*Mason!*" he'd cry, waving his Masonic papers. And then he'd make his way to the front door and call into the night: "I'm crowing on my own doorstep!"

Ellen Kent was known as a teetotaler, but she had a good time too. She liked to do a dance called the Rang Tang, which Be-Be could imitate even in her eighties: "A jig, jig, jig, and then a kick up!"

When Wheeler got sick, Eva was sent to live with Ida and her new husband, Jim Rhodes, in Charleston, West Virginia. Rhodes was a "colored" man so fair-skinned he looked white. ("She must not have liked dark-skinned men" Be-Be said to me, only a few months before she died. "Why do you say that?" I asked. "I never saw her with any," came the matter-of-fact reply.) Jim Rhodes had two artificial legs because of a coal-cart accident in the mines. He worked with his father-in-law as a shoemaker and barbered, as well, to support the family.

While Eva was with Ida she broke a dish every day, and every day Ida, thinking her daughter had done it on purpose, would whip her. Eva was incensed. "Ida gonna whip me? No indeed!" she'd say to herself as she angrily wiped away her tears. Ida, as my grandmother described her, was an impatient woman who would "just get disgusted," not so much from big things, but from little things. Be-Be thought Ida had inherited her bad temperament from her mother, Wheeler's first wife, along with her "bad" hair—her grandfather's hair was as fine and straight as Be-Be's own. My grandmother saw her mother's mother's portrait one day and thought it captured a woman so fierce she looked as if she was going to "jump out of the picture."

Whatever else Be-Be thought of her mother, she never denied that Ida was "some cook." And whatever else was lacking, food was plentiful in Charleston. There were hams and middlings, a milk cow, and butter they churned themselves. And there was a big garden, with string beans and corn.

Ida taught her daughter to sweep, clean, make biscuits, grill ham for breakfast, and fill the dinner pails for Jim Rhodes and the two boarders, who worked in the mines. "I made biscuits and made biscuits until I got it right," Be-Be told me. She baked eight or nine pies daily, mostly of apples and berries that grew nearby. Soon she wrote a tearful letter to her grandfather: "I want to come home. I don't like Ida. She whips me every day."

But Eva didn't get to go back to Covington until Ida returned home to help care for her father. "Oh, my child has come home! My child has come home!" the old man cried, when he saw his granddaughter walking in the door. While he lingered, Eva gave him his medicine—cod-liver oil—and fed wood chips to the old potbellied stove in his room.

After he died, Eva, stunned by her loss, went back to live with her stepfather and her hot-tempered mother. She slept on the sofa in the living room. It was 1900, and she was eight years old. Ida decided that her daughter should have her new husband's name and enrolled her in elementary school as Eva Rhodes.

Soon Ellen Kent came to live with them. "I had my grandma then," Be-Be told me. "We slept together, went everywhere together.

She was Mama. Ida was just another person. Some of the kids would say, 'Ida's your mother.' But I didn't like Ida well enough for that. 'No! She's *not* my mother!' I'd reply."

When she was fourteen or fifteen, Eva decided to run away, and Ida had to send a truant officer after her. He put her in a homemaking school in another part of the state for three months. "Give her up into the hands of the Lord," Ida said.

Eva had been working on and off since she was twelve years old as a dietitian in the hospital in Covington, where Ida was the cook. After her return from homemaking school, somewhat chastened, she began to put in more serious hours. Mother and daughter worked there daily together. But Ida was plagued with a series of minor illnesses and was always trying different medicines for her nerves. She and Jim quarreled more and more frequently. Finally, they separated, and he moved into town. After that, whenever Eva went into town to run errands, on her return Ida would look over from the stove or up from her mending to ask: "What did Jim say?"

Sometimes Eva would just grunt; other times she'd say "Nothing." One day she decided she wanted to get her mother's goat. When Ida asked about Jim, she replied saucily, "He don't want you no more. He's got another girl named Ida." She watched Ida carefully; maybe this time she would get a reaction out of the woman who never betrayed her hurt or sorrow, who expressed only anger and impatience. Scrutinizing that familiar face for some sign of emotion, Eva focused on a small mole on her mother's cheek, which might have been ugly on another woman but was attractive on Ida. She watched as Ida blinked only a little—the smooth brown face was impassive. If she had any feelings about what her daughter had said, she was too proud to let her see.

In fact, Be-Be knew that very afternoon, Jim had been bemoaning their separation. But my grandmother enjoyed her own story so much she could almost see what the other Ida looked like. Someone soft where her mother was brittle; someone lighter-skinned and laughing. It seemed to her that Jim ought to be able to like someone like that.

The next day Eva took the train to Columbus, Ohio, on a Sunday excursion. Returning about two or three in the morning, she saw a hearse coming from the hospital. As she walked toward home, a hospital attendant leaving work caught up with her and told her, "Your mother just died."

"She was always taking some kind of medicine," Be-Be told me. "She took carbolic acid—by mistake, some people thought. . . ." Her voice drifted off.

Ida was thirty-six years old when she died. At the funeral, Eva and Jim Rhodes stood near each other. Jim, sobbing, was inconsolable, and Eva was still in shock. Afterward, Eva tried to go back to work at the hospital, but she would find herself distracted, spending long moments standing by the window, where she could see her mother's grave in the cemetery on the hill. *Ida, gone*—she couldn't get over it. She remembered how Ida always called her "nothing but a spoiled brat," and she thought about Ida being called "the backbone of the family." If that was so, that backbone had certainly been broken now.

Soon my grandmother would leave Eva Rhodes behind, to become Virginia Eva Wheeler; she would spend some time with her aunt Lelia, in Pennsylvania, and then would head to Washington, D.C., on her own. She would never know what Ida had felt, and a kernel of anger still glowed deep down. Even in death, Ida had preserved her pride and her secrets, and she had somehow gotten the better of her.

19

Finding Frank

NOT LONG AFTER MY RETURN from South Carolina, Aunt Elsie and I were driving slowly through Washington. I knew that Frank had moved there not long after the debacle of Whipper's judicial election and that she spent most of the rest of her life there. But I was still trying to piece together what happened to her after she left South Carolina.

It was odd to think of Frank living in the city of my birth, a city I had rarely visited since childhood. My father's brothers and sisters and their children lived there, and although I felt a connection to Aunt Elsie and Uncle Albert, I hardly knew any of my many cousins.

My mood in Washington was not the best. I felt isolated, a familiar feeling since this long project had begun. My researching at the Municipal Building in Charleston had revealed another family secret, so unpleasant that I wanted to forget it.

After the entry of October 19, noting that the assassinated member of her wedding party, Senator Benjamin F. Randolph, "was buried this afternoon at Columbia," there were only two more entries in

Frank's 1868 diary. Toward the end of the book, I found two recipes, one for spiced beef: *boil a shin of ten or twelve pounds of beef until the meat readily falls from the bone*; and another for macaroni pie: *boil the macaroni in water until quite tender*. How far she had come from discussions of literature, I thought. I wondered if she had ever had time to keep a diary after 1868. A few pages on, I found a child's penciled scrawl—Winifred, who must have found her mother's diary, was practicing writing her name. Frank had apparently kept the diary handy through 1880, for written across the top of one of the back pages was: *William Rollin died morning of the 24th Feb. '80 about 2 o'clock in the 65 year of his age*.

Rollin's funeral was held at St. Peter's Catholic Church, and he was buried at St. John the Evangelist, a colored cemetery not far from his Lee Street house in Charleston. A large crowd of mourners attended, and Frank filed notice in the papers of administering the estate. She set about making an inventory of his farm animals and his properties and arranging for the sale of those items that were of no use to the family.

Then, on May 1, 1880, Probate Judge William E. Vincent of Charleston revoked Frank's right to act as executrix. Frank's petition stated that her father left Frances A. Whipper, Charlotte M. Rollin, Louise M. Rollin, and Florence N. Rollin as his heirs. (No Katie, so my assumption that Katie had died in 1876 was probably correct.) But her mother, Margarette Rollin, represented by De Saussure, one of the top legal firms in Charleston, claimed that she had not been told that Frank would be administering the estate.

Margarette had been living with her daughter Frances and her son-in-law for the last three or four years in order to save money, and witnesses testified that Rollin, in his illness, had expressed the wish not to see his wife and daughters because of the expense of the trip. Finally, neighbors had sent for Frank to come care for her father, and she had complied. Frank testified that her mother refused to go to the house after the funeral and had asked her to go and take care of the property. Whipper swore he had told Margarette everything, that it had always been understood Frank would take care of her father's estate. Margarette swore that this was not so. She protested that Frank had already sold one of the properties and was collecting the rentals on others. Whipper appealed, but the appeal was dismissed.

Frank told the court that William Rollin had wanted her to be executor of his estate; but since he had died intestate, those wishes were hard to prove. And no one wanted to say for the record that Margarette and William Rollin had separated because they no longer wanted to live together.

For Margarette, frustrated at her lack of power, estranged from her husband, unable (I deduced from the X's of her signature) to read and write, Frank's taking over her husband's estate must have been the final indignity. She may have also feared, perhaps with some reason, that Frank would use the money to pay Whipper's debts; perhaps she was given the idea by one of Whipper's many political enemies. In any event, the lawyer she had talked to felt she definitely had a case.

On September 22, 1882 (my mother would be born on this date thirty-one years later), Margarette, Frances Anne, and Charlotte Rollin were served notice that certain properties owned by William Rollin were being foreclosed. Notices were published once a week for six weeks in the *News and Courier*, and notification letters were sent to New York and Washington. The legal papers show that on August 9, 1882, Margarette Rollin was in New York and had taken up residence there. No action had been taken on her petition to administer Rollin's estate herself. There is a note explaining that "the sisters were in New York City and Frances Rollin Whipper was in Washington." The process must have become so painful (and expensive) for my great-great-grandmother and her daughter that both sides dropped the suit and left the city.

They also left the land—which was soon bought up at a low price by a third party. As I sat in Charleston's Municipal Records Department, holding the thick bundle of yellowing court papers that described the bitter family feud, I could still feel the pain of that mother-daughter struggle. It had come down to me.

My father's sister turned her car down Florida Avenue, and I marveled at how little I had known about Frank during my earlier research trip. Both John and Carrie Robertson were dead now, and I felt sad about that as I began to scan the row houses for number 511. When I spotted it, I was suddenly too shy to ask Aunt Elsie to slow down.

What I really wanted to do was stop, get out, walk up the steps, spend time there, perhaps even go inside the house again. But we continued on, and I noticed that every other building on the block was inhabited—some seemed newly renovated—while the windows of 511 had been boarded up. The building was empty. Empty! I began to fantasize that one day I might be able to buy the building back.

I had met the director of the present-day Ionia Rollin Whipper Home and learned that the organization founded by my great-aunt was still alive, reorganized as a facility for troubled girls. Perhaps the Whipper Home could use part of the house and the rest could be a repository for information about the family—a kind of living museum. The thought cheered me. A few weeks later, in Saratoga, I would mention the idea to my mother, thinking it would please her. Instead, she would shudder and tell me how much she disliked that house, how she never wanted to have anything to do with it again. I would see then what I had never been able to grasp fully before—that my passion for the past only brought up my mother's painful memories.

"She couldn't be poor in a town in which she'd been wealthy," my mother had heard her father say about his mother. It was one of those isolated sentences about Frank that I'd had to drape a whole life around. I understood it finally. Accompanied by Ionia, Winifred, Leigh, and Demps, Frank left Beaufort for Washington in 1880. She had bailed her husband out of numerous bad debts and watched as he was ridiculed and lambasted by the Democrats. She had been deprived of an inheritance that would have helped her out financially. She was saddened and humiliated by her mother's public suit. Leaving for Washington must have made a great deal of sense.

The family first moved into a brick house on O Street, N.W. Frank took a job almost immediately in the U.S. Department of Lands as a copyist, transcribing documents. It was not an exciting job; in fact, it was much like her job years before in Boston at the State House; but it was one that now, as then, she did well, and it paid the rent. The official reason for her own departure from the South, with the children, was the increasing violence against blacks there. She appeared to continue her support of Whipper's work back home in Beaufort.

"She stood by him," friends and children alike reported, echoing my grandfather's sentiments. Perhaps that is why my mother once described her as "a saint, to her children." Perhaps that is what most people have meant through the years when they've said their mothers were saints—that they stood by their difficult husbands and took care of the children no matter what. I admire Frank for managing to find a way to both stand by Whipper's ideals and be independent of him as well.

Two years later, Whipper joined the family and tried practicing law in Washington for three years, before he returned to Beaufort and politics again. In 1885, Frank lost her job because Whipper had finally been elected county probate judge in Beaufort, and she was told that her husband's office made her ineligible. The *Palmetto Post* in Beaufort reprinted an article from the *Charleston News and Courier* that typifies the insulting tone common in white post-Reconstruction newspapers:

> A telegram to the *New York Herald* of June 19th says: "The Secretary of the Interior has begun to look into the history of the appointments of some of the clerks in his departments. He removed three in the general land office today. Others removed today were women, one of whom is colored. Her husband is a local Judge in South Carolina. He was a candidate for the Republican nomination for Congress in the Black District of South Carolina, but was defeated by Smalls. This colored woman was an offensive partisan, and gave almost all of her time to talking politics. Another is a white woman." The South Carolina woman referred to is the wife of W. J. Whipper, the colored Probate Judge of Beaufort County and one of the meanest and the most vicious of all the Republican leaders in the State during "the years of good stealing."

Frank's old friend Frederick Douglass, then recorder of deeds for the District of Columbia, immediately gave her a post in his office, which she held until 1893. A snapshot of Douglass stepping out of a carriage, possibly taken in front of Frank's Sixth Street house, is in my grandfather's scrapbook.

One Washington woman who remembered the old days told my mother, "She had a veritable salon there—senators and literary people." Sunday after church was visiting day. Frank began attending St. Luke's Episcopal Church, where Alexander Crummell, the great black nationalist thinker and founder of the American Negro Academy, was presiding. (Crummell had written that "for men, for societies, for races, for nations, the one living and abiding thing is *character.*") There, she was finally confirmed; it seemed time to make that commitment now. Crummell signed her confirmation card in a bold hand.

Frank renewed her old contacts and made new friends, remembering her days in Boston. She continued to write when she could. An editor at Scribners's asked her for a story about "colored soldiers in South Carolina," and she complied, writing it from notes taken in Boston, but I have not yet located the story. She also contributed to newspapers and periodicals, using a pseudonym, which is—so far—a mystery, and she continued to work for the Republican party, still hoping they might bring political salvation. She campaigned for James G. Blaine against Grover Cleveland in the elections of 1893, but Cleveland won by a whisker. My grandfather told me that on election night, his mother went door to door, asking, "Who's winning, who's winning?"—and that around this time, perhaps that very night, she caught a chill, from which she never fully recovered.

Whipper wrote periodically, and Frank kept a close watch on events in Beaufort. Her husband was voted out of his judgeship in a rigged election at the end of 1888. Bristling at the indignity, he refused to give up his probate records, which were mysteriously missing from his office when officials went to claim them. He was summarily jailed and held in the murderers' cell. He refused to go to jail until he'd had his usual supper at a restaurant next door to his office, and once imprisoned, he wrote an account of what had happened, had it published, and made sure that Frank received a copy. It said in part:

> It is not now the office of Probate Judge, for that I have long since lost sight of, neither is it the fees or emoluments of that office that would induce me to spend a single moment in this horrid cell. . . . Could I, in my wildest imagination conclude that there was the slightest doubt of my election, or that Mr. Talbird felt that he was honestly or legally elected, I would have surrendered long ago, proudly giving him the benefit of such doubt—
>
> I have shown beyond all questions that I have not only been elected to the office of Probate Judge, but the entire county Republican ticket was elected. There is a principle underlying this struggle which I cannot forget or forsake—for it is not my cause alone, it is the cause of the voters of Beaufort County.
>
> [Our cause is] the rights of mankind, and as each ant contributes

to the little mound built by their joint industry and perseverance—so we in our feeble way hope to contribute some thing to the defence of human rights, and the upholding and rebuilding of what remains of the Republican party in South Carolina. Should we succeed in doing this, though it takes years to bring it about, we shall feel that we have attained the summit of our ambition, and feel that we have not suffered personal and pecuniary loss in vain.

When every legal means had been exhausted to secure his rights to the judgeship, Whipper decided to surrender the books. He remained in jail thirteen months, holding out longer than any of his associates. On his release, broken in health and financially bankrupt, Whipper resumed his private practice in Beaufort and was, until 1889, vice-chairman of the practically defunct Republican State Executive Committee.

Of all the prominent black South Carolina politicians of Radical Republicanism, only Whipper and Robert Smalls, his political rival, remained in the state. Both were elected to the constitutional convention of 1895, along with three other blacks from Beaufort and one from Georgetown. They were the only blacks and the only Republicans to attend, and they protested vigorously but in vain while the 154 white Democratic delegates passed a set of voting regulations designed to disenfranchise black voters. The black delegates all refused to sign the sorry document that was drafted.

Frank and her family made several moves before settling at 2304 Sixth Street in 1896. Both Winifred and Ionia were teaching by that time, and Winifred did clerical work as well while she studied for a nursing certificate. Leigh was at Howard University, making a name for himself on the football team but getting into trouble with the authorities for various infractions, some having to do with girls and parties. Frank tried to impress upon her son the importance of a good education, but it wasn't easy.

Frank herself may have taken courses at Howard Medical School. One historian states that she graduated and became one of the first women physicians in the 1880s. This is such an authoritative assertion that I want to believe it. Certainly Frank was capable enough, but despite all the lapses in information handed down in the family, I can't imagine that Sistonie would never have mentioned to my mother that her mother, too, was a physician. Or that Uncle Billy would have failed to mention it. So far I have found no record of Frank's graduation.

Lottie and Louisa, with their mother in Brooklyn, were running a comfortable and stylish rooming house on Cropsey Avenue. This was a genteel way of making a living for many black women at the time. Several years later, Lottie, by then living on State Street by herself, was a high school principal. Back in 1871, the sisters told the reporter from the *Sun* that they were afraid of the Klan and thinking of leaving South Carolina, and asked him if he knew of any suitable lodgings in Brooklyn—where they could be close to the noted speaker and humanitarian Henry Ward Beecher. I've never found a record of their deaths, so I often like to imagine Lottie and Louisa in Brooklyn, still living out their lives.

The century was almost ending. It was a time to look to the future, that future Frank had contemplated so often. Overworked and in ill health, she encouraged her daughter Ionia to pursue her medical degree at Howard. Ionia had been teaching in the school system for ten years by that time, and she entered medical school with Frank's moral and financial support. She would graduate in 1903.

The past yields only so much to the present, and much of what I found in my search for Frank was painful. Yet the story refused to end; as soon as I stopped looking actively for information, something else would turn up, like an 1880s interview with Robert Smalls unearthed by historian Eric Foner, in which Smalls said, "[Whipper] deserted his wife and lived with another woman and [word missing] wife worked in Washington. She was good to him. He doesn't appreciate her."

Smalls, the popular black hero and politician, was, according to my grandfather, his godfather. A longtime colleague, he certainly knew my great-grandfather. I had always heard that Frank left Whipper; my mother had said, "She left him and took the kids and moved to Washington. He was a drinker and a gambler." Now I gathered that she had left in 1880, he had followed, and then he left her—to return not only to South Carolina and another chance at a judgeship but, if one can believe his friend and rival's assessment, to an open liaison with another woman. This may have been one of Frank's secrets, something she never told her daughters or her son.

The man who interviewed Smalls, Frederic Bancroft, was planning a book on Reconstruction and had labeled a notebook page "Mrs. Whipper." The page was blank. Apparently he never got to interview her. That blank page was a symbol of all the dead ends I'd come up against in my search for Frank. I had glimpsed her in Boston and empathized with her most strongly there, but once she went South, I felt I had lost her to Whipper and the complexities of the times. The diary entries had become few and far between. Perhaps, after all, she had lost the truest part of herself.

In 1889, as Frank's health began to deteriorate rapidly, Winifred accompanied her mother on a boat down to Charleston. Home! I realized one day that Frank had gone home at the end, back to what she called the "sleepy hollow" of Beaufort. I remembered Sistonie's thoughts of Saratoga and Be-Be near the end of her life—something that would have been inconceivable back in the early days of their relationship—and realized that despite their differences, Frank knew that Whipper was "family."

I imagined her getting off the boat in Beaufort—there'd been no first-class passage for her this time as during the days of Reconstruction. As she described it in a letter written late in her life: "It was a time when colored passengers, no matter how cultured, refined or able to pay—whether on land or sea, were subjected to the most humiliating and degrading treatment." Nonetheless, I see her faintly smiling at the memory of her earlier legal triumph against discrimination by the captain of the *Pilot Boy*.

Winifred helped her mother off; Winifred, who would die eight years later, at thirty-seven. I have never learned much about her, save that she was a teacher and a nurse and that she jumped into that cold tub at the onset of her period.

Whipper was older now and sober, having years before had a religious experience that caused his reform from both drink and gambling. He was prey to asthma attacks that caused him to spend many sleepless nights walking the quiet streets of Beaufort. His womanizing days behind him, physically diminished but morally dignified by his time in jail, Whipper stood waiting at the dock. The look between them would have been one of profound understanding, each knowing just what the other had given, each knowing that even though their lives' dreams had been crushed, they were oddly undefeated. Frank, having stood by Whipper, could hold up her head anywhere. Whipper, knowing she'd done that for him, for their cause, could feel his own worth.

Though Smalls felt that my great-grandfather did not appreciate his wife, I believe he did, ultimately. He couldn't have helped it. I imagine him taking Frank's arm much as he had when he'd met her in Columbia on her return from Boston—that time when he'd put all the fire he could muster into one simple touch. There was no fire now, only tenderness, as he walked a short way with her to his carriage, helped her in, and drove her home. Their children would be the ones to continue what their parents had started, they might have been thinking as they rode toward the house in silence. If all went well, Leigh would be a lawyer, Ionia would be a doctor. Winifred, whose fragile health was worrisome, would keep on, God willing, as a nurse. There would one day be grandchildren, Frank hoped, who would remember all they had done and tell their children. She wanted her grandchildren to be proud of their family.

Frank died of consumption at home in Beaufort on October 17, 1901. She was fifty-six. A special service was held at her home before the church service. *The State* newspaper wrote:

DEATH OF A CULTURED COLORED WOMAN

Beaufort, Oct 18—The wife of W. J. Whipper, the eloquent negro lawyer, died here yesterday afternoon. She was about 44 years of age [*sic*]. Charleston was her native city, but her education was completed in a Philadelphia seminary. Previous to her three years' residence here she had held a government position in Washington for a number of years, where her remarkable intelligence, ability as a writer and estimable character were highly regarded.

She is survived by two daughters and one son. The daughters are also remarkably bright women, graduates of a Washington Institute, who now hold positions as teachers in that city. The son is also well educated and holds a position of trust in a New York mercantile house. The three children arrived here in response to telegrams.

The funeral services of the Episcopal church (of which she was a devoted member) were held at the house today. The interment took place at the colored Methodist churchyard.

Another obituary, in the *Charleston News and Courier*, states that Frank was given an Episcopal service at the Baptist church before being buried in the A.M.E. churchyard, and that a "Reverend Bythwood" performed the ceremony. I sought this churchyard for some years and finally came to believe it must be the same Craven Street A.M.E. graveyard where Robert Smalls was buried in 1915, after a stirring service by the same minister, Dr. Bythe Wood.

On my next trip to Beaufort, I will ask permission to set markers there for both Frank and Whipper. At Smalls's burial, Reverend Wood reminded the weeping crowd that they were there to pay last respects to "a great citizen." I wish that I knew what he said about Frank. Her adopted son, Demps, recalled that she loved Saint Paul; no doubt, one of her favorite passages was quoted at the service. Demps wrote:

> Her life was so finely sincere that it made a deep and lasting impression upon those who were privileged to have known her. I wish to record these great majestic words of Apostle St. Paul, of whom she believed and would often read: "For I am persuaded, that neither death, nor life, nor angels, nor principalities, nor powers, nor things present, nor things to come, nor height, nor depth, nor any other creature, shall be able to separate us from the love of God."

20

Ghosts

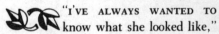"I'VE ALWAYS WANTED TO know what she looked like," my grandmother said. "Leigh talked about her all the time."

I always returned to Saratoga after my researching; this time I brought along copies of Frank's photograph. I was surprised by my grandmother's interest. "She looks just like your great-aunt," Be-Be commented.

My mother seemed pleased as well. "She looks just as I imagined her," she said, taking her copy into her room, where later, in passing, I glimpsed it on her wall. I, too, put a copy of Frank's picture on the wall of my Saratoga room, against its familiar rose-patterned wallpaper, beside a small painting I had done of myself newly pregnant ten years before.

Be-Be was beginning to have serious problems with her health. Sometimes in New York I would awaken from a dream in which she seemed to be calling me—and find that it was true, she really did need my help. That spring she appeared to me in a dream asking for water. When I called in the morning, I learned she had a fever, and I took the bus upstate right away.

My grandmother lay in bed, recovering from a broken hip. My mother had returned to Mexico some time before. A nurse came to the house every day, and George the accountant stopped by daily with *The Saratogian*, juice, candy, and companionship. He'd pour Be-Be a sherry and sit in a chair beside her, talking. More and more, we had to struggle with her over the sherry. She tended to order visitors to give her as much as she wanted. Some doctors allowed that a little sherry might be beneficial, but when she was in pain, or bored with lying in bed, she began to drink heavily. Jonathan, a white short-tailed cat that Be-Be often doctored with Mentholatum, lay purring on her bed, a permanent fixture. "He's stickin' with me," Be-Be would say.

"I never could see what Leighla saw in those Mexicans," Be-Be confided, to explain in part why she refused to go to Mexico, where my mother always said she would have been able to care for her with comparative ease. She'd been there and was unimpressed. "I don't like the beer," she said, making a face. But once, in a moment of candor, she told me that she felt she would be a prisoner down there, while in Saratoga she would always be free. In Saratoga she would always be at home.

Once, she said, she looked up from sleep and saw someone—"It could have been your aunt Sistonie"—sitting in the chair she bought long ago to rock my first son, Alessandro. She said that once a lot of other people came and gathered around in the living room and then left, saying, "It's not time yet."

During several visits, I spent long hours beside my grandmother's bed. Sometimes we talked, and sometimes she seemed to be sleeping so deeply that I could feel her going away from me. I sat writing or reading beside her. Rather than being annoyed at the old questions, I was thankful when she roused herself and looked over at me to inquire: "Are you warm enough upstairs? Have you had enough to eat? Have the boys been eating? I think I'm going to buy some new electric blankets."

Now Be-Be began to tell me things that she couldn't or wouldn't tell me before. It was all so much more vivid to her now. She told me about her mother, Ida, and an image emerged of a tall, dark-skinned, stylishly dressed woman—my maternal great-grandmother. I'd almost overlooked her in my search for Frank, my literary foremother.

Be-Be's voice was intent as she recalled telling her grandparents, "Ida come here, gonna whip me, no indeed!"

"Was she mean, Be-Be?" I asked.

"No," my grandmother answered. "She wasn't mean, I wouldn't call her mean. She had a bad temper, but she wasn't mean."

Be-Be turned her head and seemed to want to go to sleep. But I wanted to know more about Ida. Later that afternoon I asked about her again. It was then that Be-Be told me about Ida and Jim, and about the trick she played on her mother. She was gazing out the window, not looking at me, and she seemed to let the story out on a soft breath.

"They thought she committed suicide," she said at last. Her voice drifted off. "I don't know. She never showed her feelings."

I sat perfectly still, stricken, feeling as if Ida had died the day before. My grandmother had hidden her sense of guilt for almost eighty years. I realized that more than anything else Be-Be had done or not done in her long and active life, it was this one question, this one relationship, that haunted her. It was Ida who caused her to say, "The less said about me, the better."

As I thought about my grandmother's relationship with her mother, it increasingly reminded me of my mother and me. And Frank and her mother did not get along, either. Like me, Be-Be had thought of her grandmother as a mother. Didn't Be-Be see how similar it was? But I didn't ask. I was afraid Be-Be would stop talking.

Did you think it was your fault? I might have asked, but Be-Be had really already told me. In the words "I don't know" I sensed years of her puzzling it out, years of going back and forth over it. She truly didn't know.

"You only have one mother," Be-Be had said to me all my life, and I'd always turned away from the words, thinking them only a ploy to get me to make up with my mother. And now I understood that she was thinking of her own mother when she said it. She was thinking of Ida.

It would be hard to take carbolic acid by mistake, I found out. Hard, but not impossible, I suppose, if you were distraught enough. But Be-Be never knew whether she was responsible. "Any news from Ida?" we would ask the Ouija board together a few months later. But the Ouija board would remain silent.

During that same period, Be-Be gave me a cameo ring that had belonged to William J. Whipper. My grandfather had given it to her long ago. "I want you to have this," she said. I wear it with Frank's wedding ring.

I rubbed Be-Be some more with Mentholatum and remembered how I had sought it out in pharmacies all over Europe, unearthing ancient jars so that I could care for my boys just as Be-Be had cared for me. The place at the small of her back always hurt, and now there was the hip. "You've got healing hands," she told me again. She used to say I looked like her little aunt Lelia; and as I got older she said I reminded her of her aunt Emma.

Be-Be wanted to drink from a tin cup the way she used to when she was a child back in West Virginia, and I went into the kitchen and got it for her. Then I took out my yellow pad.

A certain scent of summer in this house, a museum, a tribute to time itself. Unrepaired. Though there've been changes made, [the house is] haunted with our living in it. . . . This is the home she made for me, and for a few wonderful years I felt its joys and comforts, her own enthusiasm for living and possibility handed on to me.

Last night she said, "We must get some food in here for you." Her time is mixed up. Day is night / night is day. It is her old concern. And now she bids me find the money to help pay for my car fare back. "That's what it's for, to spend when you need it," she tells me. "I wouldn't feel right if you didn't take it."

Upstairs in my room I continued to write:

It seems as if I am always returning to Saratoga. . . . My own children have been babies and young boys in this room, and in the other tiny rooms in this house. Now they are towering teenagers who do not hide from anyone; and whose heads graze the low jutting eaves. Their footsteps resound on the stairs.

"We always run real fast when we pass your room, Mommy," they told me when they were younger. "When you're not here there's the bad ghost. When you're here it's the good ghost."

Sitting in my room last night, thinking of what the boys had told me, I searched the little closet next to my bed. The one the boys always thought the ghosts were coming from. Inside, I found a box containing an old diary of mine.

Was the ghost my own lost childhood? I was startled by the melancholy of the entries in my ten-year-old's diary. Had I felt the presence of ghosts in this room myself? As an adult, I had had times when I sank into such deep depression here that I had thought of dying, of suicide. Pondering the children's words, I wondered: Who is the good ghost, and who the bad ghost? I thought of *The Uninvited*, a movie that I've loved since I was a child. My mother and I had seen it together years before. In it there is a house haunted by a bad ghost, who the heroine believes is her mother. But it turns out later that there are two ghosts, one good, one bad, and the good ghost is the heroine's true mother.

My mother's room is at the top of the stairs. In order to get to my room, I must pass her padlocked door. I always pause there—if ever so briefly.

One day I noticed that the little Morton's Salt girl had been sadly modernized. She wore a new dress and a new hairdo, but most important, the box she held was now hidden by her arm and no longer revealed an infinity of boxes.

Lying in my bed upstairs, I remembered the time years before when Fasig-Tipton had bought the house next door to 157 George Street and torn it down in order to build another stable—leaving ours, the only house completely surrounded by stables, and us, the only black family on the block. I looked up and noticed for the first time that the wallpaper in my room was faded and peeling, and that underneath it, the very walls of the house were cracking. While I was coming and going all those years, I had never noticed that the "old shack" was surfacing again, that my old home was disappearing before my very eyes.

In 1985, my father called to let me know that my mother was planning to sell the place. He urged me to do all I could to prevent it, but nothing I could do or say would persuade my mother that despite the difficulties and our differences, the house and business deserved a second chance. The children—as Be-Be was fond of saying—would soon be old enough to run it themselves. It would be a legacy for them. I offered to find a manager, to figure it all out myself. I spoke of the history of loss in our family—of how blacks have continued since Reconstruction to lose to mercenary whites property that was rightfully theirs; of how all the land owned by William Rollin along Meeting Street and elsewhere in Charleston, all the property owned by William J. Whipper in Charleston, on Hilton Head, and in Beaufort, and the Rollin sisters' houses in Columbia—all that prime real estate now belonged to white people. How even now, in the Sea Islands, developers were making poor blacks offers they could not refuse for their land. Black people were being locked out of the places where they had been born.

"I always thought that this was my house too. That it belonged to all of us. I grew up here!"

I faced her at the top of the stairs while she stood in the doorway of her room. I recognized a familiar look in her eyes—a look that seemed to say, perhaps she had been right about me all these years, that the "madness" she had always feared in me was surfacing. It was the nonexistent "madness" she had dreaded in my father, our "inheritance" from Ella, his mother.

"I don't see it that way," my mother replied, turning away.

I returned to Saratoga in the early summer of 1986. It was the first year that my grandmother was not there. Be-Be was in a nursing home in nearby Ballston Spa; the nurses had persuaded my mother that this was best. She needed continual care. My mother and I were on our way over for a visit. I was remembering how she had told me a few days before, "I just want you to know that you don't have to come up. I don't need you."

"I'm coming," I replied defiantly. "And the kids are coming too. We'll be there."

But despite my bravado, I was shaken as we entered the nursing home, not only because of the memory of the harsh conversation but because it reminded me of a dream I had had of my grandmother. I hardly had time to think of it, however, for we were already moving through the hallway and women in wheelchairs were looking at us curiously. Some nodded hello, others stared blankly. As we approached Be-Be's room, an elderly white woman was screaming in the hallway. She was tied into a wheelchair. "Please, won't somebody help me? Won't somebody let me out of here?"

I touched her arm, and she quieted down and gazed into my eyes. After a few moments, I told her, "I have to go see my grandmother—I have to go now." But as I moved slowly away, she began to scream again. "Where is that little colored girl? I want that little colored girl!"

Stunned, I sat beside Be-Be's bed, thinking that underneath it all, despite long years of effort on my part, despite centuries of effort by others, I had not grown up, the world had not grown up—I was still "that little colored girl." I tried to concentrate on my grandmother. My mother's voice was blending with the woman's strident cries. "I want to go home!" I heard her saying, loudly. "Shut up!" another patient cried; and I heard a man's voice, an attendant this time, call out, "You are home. This is home!"

My mother sat on the other side of the bed. "Carole is here!" she was saying loudly. I wanted her to speak softly. I wanted her to go away, to leave me alone with Be-Be. "Little Carole is here." It was their old term for me, and I was horrified.

Be-Be was floating in her "other" world, the one I had seen her go to from time to time recently. Her eyes focused, and yet I felt she didn't really see me. She spoke vaguely, politely, the way people do when they don't quite remember the person they're speaking to. Outside, the woman continued to scream. "I want the little colored girl! Won't somebody help me? Won't somebody let me out of here?"

As my mother and I headed toward the parking lot, she said, "She didn't recognize you, you know." I didn't reply. I knew I would never admit that. I was remembering the nightmare I had had a few weeks earlier, before I knew Be-Be was going into a nursing home.

In the dream someone shows me the papers for the house, which do not show my name. Then I ask my mother where Be-Be is. She doesn't want to tell me. I tell her that I'll find her anyway, and I do. I go to the entryway of a building like a hospital or an institution, but there are people there who don't want to let me in. Loudly, I yell out Be-Be's name and hear her reply from inside. Then I push my way in, and I discover that my grandmother is suspended—hanging in a kind of restraining harness in a stall-like room. Around her are other elderly women, all in harnesses, in other stalls. Be-Be is also gagged, but I can see her eyes, and I know she is glad to see me. The other women are glad too. They look to me imploringly.

"You're so beautiful!" I cry. "You're all so beautiful! I'll get you out of here no matter what I have to do!"

That summer I did not cook or work the service bar. I arranged for friends of mine who owned a restaurant in town to come out and help with the food. I became a hostess, a manager, like my mother. I dressed in pretty clothes and tried to take the place of my grandmother. The place looked lovely, with bright, colorful lights in the garden. I tried to think that this could continue.

"Find a place for the cats," my mother told me one day as I was passing her room. "I'm closing the house up for the winter."

"The cats?" I cried. "Where will I stay when I come to visit Be-Be and you're in Mexico? She could come home and I could be here!"

"That's not possible," she told me, and it was then that I raised my hand to her. It was then that I could do it, actually hit her, but I didn't.

She raised her hands in defense and I grabbed them. We were both horrified. "What are you doing? I'm your mother!" she cried, and I began talking, trying to explain everything, to tell her I understood her loneliness—that I didn't want it that way, that I wanted to change all that—that I wanted *life* for us all. The Spuyten Duyvil for better or for worse was the only home we had. I held on and danced her around the center of the room, uncertain what to do now that I actually had hold of her.

Finally, it came to me. "I know what it is I want to do," I said, "just once." Brusquely, awkwardly, I hugged her to me. "I love you," I said. For one split second I could feel her. We were as close as we were that night in the car in Alabama. "It's a strange way of showing it," she was saying, nervously.

Quickly, then, for there was nothing else to do, I released her and, shattered, left the room.

I continued to write in my journal:

August is over now. My mother is locking the house for the winter. It may have been the last season. On my last day before leaving 157 George Street, I climb the stairs and, remarkably, I find my mother's door standing open. She is not there. Her bags are on her bed. She is packing, getting ready to return to Mexico. I look into the forbidden room. There is the familiar gray furniture that I so loved in Riverton, there are the blue smoked mirrors, some of the old perfume bottles, bobby pins and paper clips, clippings of bullfight announcements. On the old bamboo shelves beside her bed lie some of the books she had while I was growing up—collections of poetry, Shakespeare, mysteries. The table before the window holds her typewriter and her manuscript paper.

Beside her bed, on the night table, are her cold cream and Kleenex, nail polish and polish remover. On the dresser, the television set she leaves on in the night, and the electric curlers that make a clicking sound on the mirrored surface when she is setting her hair in the mornings. Listening to that sound from my room, I can sense her mood before I hear her closing her door and locking it, before I hear her descending the stairs.

It was months ago that I found the photos she once had of me in her room—along with my bronzed baby shoes—outside in the hall. I remember words my mother had spoken to Be-Be: "How could anyone give up a child? I could never do that," and to me: "Forget about me. Just forget about me," and "I don't need you."

I wonder if it really is too late to heal the awful thing that has happened to us all.

I stand in the middle of her room and breathe. I take long deep breaths of the air in my mother's room.

21

Home

"HOME," MY FATHER HAD said to me as we were sitting on the porch of 157 George Street, "is where they can't put you out."

He had come up to Saratoga to support me through what he knew would be a difficult summer for us all. He felt that it was not his place to interfere with my mother's plans—they had been divorced for decades—but he was trying to keep communications open and, as tactfully as possible, to prevent something that was beginning to seem inevitable.

I had tried to explain to my grandmother for two years now what my mother's plans were, because only Be-Be could take steps to protect the property. But she never believed it would happen.

My father says that mother is hellbound or hellbent on selling. I awaken in my Saratoga room filled with anger and the understanding that if necessary I must let this go. Looking back over three articles I have written, I noticed with a start one day not so long ago that each of them ended with the word "home."

Later I wrote: *Entering the house, it is summer and Be-Be is not there. My mother is there alone. I have never seen her there alone before. My mother is pleasant. She has made something to eat. I eat it, aware that I am deriving a wary comfort from it. There is a fierce quiet to the place. . . . Be-Be is not here. It is a house. Not my home.*

In the aftermath of that pain-filled summer, I retreated to an old psychological place of numbing cold. Winter eventually rolled around again, and I went up to Saratoga to be close to my grandmother and to write at Yaddo.

The house is padlocked and there is no key. Be-Be, from the nursing home, asks me to get the heat turned back on, orders George, her former accountant, to give me the key even though he doesn't want to—he is following orders from my mother—and tells me to stay in the house. But the heating company will only take orders from my mother. The old house, I know, will not last the winter without some heat. Appalled, steeling myself against the cold and the anger, I enter it periodically, driving over from Yaddo. I safeguard the photographs I gave to Be-Be of the children when they were little—photographs that have been left on the damp walls. Be-Be instructs me to order a wreath for Christmas to put on the door, just as she always did in the past when she was away in Florida for the winter. When I call the florists, they think at first that I mean a funeral wreath.

Inside the house in the kitchen, Be-Be's old hot kitchen, a window has been left open. The snow and rain are coming in.

I knew that winter that the worst was happening. I was losing my home. It was a moment of what Frank would have called "ruin." I felt the way her sisters must have felt during their fund-raising visit to Philadelphia when, as Lucretia Mott wrote to her sister, they "walked out, to the garden and around."

For the Rollin sisters, home as they knew it was lost. Their childhood world of privilege had been destroyed, and their efforts to create a new society where blacks and women would be honored were failing. Walking in the Philadelphia garden, they knew they had come to a place where they could no longer pretend. Their jewelry was serving as collateral for their room and board. Their former friends were shunning them and whispering secrets behind their backs. It is this moment and others like it that last and last through the lives of all the women in the family.

It resonates in the "X" of Margarette Rollin's anger—her signature on the court papers—her conflict over the Rollin land with her eldest daughter. It is echoed in Be-Be's anger and guilt about Ida, in my mother's inability to forgive her mother for leaving her. This is the moment of not having it, of being women—colored women—up against it and, somehow, because of this, up against each other.

I have seen my mother and my grandmother sharing their morning coffee ritual in the kitchen in Saratoga. The first cup and then the important second cup. The spoons stirring. The right temperature, the right amount of sugar, the half-and-half. Just sitting there together. And yet I know that the moment was with them. It was their moment of being out in the garden. And I would share it with them for those few seconds that I lingered, eavesdropping, in the outer pantry.

And the moment was mine each August as I sat outside in the garden at the service bar in the shed, serving up liquor for the rich.

Home for my father's mother, Ella Wells, was not her house, filled with children and a difficult charismatic husband. The moment of loss was with her as she took to the streets with her babies, looking for home, a place where she really belonged. The form of what some called her "madness" was gentle and truthful. I am proud of her.

And home for Frank was not really a house, either, although she was fond of the East Bay house her father loved. Home for Frank was not so much the Rollin land that she tried and failed to hold on to, or Whipper Barony in Charleston, or even the roomy Beaufort house (where she taught Leigh the alphabet by singing him a little song), but a time of hope in the future. For Frank, Beaufort—a stronghold of blackness—must have represented the last bastion of Republican ideals in South Carolina, despite Whipper's defeats; it was the closest to home she could get before she died.

The de Caradeucs of Saint-Domingue, whose old patrician homes were shattered once, then again, by the revolutionary tide that moved from the islands to Charleston, were made of resilient stuff. Conservative to the end, they managed to preserve the memory of their island plantations. They were at home in their knowledge of the past, if not in the present. And unlike other members of the family, they were reimbursed for their losses when, in the early 1800s, the French government paid them the value of their lost property and freed slaves.

The Rollins, caught on the darker side of black and white, never found a new country to which to emigrate when war disrupted their lives in Charleston; nor was William Rollin ever compensated for the destruction of his farm. Though my mother and I have tried to lead expatriate lives, for the most part the Rollins and their descendants had to continue to make their way in an inherently hostile environment in America. Yet finally I am finding a way to accept this embattled United States, which for better and worse is mine. Although, as Frank noted in her diary, "America is not the world," I know now that this country is my home.

And the white Wheelers of whom Be-Be spoke, who came from England to a new land in the 1600s, must have longed for home, no matter what their reasons were for leaving it behind. Conditions on the coast of Virginia were deplorable for colonists. Be-Be told me that my ancestors arrived in 1607; but the date may have been 1609, when the British London Company was reorganized and more colonists were sent out to replace previous arrivals decimated by illness and battles with Native Americans—the original residents of their new home. Were some of these Virginia natives of the same tribe as my foremother Sarah? My Wheeler ancestors, refugees from a small island in the North Atlantic, must have been tough, or perhaps they were just plain lucky to survive. But though the information may exist, buried in archives, I could never trace a lineage of pride to England from the big house in which George Washington Wheeler was a preferred houseman.

Home for George Washington Wheeler was the place he built himself. "Oh, my child has come home!" he cried when my young grandmother returned. And home for my grandmother Be-Be was there, too, with her grandfather and his second wife, in the hills of West Virginia, where she could climb a tall mountain and find another mountain on the other side, where she was treated like "a little lump of gold" and always got her way.

Later, for Be-Be, home became Saratoga and the George Street house. In Saratoga, she could live the free and breezy life that suited her. And yet she worked ceaselessly to make George Street a home for us all; she knew how we all needed it.

Be-Be refused to believe that anything in Mexico, a place where she couldn't even drink the beer, could compete with Saratoga as my mother's home. But *home* for my mother was the time before she went to live with Sistonie, when she could curl up to sleep in a trunk or wait in the unhooked passenger car for her mother's show to be over, watched over by one of the other members of the Smarter Set. Whitney Tutt teasingly called her "Mother," and she called him "Baby," Homer Tutt was like a father, and there was life and love and noise and dancing on Sunday. Joy was never put off until tomorrow. There was jam today.

"We'll all end up here in Saratoga," Be-Be told my father one chaotic holiday, including him long after he and my mother had been divorced, just as she wanted to include Salvatore after he and I went our separate ways. Because she willed it so, the Spuyten Duyvil became my home as well as hers. But finally I have come to realize what seems so simple in retrospect—that it was the time spent at the George Street house when I was a child that I longed for, not the house itself. What had been lived there: that was home to me.

Even Sistonie had found a kind of home in Saratoga toward the end. But she had discovered an inner peace before that, a self-knowledge that finally enabled her to accept other people, including my grandmother. One day I took her spiritual diary down from my office shelf and opened it at random. Two years after my birth, she had written: *I had felt that being reared by intelligent Christian parents and having been born in the Church from early childhood that I was a finished Christian product. But to my great surprise when I decided that I wanted to be changed, I found that my spiritual thinking had just begun. . . . My greatest blocks were pride and willfulness. I found that I had been secretly fostering pride of family all my life and had been hiding it under the guise of indifference.*

Spirits are the feelings that survive us, and for a time the spirits of all the women in my family past and present came to reside with me in my Saratoga room, not happily. I felt only their loss there. As the only daughter of an only daughter of an only daughter, I have all my life felt the pure lineage of my mother's childhood sorrow as my own. I was never able to separate it from myself and could do nothing to assuage it.

"You only have one mother," Be-Be always said, but I have found otherwise. I dared to wonder who my mother was and found that she is many women combined in one: the recipient of an accumulation of sorrows, the secret shadowy heritage of the women who came before her. She is "C.L.," the ghost of "grandma" who made Frank shiver in Boston in 1868. She is Margarette, Frances, Charlotte, Louisa, Florence, Katie, Eva, Lelia, Mamie, Ionia, Winifred, Ida, Ellen Kent, the other Ellen, and even that strong and independent ancestor whose dreams of Africa I claim, Mama Monkee. My mother is all of these women, and so am I. I have others with me as well—Ella, Wells Lewis, Louisa, Elsie and my link to the original people of this land, Sarah, from my father's side, and all the invisible and unsung women who came before them.

Each woman longed for a lost home. Each mourned a time and place where she had been truly valued, where her true self had been honored. It seems to me that my mother was compelled to repeat the pattern of their loss by selling the Spuyten Duyvil—a potent symbol of what remained of the painful past. Although there is sadness in it, History can forgive her that.

In the nursing home, Be-Be has become more and more lucid, deprived of sherry, except for an occasional smuggled glass. "I dream of Ida all the time now. She's in my dreams. Just hovering around," she told me the other day. Ida didn't have anything to say; she was "just hovering around."

Still lucky, she has even won a pocketbook, playing bingo. She reads all the time. My mother has given her a Bible, which she is enjoying. And she likes the big-print Reader's Digests. *Someone gave her Alice Walker's* The Color Purple, *which I had given a rave review in* Essence *magazine. . . . I asked her how she liked it. I was surprised by the energy she put into her answer. "Oh, I didn't like that," she replied. "I've been down home. It was too natural. It was just like it was."*

Though I was taken aback, I felt that Walker would possibly have been flattered by Be-Be's review. I realized then that Be-Be had tried hard to create a home for us that was not "down home."

She has begun to rename the nursing home staff, much as she did with the waitresses at the Spuyten Duyvil. There's "My Standby," the one she smiles for, and there's "The Phantom Doctor," who races through, and there's "Old Stone Face" and "The Damn It to Hell Nurse," who tries to boss her around. Going to physical therapy every day, she has become stronger than before. And with clarity, she has had to come to terms with the fact that the house is gone—sold by my mother to Fasig-Tipton. "That taught me a good lesson," she said. "Always hold your own reins."

SPUYTEN DUYVIL JUST A MEMORY, read the headline in *The Saratogian*. My grandmother's first worry seemed to be for me and the children. She tried to undo it, but all she still owned was the name Spuyten Duyvil. So she signed that over to me for a dollar. The lawyer who came to the nursing home to take care of the transaction had once been a waitress and a manager at the Spuyten Duyvil. We sat at a table on the front lawn of the nursing home, and Be-Be said, "Well, where's the dollar? I need some money." I laughed and handed her the dollar. The paper we signed is called a D/B/A, which gives me the right to do business as "Spuyten Duyvil" if ever I get another property to go with the name.

My grandmother's grieving for herself has been quiet. She has kept up a good front and still tries to protect my mother from her own pain. I found some beads at a garage sale that looked like the amber ones that Be-Be used to wear and took them to her. "You should give these to Leighla," she told me.

My mother had all my old paintings and everything from my old room removed to our former bartender's garage and disposed of almost everything else in the house. She put Be-Be's bedroom set in storage and sent word through my father that I could have it. Be-Be asked me, "Where am I going to go now? I liked that old house. Leighla didn't think it was worth anything. But I liked it." And later, "You didn't deserve that, the children didn't deserve it. And no—you're right—I didn't deserve it. But maybe we can get it back somehow. Call Fasig-Tipton. I leave it to you to figure out how to do it." Be-Be was ready to climb another mountain.

Be-Be was ninety-six when she read in *The Saratogian* that Fasig-Tipton was planning on tearing down our old house. The loss hit her right away this time. "What about all the things in the house?" she asked. "What about the stove, my Revere Ware? You can't get those things every day."

"I don't know," I had to admit, "but I'm getting your bed out of storage, Be-Be. I'll get a new house to put it in."

"I don't care about the bed," she said. "It's the stove. That stove was my heart."

Not long after, I took Be-Be out to Miss Hattie's Chicken Shack for an early dinner. It was to Miss Hattie's that Be-Be would send me for steak dinners when as a child I waited for her to place her bets in Jim Scott's horse room. "Hattie makes good soup," she'd said, and that was what she wanted. After the soup, Hattie's husband, Bill, and a young assistant helped her walk slowly back to the car. "Where shall we go?" I asked.

And even though I hadn't thought about it, somehow I knew what she was going to say. We had thus far steadfastly avoided going by George Street on our periodic outings from Maplewood Manor. "I'd kind of like to go by the place," she said. "I want to see what they've done."

"But, Be-Be, what if it's not there anymore?" I asked.

"Well, then it'll just be not there. At least we'll know," she said impatiently.

Already I was turning up Lake Avenue, feeling that maybe we both could handle this now. The familiar houses, the shiny green and white stables, and then George Street, the Fasig-Tipton sales paddock, and then . . . Be-Be was leaning forward against her seat belt, and I guess I was straining to see too.

"Oh, Be-Be," I said, "it's gone. It's not there." We pulled up in front of the chain-link fence that enclosed the area where the house had been. It looked like such a small space; hardly big enough to have contained so many years, so many memories. Be-Be sat looking, soaking it in. "There's the white picket side fence," she said, pointing. She was silent for a long while. Then: "All that work for nothing. It's like climbing up a big tall mountain and falling all the way down to the bottom."

We sat a few more moments. I had my camera, and I busied myself taking some pictures of Be-Be looking and of the place where the front door had once been, as though I could raise it up from the past. Then I got back in the car and we turned up Case Street, taking in that old view we used to have from the porch.

"It's gone," Be-Be said, softly. Then she spelled it out: "G-o-n-e." Then she added, the way she sometimes did for the many old friends of hers who had died: "Gone but not forgotten."

In August, Be-Be's favorite month, I brought her to the new house I had bought with a friend, in a town in upstate New York that looks and feels much as Saratoga did when I was a child.

Finally, after all the rootlessness of the past years, after centuries of homelessness among the women in my family, I had found a place for myself, and a place for Be-Be. This was to be her first visit, and we wanted her to come and stay if she liked it. An old Victorian house, thoroughly American, it is far more solid than the "old shack" on George Street, but there is some intangible similarity between them.

This new home contained some of the familiar old furniture from Saratoga, and Jonathan, Be-Be's cat, had been waiting for her here. There were new kittens as well, and flowers out back. Inside, there was a big dining room table, at which Be-Be blessed us all, for the children were here as well. She slept well in the downstairs front room. In the morning, to my surprise—for she could not walk very well on her own—I found her standing with her walker in the kitchen, awake before me, like in the old days.

Later she sat on the sofa in the sitting room with Jonathan on her lap and spontaneously began to tell me once more the story of my mother's birth. As usual there were details I hadn't heard before, and I was jotting them down. Then I looked up at her and something happened. Time seemed to stop, and my grandmother's face seemed to be shining. I was able to see her for a second or two with a supernatural clarity.

She is really here, sitting with me, I thought. In that brief moment before the ordinary world set in again, I felt our connection through all time. I felt as if we'd always been together like this; as if we'd always be together.

My grandmother died on November 10, 1988. She had been quite healthy, and I was surprised when she was admitted to Saratoga Hospital on the day I was due to visit her at Maplewood. In the hospital, she told me of a dream she'd had the night before. She'd heard some music in the next room and gone in, to find her grandfather and her uncles singing and playing the violin as of old. Overjoyed, she joined them.

"Last hotel," Be-Be had always said wryly, nodding her head in the direction of any cemetery we happened to drive by in the last few years. She was quite definite about wanting to be buried in Greenridge Cemetery, so her "last hotel" is there, in Saratoga, her "old stomping ground."

Before and after the funeral, my mother and I both stayed at Miss Hattie's home overnight, and my mother, knowing how she had been criticized for selling the place, explained to me the situation of back taxes owed on the Spuyten Duyvil that had made her feel she had no choice but to sell. She had explained them to Be-Be recently as well, and she said my grandmother had replied, "No one knows what another person goes through."

Unless, of course, you tell them, I thought to myself, sadly. After so many secrets, and so much pain, I will always believe in the power of revelation.

My mother and I sat together at a table for two at Miss Hattie's and had an early Thanksgiving dinner. I was glad to be with her. I brought some champagne, just as we always used to have for Thanksgiving on George Street. Mother and I drank a toast. "Be-Be would love this," she said. I agreed.

I remembered with satisfaction how my son Santiago and I had driven up to Ballston Spa to get Be-Be that August, and how I'd been so nervous about it that I managed to lock the keys in the trunk of the car. Santiago had found a key that just happened to open it. I'd stood at the front desk, my grandmother beside me in her wheelchair, and watched as, for the first time since Be-Be had been at Maplewood, the nurse wrote on the sign-out chart under "Destination": *Home*.

Acknowledgments

I WOULD LIKE to express my gratitude to the following individuals and organizations who helped this book move from the realm of dreams to reality:

Julia Hotten and the staff of the Schomburg Collection, New York Public Library, as well as the New York Public Library Genealogy Department, and the Long Island Historical Society; Joy Elliott, descendant of Robert Brown Elliott, and Charles Wright, descendant of J. J. Wright. James Lecesne helped me to see Frank and to transcribe the diary.

In Philadelphia, the staffs of the Historical Society of Philadelphia, the Friends Historical Library of Swarthmore College, and Richard P. McCormick, primary scholar on William Whipper, the abolitionist. I am also appreciative of the staffs of the Massachusetts Historical Society, the Boston Library Historical Collection, and Professor Andrew Buni.

In Paris, Madame Menier, Director of the Archives Nationales de France, Section outre-mer, was most helpful. Dominique and Denis Lambilliotte helped with research, lodging, and friendship.

In Saratoga Springs, the staff of the Saratoga Springs Public Library was helpful over a number of years, and I am particularly grateful to Hattie Austin Moseley, Sarah Braveman, Sarah Foulke-Bemus, and Paul Mattfeld, who kept the faith in Saratoga.

The National Archives and Records Administration, Wilton S. Dillon of the Smithsonian Institution, Mrs. Marilyn E. Mahanand of the Channing-Pollack Theatre Collection, and the staff of the Moorland-Spingarn Collection of Howard University were very helpful. I also received assistance from the staff of the Martin Luther King Library, Dorothy Provine of the District of Columbia Government Records Department, St. Luke's Church, and Joan Hurley of the Ionia Rollin Whipper Home.

The work of many family historians contributed to the preparation of this book: Hylan Garnet Lewis, Elsie Lewis, Albert Lewis, Diane Lewis Robinson and Barbara Lewis Berger, Alessandro Lee Bovoso, Wendell Powell, Virginia Eva Wheeler, Leighla Frances Whipper, and Reverend Benjamin Whipper, Lucille Whipper, and their family of Charleston, South Carolina.

I am grateful to the South Carolina Commission for the Humanities for a grant which furthered research on the life of Frances Anne Rollin, and appreciative of former director Leland H. Cox's kind assistance and encouragement. Charles Morris of South Carolina's SCETV gave early support to my personal vision of this story. Patricia Durlach helped enormously with on-site research in South Carolina. Also helpful were Father Burn of the Catholic Diocese Archives of Charleston, David Molke Hansen of the Historical Society of South Carolina, director Allan Stokes and the staff of the South Caroliniana Collection, University of South Carolina, George D. Terry of Columbia College, the South Carolina Department of Archives and History, the Municipal Archives of the City of Charleston, the Avery Institute, the Slavemart Museum, the College of Charleston Black Charleston Photograph Collection, Robert Scott Small Library, the Charleston Library Society, St. Phillip's Church, and the Historical Society of Savannah. The Southern Historical Collection, University of North Carolina Library, in Chapel Hill, provided a particularly pleasant atmosphere for research.

Margarette Childs, Jacqueline Mattfeld, Charles Joyner, and Harry Wright were most hospitable in South Carolina. In Beaufort, I received assistance from Gearhart Speiler and the Reverend R. J. Rumley. The staff of the Beaufort Library and Ms. Berry of the Historical Museum of Beaufort were most helpful, as was the staff of Penn Center in Frogmore. A special thanks to Mrs. Adalee B. Roberts and friends who care for the forgotten cemeteries of Beaufort.

Generous support for my writing was offered by the following organizations and individuals: Philip Corner, the Dramatists Guild, the Edward Albee Foundation, the Helix Training Program, the MacDowell Colony, the Writers' Room, Yaddo, the Kioks of Sag Harbor, the Pauline Oliveros Foundation, and Catherine Williamson.

There were some guiding lights along the way: Eric Foner has been enormously helpful with suggestions and has graciously shared research with me as this work evolved. Dorothy Sterling has continued to share information and has been with me in spirit since the beginning of this project. Shortly before the completion of this manuscript, Willard B. Gatewood, Jr., sent copies of letters written by Frances Anne Rollin near the end of her life. I was as heartened and touched by these as I was when I first read Frank's diary.

Others assisted in so many ways through the years, and I thank them. They include Salvatore Bovoso, Elmore Brown, Kenneth B. Clark, Maxi Cohen, Richard Corriere, Robert Flynn, Thomas Holt, Larry Koger, Peggy Lamson, Susan Lazarus, Ron Lieberman, M. Mark, Karen Moak, Beatrice Olsen, James Roark, Camille Saviola, Ann Allen Shockley, Panaiotis, Michele Spiro, Guy Trebay, Joseph Vasta, and Valerie Wax. I am proud of my children, Alessandro, Santiago, and Antonio, whose births inspired me and made writing this book an imperative.

An amazing bit of synchronicity blessed this project. My editor, Ileene Smith, while still a student, spent a summer as a cocktail waitress at the Spuyten Duyvil in 1973. She met the women in my family and even glimpsed me in passing. The fact that we found each other years later when I was ready to write this book can hardly have been an accident. Her moments in the garden at Saratoga gave her a unique relationship to this story and made her, in a very real sense, a member of the family. Alane Mason, in addition to being a fine editor, always had a word of encouragement and a knack for sending notes that bolstered my spirits when most needed. The strong belief of these two women, along with that of my formidable agent, Melanie Jackson, saw the book through to this moment.

I am particularly grateful to Pauline Oliveros whose practice is Listening, and to my teachers, H.E. Jamgon Khontrul Rinpoche, H.E. Tai Situ Rinpoche, Master Tsu Kuo Shih, and Julie Rosa Winter.

Kingston, N.Y.
February 1991

Bibliography

Anthony, Susan B., and Elizabeth Cady Stanton, eds., *The History of Woman's Suffrage* (4 vols.), published 1881–1900 (no publisher listed).

Ballard, Allen B., *One More Day's Journey: The Story of a Family and a People*. New York: McGraw-Hill Book Company, 1984.

Barthold, Bonnie J., *Black Time: Fiction of Africa, the Caribbean, and the United States*. New Haven and London: Yale University Press, 1981.

Bennett, Lerone, Jr., *Before the Mayflower: A History of Black America*, Baltimore, Maryland: Penguin Books Inc., 1961.

Bennett, Lerone, Jr., *Black Power U.S.A.: The Human Side of Reconstruction 1867–1877*. Baltimore, Maryland: Penguin Books Inc., 1969.

Dann, Martin E., ed., *The Black Press 1827–1890: The Quest for National Identity*. New York: Capricorn Books, 1971.

Davis, Angela Y., *Women, Culture, and Politics*. New York: Random House, 1984.

Davis, Angela Y., *Women, Race, and Class*. New York: Random House, 1981.

Dobell, Byron, *A Sense of History: The Best Writing from the Pages of American Heritage*. New York: American Heritage, 1985.

Foner, Eric, *Reconstruction, America's Unfinished Revolution, 1863–1877*. New York: Harper & Row, 1988.

Fox-Genovese, Elizabeth, *Within the Plantation Household: Black and White Women of the Old South*. Chapel Hill: The Univ. of North Carolina Press, 1988.

Franklin, John Hope, *Reconstruction After the Civil War*. Chicago: University of Chicago Press, 1961.

Gates, Henry Louis, Jr., ed. *The Classic Slave Narratives*. New York: Mentor Books, New American Library, 1987.

Giddings, Paula, *When and Where I Enter: The Impact of Black Women on Race and Sex in America*. New York: William Morrow and Company, Inc., 1984.

Higginson, Thomas Wentworth, *Army Life in a Black Regiment*. Boston: Beacon Press, Massachusetts, 1962.

Holt, Thomas, *Black Over White: Negro Political Leadership in South Carolina During Reconstruction*. Chicago: University of Illinois Press, 1977.

Hughes, Langston, and Milton Meltzer, *Black Magic: A Pictorial History of the Negro in American Entertainment*. Englewood Cliffs, New Jersey: Prentice-Hall, Inc., 1967.

Jacobs, Harriet A., *Incidents in the Life of a Slave Girl*. Cambridge, Massachusetts: Harvard University Press, 1987.

James, C.L.R., *The Black Jacobins: Toussaint L'Ouverture and the San Domingo Revolution*. New York: Vintage Books, div. of Random House, 1963.

Johnson, Michael·P., and James L. Roark, *Black Masters: A Free Family of Color in the Old South*. New York and London: W. W. Norton & Company Inc., 1984.

Johnson, Michael P., and James L. Roark, eds., *No Chariot Let Down Charleston's Free People of Color on the Eve of the Civil War*. Chapel Hill and London: The University of North Carolina Press, 1984.

Jones, Agnes Halsey, and Louis C., *New-Found Folk Art of the Young Republic*. Cooperstown, New York: New York State Historical Association, 1960.

Joyner, Charles, *Down by the Riverside: A South Carolina Slave Community*. Chicago: University of Illinois Press, 1984.

Katz, William Loren, ed., *Proceedings of the Constitutional Convention of South Carolina*, Volume 1. New York: Arno Press and *The New York Times*, 1968.

Kimball, Robert, and William Bolcom, *Reminiscing with Sissle and Blake*. New York: The Viking Press, 1973.

Koger, Larry, *Black Slaveowners: Free Black Slave Masters in South Carolina, 1790–1860*. North Carolina: McFarland and Co., Inc., 1985.

Lamson, Peggy, *The Glorious Failure: Black Congressman Robert Brown Elliott and the Reconstruction in South Carolina*. New York: W.W. Norton & Company Inc., 1973.

Lightfoot, Sara Lawrence, *Balm in Gilead: Journey of a Healer*. New York: Addison-Wesley Publishing Co. Inc., 1988.

Long, Richard A., ed., *Black Writers and the American Civil War*. Secaucus, New Jersey: The Blue & Grey Press, 1988.

Mannix, Daniel P., and Cowley, Malcolm, *Black Cargoes: A History of the Atlantic Slave Trade 1518–1867*. New York: Viking Press, 1962.

McPherson, James M., *The Negro's Civil War: How American Negroes Felt and Acted During the War for the Union.* New York: Vintage Books, 1967.

Moldow, Gloria, *Women Doctors in Gilded-Age Washington: Race, Gender, and Professionalization.* Urbana and Chicago: University of Illinois Press, 1987.

Rollin, Frank A., *Life and Public Services of Martin R. Delany.* Boston, Massachusetts: Lee and Shepard, 1868, 1883.

Rosenberger, Francis Coleman, *Records of the Columbia Historical Society of Washington, D.C.* The Fiftieth Volume, Columbia Historical Society, dist. by University Press of Virginia, Charlottesvile, Virginia, 1980.

Spiller, R.E., *Selected Essays, Lectures, and Poems of Ralph Waldo Emerson.* New York: Quokka Pocket Books, div. Simon & Schuster, 1965.

Stampp, Kenneth M., *The Era of Reconstruction 1865–1877.* New York: Vintage Books, 1965.

Stampp, Kenneth M., *The Peculiar Institution: Slavery in the Ante-Bellum South.* New York: Vintage Books, 1956.

Sterling, Dorothy, *Black Foremothers: Three Lives.* New York: The Feminist Press, 1979.

Sterling, Dorothy, ed., *We Are Your Sisters: Black Women in the Nineteenth Century.* New York: W.W. Norton & Company Inc., 1984.

Strouse, Jean, *Alice James: A Biography.* Boston, Massachusetts: Houghton Mifflin Co., 1980.

Thornbrough, Emma Lou, ed., *Great Lives Lived: Black Reconstructionists.* Englewood Cliffs, New Jersey: Prentice-Hall, Inc., 1972.

Tindall, George Brown, *South Carolina Negroes 1877–1900.* University of South Carolina Press, 1952.

Walden, Daniel, ed., *W.E.B. DuBois: The Crisis Writings.* Greenwich, Connecticut: Fawcett Publications, Inc., 1972.

West, Dorothy, *The Living Is Easy.* Old Westbury, New York: The Feminist Press, 1975.

Wikramanayake, Marina, *A World in Shadow: The Free Black in Antebellum South Carolina.* University of South Carolina Press, 1973.

MAGAZINES AND OTHER SOURCES

The Atlantic Monthly. Boston, Feb. 1866, Vol. 17, No. 100, Jan. 1868, Vol. 21, No. 123.

National Geographic. Washington, D.C., May 1990, Vol. 177, No. 5.

Dissertations and Private Papers

Elsie Lewis, "Rambling and Reminiscing with Elsie Up and Down Our Family Tree," with partial research by Barbara Lewis and Diane Lewis Robinson. Also see Tape, HG, LEWIS AND ELSIE LEWIS

"Elsie on Early Memories," 3/1/80, and Ione Tape "Aunt Elsie Washington," March 1988.

"The American Negro, His History and Literature," Proceedings of the Constitutional Convention of South Carolina, Vol. 1, Arno Press, Inc. and *The New York Times,* New York, 1968.

Richard P. McCormick, "William Whipper: Moral Reformer," Pennsylvania History, 1976.

George D. Terry, "From Free Men to Freedmen: Free Negros in South Carolina, 1860–1866." December 1975.

"The Ellison Family Papers." Manuscripts Collection, South Caroliniana Library, University of South Carolina, Columbia.

"The de Caradeuc Papers." Southern Historical Collection, University of North Carolina Library, Chapel Hill; Historical Society of Savannah, Georgia and the Historical Society of South Carolina, Charleston.

"The Leigh Whipper Papers." Moorland Spingarn Collection, Manuscripts Department, Channing Pollack Collection, Howard University, and Schomburg Collection, the New York Public Library.

"The Whitefield McKinlay Papers." Carter G. Woodson Collection, Library of Congress.

"Daniel Murray Papers." State Historical Society of Wisconsin, Madison.